James M. Gustafson's
Theocentric Ethics

edited by
BECKLEY
Harlan R.
and
SWEZEY
Charles M.

James M. Gustafson's Theocentric Ethics:
Interpretations and Assessments

☐ MERCER ☐

ISBN 0-86554-307-0

James M. Gustafson's
Theocentric Ethics:
Interpretations and Assessments
Copyright © 1988
Mercer University Press
Macon, Georgia 31207
All rights reserved
Printed in the United States of America

□ □ □

The paper used in this publication meets
the minimum requirements of American National Standard
for Information Services—Permanence of Paper
for Printed Library Materials, ANSI Z39.48-1984

□ ⧆ □

Library of Congress Cataloging-in-Publication Data
James M. Gustafson's theocentric ethics:
interpretations and assessments
edited by Harlan R. Beckley and Charles M. Swezey.
      pp. 255   15 x 23 cm.   6″ x 9″
Papers from a symposium held in Lexington, Va., Sept. 26-28,
1985.
   ISBN 0-86554-307-0 (alk. paper)
      1. Gustafson, James M.—Ethics—Congresses.   2. Christian
ethics—History—20th century—Congresses.   I. Beckley, Harlan, 1943– II. Swezey, Charles Mason, 1935– .
BJ1251.J35   1988   88-21836
241—dc19   CIP

Contents

Introduction

On 26–28 September 1985, a symposium was held in Lexington, Virginia, on James M. Gustafson's *Ethics from a Theocentric Perspective.* Eight scholars were invited to analyze and assess Gustafson's proposal and to indicate its significance for constructive work in theological ethics. The papers and edited discussions in this volume, including Gustafson's Response, are taken from this conference. Gustafson subsequently contributed the Afterword.

The order of essays in this volume, like the schedule of lectures at the symposium, follows Gustafson's two volumes in moving from theology to ethics. The only change from the sequence of lectures, placing John Howard Yoder's essay prior to Robert O. Johann's, has been made in accordance with this guideline. The essay by Robert N. Bellah follows those by Johann and John P. Reeder, Jr., because it focuses on another aspect of Gustafson's ethics, that is, his criticism of culture or ethos. The last two critics' essays are from philosophers (Robert Audi and Mary Midgley) who treat issues that relate theology or religion to ethics, and science, but with widely differing interests and styles.

The discussions following each of the articles reflect the dynamics of the symposium. They build upon previous papers and discussions and culminate in the panel discussion among the lecturers. We have selected discussion materials that clarify the authors' interpretations of Gustafson or compare and contrast their own positions with Gustafson's. The discussions are not verbatim transcripts; we take responsibility for adapting extemporaneous speech to a written format without altering content.

The symposium was cosponsored by the Department of Religion at Washington and Lee University and the Institute for the Advanced Study of Religion at the Divinity School of the University of Chicago. The Philip F. Howerton Fund for Special Programs in the Department of Religion at Washington and Lee provided support for the symposium and for editing this volume. Gratitude is also due to the planning committee, which included, in addition to the editors of this volume, Minor L. Rogers, William Lad Sessions, and David W. Sprunt of Washington and Lee University; James F. Childress and David Little of the University of Virginia; and Robin W. Lovin of the University of Chicago, who was also the liaison with the Institute for the Advanced Study of Religion. Nancy W. Hanna, administrative assistant to the program for Society and Professions at Washington and Lee, provided valuable editorial assistance.

Ethics from a Theocentric Perspective is a far-ranging revisionist proposal for theological ethics. Drawing on a variety of sources and disciplines, Gustafson sets forth a view of God, a polemic against anthropocentrism, a model of moral discernment, and much more. The two volumes have elicited responses from several points of view. Those invited to present papers at the symposium represent different disciplines—theology, philosophy, and social science—and also approach their assessments of Gustafson's work differently.

It is not surprising that the lecturers have varied judgments about the worth of Gustafson's proposal. These judgments depend in part on their interpretations of his argument. The diversity in judgments and interpretations appears to reflect the lecturers' different normative positions as well as their different disciplines and approaches.

Despite these variations, all of the authors work within a view that morality and ethics depend in one manner or another upon basic beliefs about the way things ultimately are. Their judgments and interpretations may focus on either theology or ethics, but no author treats one without referring to the other. Further, the relation between ethics and theology is explored in light of how knowledge is possible. Therefore, three related themes recur throughout this volume.

In the area of epistemology, the authors consider the status of claims for knowledge, the kinds of arguments appropriate to that knowledge, the use of various sources and the role of piety in coming to knowledge, as well as how theologians can converse with others and the extent to which communication is possible. They also attend to theology, especially perceptions of God and God's relation to humanity and the world. Finally, they consider ethics. They evaluate stances toward the world, ethical theory, and the process of moral discernment. It is possible to show that each essay makes at least implicit judgments about aspects of these three related themes. Attention to these themes will alert readers to issues raised by Gustafson and to some of the differences in the authors' interpretations and evaluative judgments.

Gordon D. Kaufman largely agrees with Gustafson's ethical procedures and endorses his intention to develop an understanding of God that will sustain a theocentric ethics. Kaufman, however, believes that Gustafson fails to fulfill this intention. Gustafson's naturalistic conception of deity does not cohere with a view, which Kaufman thinks Gustafson's project correctly implies, that God is the "ultimate point of reference in terms of which all else is understood." As ultimate reference, God must interact with history and culture.

The incoherence arises from Gustafson's attempt to combine an understanding of God as Other from the Reformed tradition with a natural piety that eliminates anthropocentric and anthropomorphic language about God. Kaufman identifies Gustafson's concept of God as Other with Karl Barth's notion of Wholly Otherness. This view of God presupposes a metaphysical dualism characteristic of the Reformed tradition. Metaphysical dualism separates God from humanity, and this separation is overcome only by a doctrine of revelation, which Gustafson rejects. For Gustafson, piety is a response to the powers of God known through the natural world, so that his appeal to the theistic elements in the Reformed tradition is merely a "personal preference." Without these elements, his intention to understand God as interactive and interdependent with the world and humanity has no basis.

As a result, Gustafson "presents a God that seems little more than a kind of reification, into a unified structure, of natural powers and orders." Kaufman questions whether this God is "anything more than what is generally called 'nature.'" Stripped of personal and agential metaphors, this God is indifferent to the distinctively human. Gustafson's intention to construe all of life in relation to God leads him to use personal metaphors such as Creator, Governor, Judge, and Redeemer, but "he has not articulated a conception of God which can make these convictions intelligible." Gustafson is unsuccessful in providing an understanding of God that grounds theocentric ethics.

Kaufman proposes a solution that seeks to retain the intentions of Gustafson's program. An imaginative construction of the idea of God as "an ultimate grounding in reality, not only of the physical and vital dimensions of human life, but of the spiritual and moral dimensions as well" would depict God as One who interacts with humans in history and culture. Unlike a simply naturalistic conception of God, it provides a "unifying focus" for "devotion and service" that enhances and reinforces human morality without anthropocentric effects. Symbols from the tradition are used in the task of imaginative construction because they ground the distinctively human and nurture morality, not because they mediate knowledge that corresponds to the way things truly are in the world. Kaufman believes this method avoids Gustafson's failure to give sufficient reasons for appealing to the tradition.

Edward Farley also criticizes Gustafson's proposal with the intent of improving it. His concern is not with an incoherence in Gustafson's understanding of God but with "breaks" in a genetic argument. This argument moves to an understanding of God by exploring the "'conditions of possibility' of theocentric piety" in the following four spheres of experience: human historical being, human religiousness and piety, the traditioning of the Christian community, and reflection about world processes. Farley distinguishes this mode of argument from precritical appeals to the authority of Bible and tradition and from natural theologies developed independently of specific religious traditions. In contrast with "merely symbolic monotheism" that "eschews the truth question," Farley sees Gustafson as an "objectivist" seeking knowledge about God's relations to the world that corresponds to the way things truly are. This intent, combined with his tentativeness in treating the Jewish and Christian traditions as sources of truth, creates the "breaks" in his argument.

Due in part to suspicions about anthropocentrism and precritical stances toward authority, Gustafson views the Judeo-Christian tradition as a social scientist. It is a "matrix and framework for knowing" but not a source that "mediates the way things are." Thus, his appeal to the tradition to back piety's monotheistic claims has no warrant. It looks like fideism. His argument also neglects the centrality of the experience of redemption in the Jewish and Christian traditions. Gustafson reduces redemption to an enlargement of the scope of responsibility; therefore, he does not draw upon how it alters the content of morality in the tradition.

The absence of moral content in God's redemptive activity has consequences for ethics. The world processes through which one discerns signs of God's activity include the human arenas of culture, history, and society, as well as nature. For Farley, Gustafson does not identify God with nature. By not showing how redemption alters the content of morality, however, Gustafson has no way to distinguish God's purposes from world processes. Since the basis of moral discernment is "more or less coincident with world process," what is morally good or worthy cannot be known theologically. Farley suggests a way can be found within the genetic argument to defend Western religious traditions as a source of truth. Since the experience of divine redemptive activity in these traditions is "more determinate than world process," it would provide theologically informed ethical criteria. Gustafson could also be less skittish about claiming universality for the knowledge of God mediated through the tradition.

Kaufman and Farley criticize aspects of Gustafson's work to improve it. John Howard Yoder is more critical. Yoder believes Gustafson abandons the decisive disclosure of God's purposes for an "uncritical cosmological argument for a different God," which cannot convince the audience to which his book is addressed. Furthermore, he does not really engage the Reformed tradition, the point of departure to which he affirms an allegiance.

According to Yoder, Gustafson abandons the central assertion that God chose to associate His cause with the events culminating in the incarnation.

For the Reformed tradition, which Yoder seeks to represent, these events are the measure of what God enables and requires. Without criteria for cross-disciplinary conversation, Gustafson invokes science with trusting simplicity and thereby subordinates the "complexities of the historical deposit to the screening of a modern cosmology." Gustafson draws conclusions about God from science without distinguishing its firm empirical conclusions from its extrapolated world views. Yoder denies a fundamental disjunction between historical and cosmological realms, but he maintains that the conclusions of science are "of only very indirect relevance to determining what constitutes the fulfillment of the promise made to Abraham." Gustafson's argument simply bypasses the confession that Jesus is Lord. He also selects arbitrarily from the biblical witness, heedless of ways that have dealt with the diversity of Scripture without denying its authority. For Yoder it is less anthropocentric to let "God set the terms of our knowledge of Him than when Man the measurer claims for himself the authority to set those terms otherwise."

Yoder also objects to Gustafson's "comparative-descriptive method." Gustafson only locates his normative position by comparison and contrast with other views. He provides no argument for it. This method implies agnosticism about the truth. Yoder cannot tell whether Gustafson "thinks his major moves *ought* to convince me that they are in some way 'true,' in the classical sense that I should follow him in them." If so, Gustafson has substituted "the meta-logical consistency of the thought system in its own interior coherence" for "the dialogical vulnerability with which the ethicist remains accountable to the community, whose logic and language it is not her or his vocation to replace." This method also allows Gustafson to abandon the epistemological centrality of the incarnation without giving reasons. It releases him from "the burden of particular identity" that requires theologians to offer warrants that could call others in their tradition "to hear and change."

Yoder suggests that Gustafson's motive for abandoning "the particular burden of identity" may be his aspiration to develop a theology that overcomes the boundaries of particular communities. By a process abstracting from history, for example, Gustafson relativizes the Reformed tradition's claim for the unique dignity of Jesus as a prophet, priest, and king. Gustafson's intent seems to be to persuade people "in the wider 'public' arena," but his "modern and individual" synthesis does not register the evangelical option. This option strives towards communication and reconciliation not by jettisoning particular identity, but through changes in the language of the "target" culture, enabling it to carry the "good news."

Yoder concludes that this epistemology undercuts the theological context for ethics. For example, because Gustafson relativizes the Reformed view of Christ: (1) Scripture no longer provides "morally adequate knowledge of what

God enables and requires" (Christ as prophet), (2) a redemption that enables moral knowledge freed from the "noetic effect of sin" is downplayed (Christ as priest), and (3) the political aspects of ethics are de-emphasized (Christ as king). Further, restricted by his scientific world view, Gustafson's definition of God is deprived of "personlike metaphors" so that language about glorifying and obeying God is "an excessive and substantively empty metaphor."

From a quite different perspective, Robert O. Johann praises Gustafson for developing a "revolutionary" theory of moral reasoning that rehabilitates the notion of conscience by moving beyond the objectivist-subjectivist debate in ethics. Objectivists posit a determinate moral order that can be discovered by purely cognitive reason. Principles or standards derived from this antecedent order are the basis for deducing what is morally right and form the content of conscience. Subjectivists assert that the choice of moral principles is arbitrary and deny the existence of an objective moral order. They conclude that conscience is wholly subjective, divorced from reason, and founded on mere inclination. Both parties err in conceiving of reason as "purely cognitive and separate from appetite."

Gustafson goes beyond this debate with his conception of rationality. "[R]eason gives order and form to our natural impulses and desires while these in turn give content to reason's quest for sense." Reason is not the faculty of a disinterested spectator impartially seeking knowledge of an antecedent moral order. It is naturally biased toward making sense of the whole of experience by organizing it into a moral order that moves "toward the possibilities for being inherent in experience." The natural ground of conscience is not mere desire but desires ordered by reason's quest for sense. In this quest conscientious agents inventively reorder a given situation toward wholeness, much like a discerning biographer orders the data of a subject's life. Unlike subjectivists, Gustafson provides a model of moral deliberation through which a rational and objective moral order emerges. Unlike objectivists' perception of the moral order, Gustafson's perception does not preexist "its elaboration by human deliberation and judgment."

Johann states that Gustafson's ethics, like his theology, is a human construct in the interest of greater sense. Practical reason's interest in sense is also an interest in God, "the name for the ultimate source of the possibilities for being inherent in experience." What is known about God emerges from reason's quest rather than being grasped by the discovery of an antecedent order. Gustafson's understanding of reason's quest incorporates a theocentric perspective. It moves towards the possibilities for being in the whole of experience instead of making human well-being its final norm. Johann applauds this inclusivism, yet he objects to Gustafson's inference from the sciences that God does not have human well-being at the center of His concerns. This effort to conform morally to an antecedent factual order retains vestiges of the objectivists' view of reason. For Johann, "we find out God's will by determining what it makes overall sense to do; we do not find out what it makes sense to do by first ascertaining His will."

Johann criticizes those aspects of Gustafson's theocentric perspective that retain objectivist claims. They are inconsistent with his concept of practical reason. Further, since practical reason is the measure for understanding God, Johann, in contrast to both Farley and Yoder, does not need to consider the role of religious tradition in Gustafson's argument. He does not ask Gustafson to treat the tradition as a determinate source for the knowledge of God.

John P. Reeder, Jr., also focuses upon the ethical component of Gustafson's argument. Reeder observes that Gustafson understands all ethical theory to be embedded in "webs of belief " about human existence and its contexts. For Gustafson's ethics, this web of belief includes a theological component. Reeder's interpretation of Gustafson's epistemology as a pragmatist alternative to objectivism and relativism differs in some respects from all of the authors discussed above.

Reeder's interpretation is similar to Johann's in that Reeder does not think Gustafson construes moral statements as corresponding to an immutable moral order; "we never transcend our historical constructions." Unlike Farley, Reeder is unwilling to interpret Gustafson as intending a transparticular truth beyond historical conditioning. Yet, in contrast to Johann, Reeder sees Gustafson as drawing upon the tradition and other sources to explain and justify belief in a "framework constituted by God's purposes." For Reeder, Gustafson begins with "experience as interpretation, as a cultural system of meaning," but human experience is sufficiently common to provide some basis for cross-cultural communication. We work from the perspective of particular traditions, but they are not "hermetically sealed systems." In forming a web of belief, one aims at a coherence tested against multiple traditions as well as by what one knows of the present. This understanding of Gustafson's argument allows Reeder to interpret him as appropriating the Christian tradition as part of an argument without defending it as the sole determinative source of truth.

Reeder views Gustafson's pragmatist argument as forming an ethical theory that consists of three dimensions. A commitment to God's purposes for the good of the whole of creation and functional requisites for human society each informs substantive notions of the mutual well-being or flourishing of the parts (including humans) and the whole of creation. In the first dimension, distinctively theocentric beliefs are joined with other beliefs to form a rationale for the content of the commitment. The other two dimensions are not based upon distinctively theological premises, but they can be interpreted theologically.

Reeder believes there are prospects for agreement on, though not universal assent to, the moral content in each of these three dimensions. Agreement on the substantive standards of mutual flourishing is most problematic. Because the goods required for flourishing or well-being are incommensurate and may conflict, Gustafson rejects an overarching principle to order and distribute them. He refuses to be bound by either a Rawlsian inviolability of "the right" or a utilitarian maximization of "the good." Moral judgments are like the work of an artist who combines various elements. Even agreement on what goods to consider is difficult. Despite these difficulties, Gustafson's ethics provide resources for "dialogical convergence as well as divergence." We can draw from multiple traditions to "understand others, compare, criticize and be criticized, offer reasons and arguments, convince and be convinced, all without supposing there is a neutral ahistorical framework." Gustafson's pragmatist epistemology allows this possibility, but no more. Unlike Yoder, Reeder views Gustafson's pragmatist epistemology as providing legitimate possibilities for theological ethicists to communicate with others.

Reeder believes Gustafson's commitment to the good of creation and his attention to the requisites are the right foci for ethics. Unlike Farley, Reeder does not suggest that knowledge of God's purposes can provide more than a commitment to the good of the whole. Where Gustafson identifies substantive notions of the good, Reeder hopes that a way may be found to eliminate irreconcilable moral conflicts, but if Gustafson is right, he agrees that the task of ethics is "to concentrate on the concrete, to enlarge our sensitivities, and to do what good we can."

Robert N. Bellah is not nearly so affirmative; he offers an alternative to Gustafson. Bellah finds that a sense of "calm detachment" mutes the prophetic criticism one would expect from a theocentric perspective. Gustafson's process of ethical discernment is "subtle and persuasive," but his criticism of culture is "surprisingly hesitant, gentle, and in the end peripheral." Although Gustafson recognizes the validity of a prophetic approach, his emphasis upon "complex patterns and processes" seeks a "better balance in specific contexts" and supports "specific policy suggestions more than sweeping cultural criticism." Furthermore, Gustafson's critique of religious anthropocentrism seeks "to correct historic Christianity by the standard of a natural piety." This cleansing eliminates traditional beliefs—for example, the incarnation of God. Jesus "incarnates theocentric piety" only as an exemplar calling us to "a piety toward the whole of being that gives us no special claim." This "cosmic piety" makes Gustafson "somewhat remote from the conflict of human interests and values," emphasizes "the complexity of all issues," and mutes "his role as a critic of secular culture."

Bellah's dissatisfaction concerns Gustafson's theory of religion and his theology. Gustafson's emphasis upon experience as a basis for religion allows a piety based on contemporary science to correct religion as shaped by the Christian tradition. Both Bellah and Gustafson view religion as formed by experience and by the language of traditions, but Bellah gives priority to the latter. Gustafson's approach to religion makes sense to Bellah as a modern intellectual, but Bellah is more confident of the "first-order language" of the Christian tradition than of "the experience of living in the modern world." An understanding of religion that emphasizes the power of tradition to shape experience would rectify Gustafson's tendency to resolve conflicts between modern science and "first-order religious language" in favor of the former. It would also ground a more prophetic stance toward secular culture. The theological source of Bellah's dissatisfaction is Gustafson's preference for the Reformed tradition. The remoteness and austerity of its idea of God leads to the "Stoicism toward which Gustafson is tempted." For Bellah, by contrast, a "vital incarnational piety, rooted in a living sacramental practice of the church" would "mitigate the harshness" of that tradition and necessitate a "sharp criticism of contemporary secular culture."

Gustafson's epistemology is too independent of the "first-order language" of the tradition. Unlike Yoder's similar criticism, Bellah's critique is based on a theory of religion and not on a theological defense of God's disclosure in the incarnation. Combined with a theology based on the Reformed idea of God, this epistemology mutes the prophetic element in Gustafson's ethics. Bellah thinks that Gustafson's proposal is deficient epistemologically, theologically, and ethically.

Robert Audi focuses on "Gustafson's view of the connections between theology and the sciences and of both to ethics." Unlike Yoder, who thinks science is only indirectly relevant to God's disclosure, Audi argues, "[I]f nature is ordered by God, our understanding of it can aid us in understanding God." Audi also thinks Gustafson establishes criteria for using the sciences that reject any demand that scientific data "be the major basis on which people come to believe in God, or the major source of attributions of divine properties." Theological statements are justified only within natural piety. Though piety may be evoked by science, it precedes testing what one says about God on the basis of the sciences. For Audi, then, natural piety is not based upon the natural sciences, as Bellah sometimes suggests, and Audi does not see Gustafson invoking the authority of science with trusting simplicity.

Audi's concern is whether Gustafson goes too far in rejecting and modifying traditional beliefs due to their supposed incongruity with the sciences. He questions whether Gustafson's proposal is incompatible with traditional theism. Most especially, he asks if Gustafson's legitimate rejection of anthropocentrism leaves room for personal conceptions of God and any basis for attributing agency to God. Some statements by Gustafson reinforce this impression, yet he also speaks of God as "enabling and requiring" and uses other terms expressing agency. If these terms are to be intelligible for morality, "*some* broadly personal divine characteristics" must be permitted, especially a kind of agency. Audi does not believe Gustafson identifies God with nature, but he is discontent with Gustafson's tentativeness about ascribing agency to God. One does not have to regard God as like us, only infinitely greater, Audi argues, in order to establish "limited similarities between the human and the divine" within Gustafson's theocentric framework. Audi argues that a theocentric perspective can also sustain other elements of traditional theism that Gustafson is reluctant to affirm. He concludes that Gustafson's theological framework is "quite suited to offering us a possible way to retain both a scientific habit of mind and a theistic world view."

Audi thinks that Gustafson should address more fully the ways in which science and a theocentric perspective can provide a framework that helps formulate and refine moral principles. Gustafson's framework, for example, encourages respect for the environment, nurtures respect for persons, and adopts tolerance. Audi also argues that a "fallibilistic epistemology" that supports tolerance can be maintained apart from Gustafson's rejection of ontological realism (the view that there are objective truths about reality). According to Audi, affirming realism in science, metaphysics, and ethics need not be inconsistent with Gustafson's rejection of "naive epistemological realism" (the view that "certainty is often obtainable even on complicated matters"). In ethics, ontological realism claims that there are "universal human ideals and cross-culturally valid moral truths which may be progressively clarified." Unlike Johann (and probably Reeder), Audi believes Gustafson can hold to ontological realism while maintaining much of his present epistemology and theology. Indeed, Audi believes that certain elements in Gustafson's ethics imply a moral theory that is cross-culturally valid.

Mary Midgley observes that her criticism of the view that man is the only thing of value has brought her to the borders of the territory occupied by religions, and she sets out to explore and map this territory. She suggests that an accurate perception of human nature in relation to the universe accounts for some nontraditional forms of religion. Humans are part of a larger pattern through which they are related to each other and to the rest of the natural order. They are equipped by their natural feelings to see themselves as part of this larger whole and to respond to it with wonder, reverence, and gratitude. How does this occur? They discover that these patterns, which are essential for mature human life, require humans to value things beyond their own individual wills and even beyond the human species. They also come to realize that their motivation for these valuations, and the objects that move their motives, are givens and not entirely in their control. Sensing the givenness of what they discover in these wider patterns, humans come naturally to revere aspects of these patterns. This reverence is a basis for developing a view of the world and the place of humans in it. Using general ideas, facts are selected and assembled to form world pictures and belief systems.

One world view that borders on the territory of traditional religions is pantheism, a view Midgley finds congenial. It sees the giver of the world so impersonally that the word *god* may be out of place. But pantheistic views are "real faiths," asserts Midgley, and the word *god* is invoked with good reason to indicate a deeply religious awe and wonder. A bit further beyond the borders of traditional religion, Midgley also finds religious elements in the attitudes of good and serious scientists. Their view that humans are not the greatest thing in the cosmos evokes a sense of awe and wonder; for some this veneration is a foundation for religious or mythological world pictures. Here Midgley accounts for the roots of belief systems that Reeder claims overlap with Gustafson's theological rationale for valuing the good of the whole.

Midgley sees this awe as the opposite of "reductive humanism." It intends to celebrate and to increase the glory of human life, undistracted by reverence for God or Nature, but when these go, valuable elements in human life also disappear. Detached from larger patterns, humans are isolated from the heavens and the earth as well as from other humans. The individual will and intellect are celebrated at the expense of natural feelings for other values. By outlawing reverence for anything beyond the autonomous human will and intellect, and by concentrating on particular facts, reductive humanism intends to eliminate religion and metaphysics, but it actually generates strange belief systems. In the name of science, reductive humanism produces wild cosmic fantasies about a dazzling human future. The needed corrective to this "superstitious humanism" is to stop locating the meaning of life solely in some distant future and to look for it in the whole pattern of the past and present and in eternity.

This absurd exaltation of mankind has also infiltrated the territory of traditional religion. Gustafson recognizes and addresses this problem just where it has become an emergency; our species has begun to threaten its environment and needs restraints. Although Midgley applauds Gustafson's criticism of anthropocentrism, she avers that this term may not convey the severity of the problem. Reductive humanism not only portrays the universe as centering on the human will and intellect, it also "exalts them to the point of apotheosis," reducing other values to instrumental status. Nonetheless, the convergence between a theocentric perspective and some territories bordering on traditional religion indicates a common and urgent cause to reshape the conceptual schemes that block an adequate response to the central trial of our age.

Gustafson responds to the articles, first at the symposium and then in an Afterword. His Response treats various aspects of the interpretations and criticisms in light of several crucial issues. This procedure relates the authors' positions to each other and to his own in order to clarify points for further discussion in the field of theological ethics. He writes that "although there are well-developed critiques as well as fundamental rejections" of his proposal, "the coherence of the work as a whole has not been seriously challenged." His Afterword, written several months following the symposium, offers "reflections on items on which I am now prepared to make clarifications and amplications." In doing this he also draws attention to themes in his proposal that have been overlooked.

Readers will make their own assessments of Gustafson's revisionist proposal and his responses. Whatever their assessments and their views of his interpreters, the related concerns of theology, ethics, and epistemology will continue to be pivotal for theological ethics. The symposium certainly exhibits diversity in points of view, but it also shows how common and crucial concerns are approached differently. The hope of the planning committee is that the symposium will not only aid in assessing Gustafson's proposal, but will also contribute to the larger discussion of substantive concerns in the field.[1]

Harlan R. Beckley
Charles M. Swezey

---

[1]The symposium has generated other publications. Elmer W. Johnson, vice-president, group executive, and general counsel of General Motors Corporation, addressed the symposium in a talk expressing appreciation for Gustafson's work. Johnson's address, "The Style of James M. Gustafson and the Process of Moral Discernment," appears in *Criterion* 25:2 (Spring 1986): 1-5.

William Schweiker, assistant professor of theology and ethics at the University of Iowa, analyzes the proceedings of the conference in "Theocentric Ethics: 'God Will Be God,' " *Christian Century* 103:2 (15 January 1986): 36-38.

Paul M. Gustafson, professor of sociology, emeritus, at Hiram College, perceiving a need for more sociological analysis of his brother's work, compares and contrasts it with Weberian thought in "A Sociological and Fraternal Perspective on James M. Gustafson's Ethics." This essay appears in William H. Swatos, Jr., ed., *Religious Sociology and the Sociology of Religion* (Westport CT: Greenwood Press, 1987) 57-68.

How Is <u>God</u>
to Be Understood
in a Theocentric Ethics?

I n his *Ethics from a Theocentric Perspective,* James Gustafson has set out both a theology and an ethics; or rather, he has argued for the intimate interconnection that obtains, and must obtain, between theology and ethics. He presents a conception of God that he intends to be appropriate for modern life and thought, and he simultaneously attempts to show the significance of this conception for the hard choices of daily living, for human moral existence. We are all heavily indebted to Gustafson for setting out for us such a full-orbed moral and theological perspective, and I am sure many of us will continue to meditate on its richness and wisdom for a good many years to come.

In the second volume of his work, Gustafson mentions four "base points" with which, in his view, an adequate theological ethics must deal:

(a) the interpretation of God and God's relations to the world and particularly to human beings, and the interpretation of God's purposes; (b) the interpretation of the meaning or significance of human experience—of historical life of the human community, of events and circumstances in which persons and collectivities act, and of nature and man's participation in it; (c) the interpretation of persons and collectivities as moral agents, and of their acts; and (d) the interpretation of how persons and collectivities ought to make moral choices and ought to judge their own acts, those of others, and states of affairs in the world.[1]

It is his intention, in the work under consideration here, to present a theological ethics that deals with all four of these base points, and he believes he has "largely . . . fulfilled . . . [these] requirements."[2]

In view of the comprehensiveness of Gustafson's work, it will be impossible for me to give an adequate overview of his theologico-ethical position or to assess critically even a majority of his most important contentions; I shall have to be very selective in what I treat. I would like to focus my attention primarily on what Gustafson himself regards as the heart and foundation of his position, namely his understanding of God.[3] My failure to take up other topics considered at some length in this book should not be interpreted as in any way a judgment that they are not of importance or have not been treated wisely or effectively. Many of these other important questions taken up by Gustafson will doubtless be addressed by other contributors to this symposium.

I

Let us begin by attempting to clarify what Gustafson understands by "theocentrism" and why he regards it as important for ethics. Although, as he says repeatedly, his position is rooted in the piety of the Reformed theological tradition,[4] Gustafson does not regard his position as grounded simply on a religious confessionalism. Rather, his dominant concern—that the pervasive anthropocentrism of our religious traditions and moral theories has become increasingly untenable—grows largely, I think, out of contemporary scientific knowledge of the bases of human life and contemporary ecological consciousness of the interconnectedness of all forms of life. Knowing, as we do, that human life has grown up through a long evolutionary process on earth,

---

[1]James M. Gustafson, *Ethics and Theology,* vol. 2 of *Ethics from a Theocentric Perspective* (Chicago: University of Chicago Press, 1984) 143.

[2]Ibid.

[3]See, for example, ibid., 2:98.

[4]See especially, James M. Gustafson, *Theology and Ethics,* vol. 1 of *Ethics from a Theocentric Perspective* (Chicago: University of Chicago Press, 1981) ch. 4.

made possible by fortunate coincidences of certain physical and biological conditions, it is no longer reasonable to think of humans as the apex and center of God's creation. Ethics (whether religious or secular) must now be done in a way that is continually sensitive to our situatedness in the natural order. It may no longer be worked out largely in terms of traditional religious concepts, values, and claims (as with much theological ethics) nor on the basis simply of reflection on and analysis of rightness and goodness, obligation and value (as with much philosophical ethics). More careful attention must be paid to the actual physical, biological, social, and historical contexts within which human life, and the specific problems to which humans must address themselves, fall, if ethics is to provide effective guidance for the ordering of human affairs today. It is one of the great merits of Gustafson's work that he shows so convincingly how inadequate it is to think of moral reflection as a relatively autonomous activity, something that can be carried on without much attention to questions about human nature, about the world within which human life falls, and about the ultimate reality with which human beings must come to terms—that is, without close attention to the natural and metaphysical foundations of human existence.

It is Gustafson's contention that every moral position is in fact based on certain anthropological and metaphysical premises (though these are certainly not always made explicit and acknowledged).[5] His development of the theocentric foundations of his own position is thus not something extraneous or dispensable, imposed on him because he is a theologian or a religious person;[6]

---

[5]Though *ought* must not be confused with *is,* for Gustafson it is very clear that it cannot be properly understood or conceived independent of "the facts," and that every ethics is always based on and presupposes some particular understanding of human nature, its capacities, and its needs. See, for example, his analyses of utilitarianism and Kantianism (*Ethics,* 2:100-41). "The patterns and processes of interdependence of life in the world are *a basis, foundation,* or *ground* upon which ethical reflection is further developed, and which must be taken into account in determining the values and principles that are to guide human ends and action. From this basis, foundation, or ground, further considerations are developed; the patterns are not sufficient to determine what we are enabled and required to do. They are *necessary conditions* for human action, and they are necessary conditions for what human beings value. One adduces them to support and justify values, ends, and principles, but in and of themselves they are not sufficient justifications. They are the 'is' on which 'oughts' depend, though the oughts are not deduced simply from an 'isness' " (ibid., 2:295).

[6]Gustafson's argument is really rather ambiguous (confused?) on this point, and

it is, rather, the carrying through of a responsibility that properly falls on every ethicist. For Gustafson God is not an extra and dispensable reality of interest only to "faith"; rather *God* is our name for the ultimate reality with which humans must come to terms in life, "the power that bears down upon us, sustains us, sets an ordering of relationships, provides conditions of possibilities for human activity and even a sense of direction. The evidences from various sciences," he says, "suggest the plausibility of viewing God in these terms."[7] This sort of theocentric move, therefore, can properly be understood as essentially an extension—suggested to and reinforced by our "natural piety"[8]—of our various modes of knowledge about ourselves and our world. We humans are subject to a natural tendency—what Gustafson calls the human "fault"[9]— to define our problems and our concerns too narrowly, in terms of our immediate interests and needs (egocentrism), or of the needs and interests of our own social class or group, or our own society or cultural tradition (ethnocen-

---

this, as we shall see, is a root of a major problem with it. Sometimes he seems to ground talk about God (and thus his theocentrism) on some very vague claims about "religious experience" (*Ethics* 1:129ff.): this is something "beyond the means of scientific investigation and proof " but is nonetheless not an "idiosyncratic projection of human imaginations," although it is affirmed "for reasons of heart and mind" (ibid., 1:135); it is truly an experience of "others" now "construed" or "seen" (by "hearts and minds nurtured in the language of monotheistic piety") "as various manifestations of the *Other*" (ibid., 1:136). These sorts of passages suggest that Gustafson's position is basically a confessional one and that he cannot make claims for it in the arena of public discourse. But that sort of narrowness seems to me to be against the basic intentions of his work, because he does not hesitate to amend or even truncate what many have regarded as central traditional theological claims on the basis of modern scientific knowledge and secular philosophical reflection (see, for example, ibid., 1:178ff., 251ff.). He certainly does not claim to ground his position on "revelation" (this point is not discussed systematically, but is entirely consistent with Gustafson's thoroughgoing rejection of anthropomorphism in conceiving God [cf. his "A Response to Critics," *The Journal of Religious Ethics* 13:2 (Fall 1985): 197-98]). I have chosen, therefore, to interpret him as commending theocentrism as an ethical stance that should be considered on its merits in public discourse, not as a position of interest simply to "Christians" or other "religious folk."

[7]Gustafson, *Ethics*, 1:264.

[8]The grounding of theological claims in "piety" is very complicated in Gustafson. See my discussion below.

[9]See especially Gustafson, *Ethics*, 1:293ff.

trism), or of our own species (anthropocentrism). This tendency leads us to misperceive the full complexities of the actual situation in which we live and to improperly set our goals and direct our energies. In contrast with this, "A theocentric construal of the world expands the human perceptions of the wholes of which persons are parts; it is spelled out in patterns and processes of interdependence of life which are the basis for human values and moral principles. . . . And since life is interdependent with the ordering of nature, there is proper concern for the common good of all of life on the planet."[10]

The central moral question that needs to be posed in every situation, then, is not what does the categorical imperative require here, or what is required by the principle of utility or the pursuit of *eudaimonia*. It is rather, " 'What is God enabling and requiring us to be and to do?' The most general answer is that we are to relate ourselves and all things in a manner appropriate to their relations to God."[11] Gustafson articulates this imperative nicely in the language of piety by means of a paraphrase of Romans 12:1-2.

> Individually and collectively offer yourselves, your minds and hearts, your capacities and powers in piety, in devoted and faithful service to God. Do not be conformed to the immediate and apparent possibilities or requirements of either your desires or the circumstances in which you live and act. But be enlarged in your vision and affections, so that you might better discern what the divine governance enables and requires you to be and to do, what are your appropriate relations to God, indeed, what are the appropriate relations of all things to God. Then you might discern the will of God.[12]

When articulated in this manner Gustafson's position may sound very like traditional Christian piety. But that would be a mistaken understanding. In traditional Christian faith, who God is and what God is doing are worked out in close relation to what is regarded as "God's revelation" in the Bible. God is thought of as an *agent*—as one who can be properly characterized by such personalistic and political metaphors as "creator" and "king," "father" and "judge"—and God's relations to humans are understood principally in terms of such activities as ruling and governing, commanding and forgiving, healing and loving. In Jesus Christ, God has supremely revealed Godself to humanity, and through faith in Christ and discipleship to Christ humans can discern God's will and are motivated to carry it out in their decisions and ac-

---

[10]Gustafson, *Ethics,* 2:247; for a fuller discussion see especially 1:307ff.

[11]Gustafson, *Ethics,* 1:327.

[12]Ibid., 1:327f.

tions. None of this, however, properly characterizes Gustafson's understanding of God or his conception of how we relate "ourselves and all things in a manner appropriate to their relations to God." This is because the biblical picture of God and many of the traditional Christian claims based upon it are (according to Gustafson) very misleading in certain crucial respects. They are, in fact, fundamentally anthropocentric in their orientation.

> The dominant strand of piety and theology . . . has focused on the grandeur of man, on the purposes of the Deity for man, and primarily on the salvation and the well-being of man. . . . Indeed, in some cases the divine purposes seem to be exclusively oriented toward human benefits: the salvation of man is claimed to be the ultimate intention of God. . . . Religion itself becomes excessively anthropocentric, Ptolemaic; God is thought to exist and act almost exclusively for the benefit of man. The Christian story, beginning with the Apostle Paul, has intensified this concentration.[13]

A main point of Gustafson's work, however, is

> to propose an alteration of the egocentric, anthropocentric concern of Christian piety and Christian theology. The salvation of man is not the chief end of God; certainly it is not the exclusive end of God. Concern for human salvation must be placed in a wider context than that of Ptolemaic religion. The preoccupation with self has to be altered: the proper orientation is not primarily toward self but toward God—to the honoring of God, and to the ordering of life in relation to what can be discerned of the divine ordering. . . . Human purposes and human conduct have to be evaluated not simply on the basis of considerations derived from reflection about what is good for man. . . . [W]e are to conduct life so as to relate to all things in a manner appropriate to their relations to God.[14]

What then is the divine ordering of things, and how do we come to know it? "God orders the life of the world through the patterns and processes of interdependence in which human persons, institutions, communities, and the species participate."[15] These patterns and processes of interdependence are experienced in everyday life and they are studied in detail in the natural and hu-

---

[13]Ibid., 1:109-10; for elaboration see the entire section from 1:88-113; also 1:178-93.

[14]Ibid., 1:110, 113.

[15]Ibid., 2:298.

man sciences; so ordinary human experience, corrected, supplemented, and greatly expanded by scientific knowledge, is the principal source of our knowledge of the ordering activity of God. Since moral questions are always specific and particular, it will be "the very specific circumstances in which human relationships and actions occur" to which we must primarily attend, not general philosophical questions about God's relations to such broad areas as "nature, history, culture, society, and selves in general or in the abstract."[16] Thus, for example, Gustafson points out that the moral issues connected with marriage and the family can be properly understood only if we remember how the "divine empowering and ordering of life" takes place here in and through "biological relationships first of all."[17] But social customs and institutions are also deeply involved, as well as personal affections, interests, and aspirations. All of these matters must be taken into account as one seeks to understand the divine ordering in this sphere of life and attempts to address questions about chastity, monogamy, procreation, duties of marital partners toward each other and toward their children, birth control, and so forth. Moreover, since many of these circumstances (both biological and social) may change over the course of time, and since our psychological, sociological, and biological knowledge concerning them is certainly changing, it is not to be supposed that any fixed or final conclusions are ever reached about this ordering activity of God.[18] For this reason, an ongoing attempt to "discern" what God is doing—that is, what sort of ordering activity is actually going on in the situation under consideration—is required of persons or communities attempting to live out of and on the basis of a theocentric orientation.[19]

Theocentric ethics, thus, does not depend particularly on maintaining a personal relation to God or Christ, or on commitment to biblical faith, or even on claims to some kind of definite or certain knowledge of God, though any or all of these may be in some ways involved for particular individuals or communities. A theocentric orientation is essentially a particular way of "construing"[20] the ordering we actually find in human experience and in the world; and our living and thinking (including living and thinking ethically and theologically) primarily involve careful attention to, and sensitivity with

---

[16]Ibid., 1:209.

[17]Ibid., 2:159.

[18]Ibid., 2:293ff.

[19]See especially ibid., 1: ch.7 and 2: chs. 5-8.

[20]Ibid., 1:136, 208, and passim.

regard to, the actual structures and orders, processes and events, within which we live and with which we continuously interact. In many respects, it would seem (as Gustafson himself recognizes[21]) that this theocentric perspective is more closely related to Stoicism in its main bearings than to traditional Christianity—at least insofar as Christian faith and ethics have been heavily shaped by a highly personalistic (and anthropocentric) orientation.

The perspective Gustafson has worked out has much to commend it. (1) In its emphasis on theocentrism in ethics, Gustafson's framework systematically directs attention toward overcoming every sort of provincialism and narrow vision in our thinking about the policies we should adopt in ordering our lives and our communities, and about what we should do in the implementation of those policies. Our growing awareness of the many ways in which we have been polluting and poisoning our environment, as well as of the depletion of many of the natural resources on planet Earth, due to our nearsightedness, our ignorance, and our greed, has made it evident how important it is that we learn to take a wider view of human activities and their effects than our traditional anthropocentrism, and our individualistic egocentrisms, have encouraged. A theocentric perspective, which calls us to take the widest possible view and then to relate appropriately to that view ourselves and the other realities with which we interact, directly addresses in a very profound way these ecological issues.

(2) Gustafson's position is not in any way bound by dogmatic or other arbitrary constraints on ethical reflection and moral action, whether religious or secular. All moral principles and rules inherited from the past are to be taken seriously as guidelines, as we reflect on and act within the complexities of modern life, but none is absolutely binding or unchangeable. This leaves Gustafson completely open to the use of modern scientific knowledge of the world and understanding of human affairs, and it frees him from the dangerous parochialism characteristic of so much dogmatic (religious or secular) ethics.

(3) Gustafson has thus developed a framework that (a) encourages complete openness to all the details and complexities of each concrete moral situation we confront; (b) calls for the employment of all the richness and wisdom of the various traditions of human religions and moral reflection that might bear on these issues, together with such knowledge and insight as the physical, biological, and social sciences might afford; and (c) demands that all of this be set in the widest possible context, so that unforeseen side effects and other unfortunate consequences will be taken into account as fully as possible.

---

[21]See ibid., 1:89, 190.

The wisdom and insight this conceptual frame for moral reflection facilitates is readily seen in the judiciousness and understanding Gustafson is able to bring to the analysis of the several concrete moral issues he takes up in the latter half of volume two. There is a great deal, indeed, that commends Gustafson's theocentric perspective in ethics.

II

Though there are many points here and there where I could quibble with Gustafson (I am quite unhappy, for example, with what seems to me a particularly perverse treatment of Kant[22]), I do not want to take issue with the main outlines of the ethics he has sketched; it is a position with which I am in substantial agreement. I do have some problems with the theology that undergirds and grounds the ethics, however. The central issue can be articulated like this: Why has Gustafson presented his ethics as a specifically *theological* position? Why has he not set it out as a form of ethical naturalism? Is *God* really as important to Gustafson's scheme as he claims? Would not a naturalism developed with ecological sensitivity provide essentially the same framework for ethical analysis and judgments as Gustafson's so-called theocentrism?[23] A second closely related question is: Has Gustafson formulated his conception of God adequately for his purposes? Can his conception of God as "the great Other" toward which piety is to be directed really perform the functions required by his overall position, or would a God conceived in much more interactive and interdependent terms be more suitable for his concerns? Let us look briefly at these issues.

Despite his interest in the anthropocentrism/theocentrism problem, Gustafson founds his argument about God not primarily on a conceptual analysis but rather on the role he thinks piety plays (and should play) in human life. There is a "natural piety"[24] found in most religious traditions, and among many secular people as well, that is grounded in "basic intuitions . . . that human life is part of and depends upon realities grander, more majestic, more awesome than humanity itself."[25] By *piety* Gustafson does not mean pious-

---

[22]See especially ibid., 2:116-41.

[23]Gustafson himself admits, "The enlargement of vision that a theocentric perspective enables certainly can be achieved, at least in considerable measure, from non-theological perspectives" (ibid., 1:308).

[24]Ibid., 1:159, 165, 258.

[25]Ibid., 1:108.

ness, sanctimoniousness, or a particular intensity of religious emotion, but rather "a sense of dependence on, and respect and gratitude for, what is given,"[26] "a settled disposition, a persistent attitude [of awe and respect] toward the world and ultimately toward God."[27] Gustafson makes it very clear that it is *piety* in which he is interested here, not "faith" or "belief."[28]

> Faith as a measured confidence in God is part of piety, but faith in the benevolence of God to fulfill human purposes as we desire them to be fulfilled in all respects is not part of piety. Faith as fidelity is central to piety. It is an alignment of persons and communities with the "coercive and persuasive powers" that order life. . . . Faith, as excessive trust [however], puts God primarily in the service of humans.[29]

Gustafson seems ambiguous on the question of whether it is God who calls forth this natural piety, or whether it is the awesomeness and glory of the various powers we experience in the natural world. Sometimes he suggests that it is an awareness of God, a "sense of the powerful Other . . . [that] evokes piety; a sense of awe and reverence, the senses of dependence, gratitude, obligation, repentance, possibilities for action, and direction."[30] But more often he speaks of piety as "a response to the powers of God . . . *known through the natural world*,"[31] and it seems that any profound sense of human dependence on and awe before the great sustaining powers of nature would qualify as piety.

Why, then, does Gustafson regularly make additional reference beyond nature and its powers to God, the reference that makes his position specifically theological? His ethics as such does not seem to require such reference, and he rejects talk about divine revelation. Nor does our natural piety require this sort of reference; indeed, according to Gustafson, talk about God is only one among a number of ways to interpret or "construe"[32] such piety. We do not, he says, directly experience "the powers of God ordering nature, but [we have]

---

[26]Ibid., 1:61.

[27]Ibid., 1:201.

[28]Ibid., 1:201 and 257.

[29]Ibid., 1:203.

[30]Ibid., 1:167.

[31]Ibid., 1:165. My italics.

[32]Ibid., 1:136, 206ff., 225ff., 237.

experiences of the natural world that evoke affectivities that can be religiously significant. The intellectual construal of the theological significance of the objects that evoke the affectivities . . . is a further step."[33]

Why, then, construe our experience and the world in this particular way rather than some other way? Gustafson has no very good answer to this question. It is his own personal preference to think in the theological terms provided by the Protestant Reformed tradition,[34] but he is unable to give particularly convincing grounds for commending that tradition to others. "The religious heritage to which we consent," he says, "arose out of the construal of the world in dispositions and attitudes of awe and respect, out of experiences of the natural world, historical events, and so on, in a religiously affective way."[35] (But this would be true, of course, of practically every other religious tradition as well.) It is out of this mixture of "construal" and "experiences" and "affectivities" that knowledge of God arises. "A knowing came through religious affectivity, a knowing that was confirmed or disconfirmed, sustained or revised, of the presence of God in and through human experiences."[36] All of this remains very vague and sketchy. Although it may provide a sufficient basis for Gustafson's own personal "consent"[37] to the Reformed tradition, it certainly does not present adequate grounds for his foundational claim that ethics should be conceived theocentrically rather than naturalistically. This is an especially serious matter when we remember that the main lines of what Gustafson is contending for ethically could, apparently, be worked out quite adequately in strictly naturalistic terms. Is Gustafson's theism, then, essentially confessional after all, a basically sentimental attachment to God-talk for which publicly convincing reasons cannot be given, or has something gone wrong with the argument?

I think something has gone wrong with the argument. At some points, as we have just seen, Gustafson recognizes that experience and piety alone do not provide sufficient grounds for construing everything theistically, and theology must therefore be understood as essentially an activity of imaginative construction.[38] But he really does not proceed from this insight to an exam-

---

[33]Ibid., 1:208.

[34]Ibid., 1: ch. 4.

[35]Ibid., 1:234.

[36]Ibid., cf. 1:189, 195ff., 225ff.

[37]Ibid., 1:232ff.

[38]Ibid., 1:229, 322-23.

ination of the grounds and procedures for such constructive work; indeed, he seems to regard such "methodological" problems as relatively unimportant for his enterprise.[39] Thus, instead of addressing himself directly to the question of why we can and should construe the world theocentrically, he talks about his own basic "conviction"[40] that theology is fundamentally a sort of simple and direct "reflection" on "experience"—a conviction that is actually inconsistent with his understanding of theology as imaginative "construal"—and seems to suppose that nothing more is required to ground his central claims about God. What is missing throughout Gustafson's book is (a) an adequate justification for moving beyond talk of nature or the world to talk about God, and (b) an adequate justification for characterizing God in the way Gustafson wishes to do.

I think Gustafson may have been led astray from this task precisely by his own combining of the Reformed tradition (which is so important to him) with qualifications demanded by his strong criticism of its anthropocentrism and anthropomorphism. I do not want to disagree with that critique itself. In my opinion Gustafson is correct in his claim that traditional Christian faith and piety have been very human-centered and utilitarian, and that an orientation of that sort is not helpful in dealing with the central problems of modern life. I agree also with his contention that we should look to the theocentric strands of the Christian tradition in attempting to construct a viable framework for the orientation of life today.[41] However, the powerful sense of the reality, majesty, and power of God characteristic of the Reformed tradition has led Gustafson, I think, to overlook the fact that this Calvinistic sort of God-talk becomes highly problematical when the radically dualistic metaphysical assumptions on which it rests are given up, as they most certainly are in Gustafson's quite modern world. He seems to take it more or less for granted that it continues to be intelligible and justifiable to talk of "the experience of *an Other* present in, through, and beyond particular experiences";[42] the important thing is that we not do so anthropocentrically. In this concentration on the problem of anthropocentrism, he fails to notice that the particular theistic branch on

---

[39]Ibid., 1:64-68.

[40]Ibid., 1:115ff.

[41]For my own most recent efforts to work along these lines, see *Theology for a Nuclear Age* (Philadelphia: Westminster Press, and Manchester: University of Manchester Press, 1985) see also *The Theological Imagination* (Philadelphia: Westminster Press, 1981) esp. chs. 1-3, 10.

[42]Gustafson, *Ethics,* 1:148. My italics.

which he has been sitting has itself been sawed off by his movement into the ecologically interdependent modern world.

The strongly theocentric emphasis Gustafson finds in the Reformed tradition, and which is so much to his liking, was made possible by dualistic metaphysical assumptions—that the Creator and the creation, God and humanity, were utterly distinct sorts of reality to be sharply contrasted with each other. God is self-existent, completely independent and free of all other beings, the source and foundation of all else that exists; the entire created order including humanity, in contrast, is derivative from God's activity and depends absolutely on God in all respects. God thus is (as Barth so often emphasized, especially in his early writings) "wholly other" from humankind. That it is this strongly dualistic way of thinking from which Gustafson derives his theocentric emphasis can be easily seen in his insistence that "religion is grounded in experiences of 'others,' "[43] and that, above all, it should be "directed toward *the* Other,"[44] since consciousness of this "powerful Other" evokes a very profound sort of piety.[45] However, if we take the notion of God's "wholly otherness" from us seriously (as Barth in his commentary on *Romans* showed, and repeatedly reaffirmed in the *Church Dogmatics*), it is clear that there can be "no way from man to God," no natural knowledge of the divine being: only through God's own initiative in coming to us in revelation can God be known at all, can it even be known that this "wholly other" God exists. Apart from such revelation we humans are utterly alone in the world.

I cannot expound Barth's argument in detail here, but I think it is a substantially correct reading of the logical implications of founding one's conception of God on the notion of *otherness*. This conceptual dualism, of course, when it is taken for granted, facilitates a profound sense of God's utter reality and power, and thus it can evoke, as Gustafson says, a very deep piety. But all this is bought at the expense of understanding our knowledge of God to be grounded almost totally on revelation, on God's own movement to bridge the chasm that divides the divine reality from us. If, for whatever reasons, one gives up the notion that our knowledge of God is rooted primarily in God's revelation to us—and Gustafson assuredly does this—then there no longer remains (even for piety) a "powerful Other" about which we can speak or before whom we might bow in awe. Our conception of God, if we wish to retain such a conception, will need to be grounded on a significantly different notion than "otherness," and our piety will also need a differently conceived focus.

---

[43]Ibid., 1:134-35.

[44]Ibid., 1:136. Gustafson's italics.

[45]Ibid., 1:167.

In order for the program Gustafson has proposed to work, a substantially different conception of God than he has sketched is required, since he is especially interested in emphasizing not merely human *de*pendence on the natural orders within which we live and on God, but also our *inter*dependence with these.[46] This means that God must be understood as being somehow interactive and interdependent with us, not simply over against us as the dualism underlying the model of otherness suggests. Gustafson seems to commend process theology for seeing the significance of this point and addressing it;[47] nevertheless, he retains the notion of radical otherness in working out his own position, particularly when he is expressing himself in the language of piety.[48] This is not surprising, since Gustafson's thinking about God is so heavily informed by the Reformed tradition, but it means that there is a profound tension—if not incoherence—between the basic scientifically informed understanding of humanity-in-the-world, which governs most of his thinking about human moral existence and its context, and the conception of God that he regards as the heart of his theocentric ethics. Thus, the question of who or what God is, as well as the question of why Gustafson engages in God-talk at all, is left in a very undeveloped fashion. In both cases this is largely, I think, because Calvinism's heavy emphasis on God's radical otherness from humanity—apprehended and deeply appreciated in Gustafson's own personal piety—has led him to suppose that these are not matters to which he must give serious attention.

Due to Gustafson's failure to investigate carefully the obtrusiveness of these conceptual presuppositions of his piety and his reflection, the already strong Calvinistic emphases on God's otherness become even further intensified in his work, as he attempts to eradicate the anthropocentrism and anthropomorphism of traditional Christian views. Christian themes about God's love or special care for humanity, or about humanity's being distinct from all other creatures by virtue of bearing the divine image, or about humanity's occupying some special place or distinction in nature, all become unacceptable to him. In his zeal for God's utter independence from everything human, Gustafson does not hesitate to declare that the "ultimate power is not the guarantor of human benefits";[49] "the divine governance through nature is not

---

[46]Ibid., 1:282-93; also 2:279ff.

[47]Ibid., 1:56ff.

[48]For example, see ibid., 1:318ff.

[49]Ibid., 1:99, cf. 1:112.

necessarily beneficient."[50] "Piety stands in awe of the powers that bear down on us and sustain us; it does not trust them to fulfill all our perceptions of the human good."[51] "I do not say God is against man," he writes,[52] but one can properly say that "God is for man" (a central Barthian phrase) apparently only "in the sense that the possibilities of any human flourishing are dependent upon what we have received and on forces that are not ultimately under our control"[53]—a very limited, indeed essentially negative, affirmation. In Gustafson's version, God appears to have no special concerns for human well-being and seems to be totally impersonal. God is neither a moral reality nor a guarantor that we live in a moral universe;[54] and it is questionable whether or not God should be conceived as in any real sense an agent with intelligence and intentions.[55] Gustafson seemingly will allow a certain "purposiveness" in God, of a sort similar to the end-directed activity of animals,[56] but this is as close to the idea of God's agency as he is willing to move. It is clear that the otherness of God from humanity is carried much further in Gustafson than in the Calvinistic dualism from which he begins.

Given the conception of God to which he finally comes, Gustafson's unwillingness to use a straightforward ecological naturalism as the basic framework for his ethics seems even more difficult to understand. What can the introduction of the notion of God—conceived in this completely dehumanized and depersonalized way—do for Gustafson that the notion of nature cannot do as well? Is God here any other or more than the structure of natural powers, processes, and events that has brought us into being and within which we live, that is, anything more than what is generally called "nature"?

III

I do not believe Gustafson has any adequate answers to these questions, but I would like to suggest to him a way to deal with them. Although I agree with the basic thrust of Gustafson's critique of the anthropomorphism and an-

---

[50]Ibid., 1:272.

[51]Ibid.

[52]Ibid., 1:181.

[53]Ibid., 1:182.

[54]Ibid., 1:264ff.

[55]Ibid., 1:268-73.

[56]Ibid., 1:270ff.

thropocentrism of traditional Christian theology and ethics, I think he has overreacted to these problems. Instead of searching out the positive value and meaning that may lie beneath these inadequate ways of speaking and thinking, he has tried simply to cut them out. That is why he is unable to give an adequate account either of why it is important that ethics be theocentric and not just naturalistic, or of the sort of God who is appropriate to the theocentric ethic he wishes to develop. Gustafson wishes to continue to think of God as our "creator," "sustainer," and "governor,"[57] for these symbols express well our consciousness that we have been given our very being by "creative powers"[58] we do not control, and that we could not continue to exist if we were not sustained by the ongoing "ordering of the universe, of life on this planet, and of human relationships . . . by natural, social, cultural, and historical processes."[59] But Gustafson has not articulated a conception of God that can make these convictions intelligible. The God he has described cannot be understood as significantly present in or working through those powers that have actually brought humans *qua their humanity* into being and that continue to sustain them in being.

The God Gustafson describes—and which I would be inclined to call simply "nature"—is essentially the structure and order of inanimate being and of life that we find in the world around us (and also in our own existence). It is not at all clear, though, how this particular structure, without very important additions, can be understood as the source and ground and continuing sustainer of that which is *distinctive to our humanity,* that is, of that which distinguishes human being from other modes of life and reality—for example, self-consciousness, intentionality and choice, language, imagination and creativity, the ability to take responsibility for ourselves and our actions, the desire to make and keep promises and other personal commitments, the capacity to live together in love and loyalty and forgiveness in communities governed by freedom and justice. These qualities of our existence that are most characteristically human and humane, and which we cherish above all others as those things "that make life worth living," are just the ones to which Gustafson's God remains completely unrelated, for Gustafson's God has no significant connection to or interest in the process of history and the distinctive forms of order and value and meaning that have emerged in history. It is precisely to the movements and developments, triumphs and tragedies, of

---

[57]Ibid., 1:236-42.

[58]Ibid., 1:238.

[59]Ibid., 1:239.

history—where we are most profoundly involved as moral beings and where that which is of deepest and most fundamental importance to us as humans happens—that Gustafson's God maintains a magnificent and total indifference.

But it is in and through historical and cultural processes that we have emerged from mere animality into our humanity, and without the continuance of historical, social, and cultural institutions and patterns of order human life could not go on. Gustafson seems to recognize this at times, as when he refers to God's involvement in the ordering of life through social, political, and economic institutions and processes.[60] However, he often seems quite uncertain that God is really active in these historical processes and institutions,[61] and then references to human "stewardship" (rather than God's activity) become prominent in his language.[62] It is difficult to see how the sort of God Gustafson has actually described—one who is totally indifferent to everything distinctively human and to much that is precious and valuable to human beings—could be involved in any significant way in social and cultural modes of ordering activity. Thus, in completely discarding everything he thought to be anthropomorphic or anthropocentric in God, Gustafson has made it impossible to understand how God can be significantly involved in central, defining features of human existence.

Is it really plausible or reasonable to expect humans to glorify, respect, worship, rejoice in, and possibly even love such a God as this, who does nothing to sustain us in our distinctively human ventures? I do not think so. And there is a very good reason for this, entirely independent of our proclivities for anthropocentrism: it is not really possible to see this God as the reality that in fact gives us our being as distinctively human, nor does this God in any way help support us and sustain us in our humanity per se, in the moral, social, and cultural ventures without which human life would not be itself. This God is not, thus, either our creator or our sustainer, not to mention our redeemer; why should we worship and bow down? Would it not be idolatry to bow before such a God as this?

The deepest reason for the sometimes crass anthropocentrisms and anthropomorphisms found in the traditional understanding of God—which Gustafson rightly criticizes severely—is not simply that we humans desire to glorify only ourselves, though undoubtedly that motive has also often been

---

[60]See, for example, ibid., 2:160ff., 166ff.

[61]For example, ibid., 2:220-21.

[62]Ibid., 2:234-50, 279ff.

present. The deepest reason is that human beings, when they first became conscious of their distinctiveness within the natural order, found it impossible to imagine or understand the source and ground of this distinctiveness without resorting to quasi-human images and metaphors. They did indeed have a natural piety—as Gustafson so correctly emphasizes—for that which gave them their being and continued to sustain them in being. But how was that awe-inspiring *x,* which was to be the object of their worship, respect, and love, to be conceived? Though metaphors of rocklike stability and of brilliant light, of enormous power and great vitality, could express part of what needed to be said, it seemed necessary to complement and complete these metaphors with others drawn from the distinctly human spheres of spirit, morality, culture, agency. Omitting these, the object of their adoration and devotion, instead of focusing their interests, activities, and passions on those things that would help to evoke their fullest humanity, would have contributed instead to their degradation and dehumanization. (It is this issue that is in part at stake in the Old Testament struggle between Yahweh and the nature gods.) If the God humans worship cannot be conceived as significantly undergirding the moral and spiritual dimensions of human existence, the worship of God will undermine those dimensions and contribute to the destruction of the human; and what we took to be God will have turned out to be an idol.

We do not need to go to the anthropocentric and anthropomorphic lengths of the Christian tradition in order to affirm that it is important that God not be conceived as irrelevant to or unconnected with that which is most significant and precious to us as human beings. But this implies that purely naturalistic metaphors such as structure, process, event, and even life will not be sufficient for developing an adequate conception of God. We will have to go beyond these, using metaphors drawn from history, culture, and personal existence as well. Of course, as Gustafson rightly sees, it is a mistake to maintain that God is chiefly concerned with our distinctively human interests. Inasmuch as the orders of nature underlie and ground the structures of history and culture through which we have emerged into humanity, he is quite right in giving a certain primacy to naturalistic metaphors. But he is mistaken in supposing that it is unnecessary to go beyond such metaphors in our theological construction. For it is in just such a going beyond—however carefully restrained and constrained we may today feel this must be—that the concept of God is distinguished from the concept of nature; and it is this that gives God that special significance for humans that nature (of itself alone) can never have. Were Gustafson to take up the task of articulating more precisely just what sort of going beyond nature is required to create and sustain humanness, he might find it possible—even necessary—to give a larger place to such central Christian metaphors as love.[63]

It is Gustafson's failure to articulate clearly how we are to understand this going beyond nature's powers and orders in our conception of God that accounts for the significant ambiguity in his theocentric position. Gustafson rightly believes that a theocentric framework for ethics has important values that a strictly naturalistic frame cannot claim. This is why he has taken the trouble to write these two volumes; and it may also be the reason why, despite his great efforts to overcome the anthropocentrism and anthropomorphism of the tradition, in the end he thinks it is appropriate and important to continue to use such personalistic symbols as "creator," "governor," "judge," and even "redeemer,"[64] at least in personal meditation and in public worship.[65] It is really quite difficult to understand this conservatism about traditional symbolism in light of the powerful critique of just this kind of imaging and thinking that he makes throughout his book. The explanation for it, in my opinion, is that Gustafson senses that something quite important is being conveyed in these ancient symbols, something that cannot be fully captured in the structuralistic conceptual formulations he has developed, and he wishes somehow to retain that. Hence he has set forth a "theocentric" rather than a simply "naturalistic" ethics. All this is certainly to Gustafson's credit, but it leaves his position in a great deal of tension and ambiguity.

In my remarks here I have tried to indicate briefly the important positive theological meaning carried by the anthropocentric and anthropomorphic features of traditional talk about God, even while acknowledging, with Gustafson, the dangers and destructiveness into which these distortions can lead us. If a conception of God can be articulated that takes this positive significance fully into account without falling into the anthropocentric traps into which (as Gustafson shows so well) the tradition often fell, it should be possible to overcome the enormous tensions—even contradictions—found in the present work between what is appropriate in worship and what is tolerable in theology. If such a conception cannot be worked out, and the life of worship and the life of the mind are each continually undermining the other, it would seem that a truly theocentric framework for life and thought is no longer possible in today's world.[66]

---

[63]Cf. ibid., 1:236.

[64]See ibid., 1:236ff.

[65]Ibid., 1:250-51, 278-79, 317ff.

I have been arguing thus far that the idea of God is the notion of an ultimate grounding in reality, not only of the physical and vital dimensions of human life, but of the spiritual and moral dimensions as well. This position makes it possible for an orientation centered on the idea of God to take with complete seriousness, and to give its full value to, that which is distinctive about our humanity, as well as that which we have in common with other living beings. Through undergirding and supporting human existence in its totality, faith in God or piety toward God also undergirds and supports human moral existence, and it helps motivate moral seriousness in life. In contrast with this, a purely naturalistic framework for orienting life—or a theistic scheme that, like Gustafson's, attempts to define God in exclusively naturalistic terms—since it fails to relate to what is uniquely and distinctively human, remains seriously defective as a framework for orientation.

The symbol *God,* properly articulated, provides a unifying focus to which selves and communities can give themselves in devotion and service, as they seek to live and act with integrity in a world of enormous complexity and diversity. The many powers, values, and goods that we experience push and pull us in all directions, threatening us with disintegration. However, if we can orient ourselves in terms of a single center working through and ordering all these finite values and powers, our selves and our actions are given a kind of consistency, wholeness, and integrity that they could not otherwise have. Thus, a theocentric ethic can enhance and reinforce human agency, and also human morality and responsibility, in ways that an ethic, which knows only the great variety of powers, structures, and processes of nature, cannot.

IV

It is time to bring these remarks to a conclusion. In his *Ethics from a Theocentric Perspective,* James Gustafson presents a wide-ranging interpretation of human life in the world and under God, and within this context he develops a distinctive conception of how ethics is to be done. There are many important themes in this work that I have not been able even to touch upon here; in particular, I have said virtually nothing about the understanding of ethics proper, and its procedures, that Gustafson works out, and I have not been able to take up the four major examples of contemporary moral issues through which he attempts to show the practical usefulness of his ethical stance. In these matters I find myself largely in agreement with Gustafson's work; his discussion of

---

[66]I have attempted to sketch more fully, though still very briefly, the sort of understanding of God that I have in mind here, in chapter 3 of *Theology for a Nuclear Age.*

concrete issues seems to me extraordinarily wise and insightful. To the extent that the proof of ethics is to be found in its practical applicability, Gustafson's program, in my opinion (at least with reference to these four examples), must receive very high marks. Criteria other than practical usefulness, however, must be brought to bear in any evaluation of a systematic work in ethics and theology: the comprehensiveness and completeness of the picture it presents, the overall coherence of that picture, the adequacy with which the basic themes of the work are articulated, and so forth. It is to these sorts of issues that I have, for the most part, directed my attention.

A distinctive and important claim of Gustafson's is that every ethics must be (and in fact is) built on certain anthropological and metaphysical presuppositions or foundations; a theocentric framework, he argues, that makes God the ultimate point of reference, in terms of which all else is understood, can deal with these issues in an extraordinarily apt and able way. Many features of the traditional conception of God, however, and of traditional Christian faith and piety, seriously obscure this point, especially when modern understandings of the place of human life in the universe are taken into account. Therefore, Gustafson finds it necessary to perform radical surgery on traditional views in order to work out a theocentric framework adequate for today's world. I find myself in substantial agreement with these basic aspects of Gustafson's program. His powerful attacks on the essential anthropocentrism (and even egocentrism) of traditional Christian faith and of most Western moral reflection are well placed, in my opinion; and I agree with him that a radically theocentric perspective is the most adequate vehicle for providing us with the wide vision and understanding we need today, as well as for motivating us to act appropriately in our actual place, as humans, in the world. With Gustafson's basic theological and moral intentions, therefore, I find myself in substantial agreement, and I want to thank him personally for presenting us with this comprehensive statement of what is involved in a theocentric orientation toward life today.

As my remarks have shown, however, I have some serious problems with the way in which Gustafson has worked out the conception of God that is at the very heart of his systematic perspective. It seems to be deficient in important ways. In his zeal to eradicate all remnants of anthropocentrism and anthropomorphism and to emphasize our human situatedness in nature, Gustafson presents a God that seems little more than a kind of reification, into a unified structure, of natural powers and orders. Two sorts of criticism need to be brought against this understanding of God. First, it is difficult, if not impossible, to see how such a God significantly relates to, and can be understood to provide an adequate foundation and support for, those dimensions of human life that distinguish it from other forms of life and being and that are most precious to us as humans: powers of understanding, imagination, and intellect; moral and cultural values such as truth and justice, freedom and creativity, loyalty and responsibility; and yes, the profound personal and spiritual meaningfulness of such virtues as faith, hope, and love. It would be wrong—demeaning to us as humans—and I think it is probably impossible, for us to devote ourselves to a God so unconnected with matters of the highest importance to us. Second, this conception of God in fact introduces a serious incoherence into Gustafson's own program; for, as he shows in his analysis of certain moral issues, he wants to think of God as the source of, as continually active in and through, and as a support for precisely those social and cultural orders, institutions, and processes that create and sustain us as distinctively human. But a God capable of such activities as these cannot be constructed from exclusively naturalistic materials. Without moving back into anthropocentrism, or employing crude anthropomorphisms, it will be necessary to give a more significant role to metaphors drawn from historical and cultural experience than Gustafson has been willing to do.

I want to emphasize that I do not regard these criticisms as fundamentally destructive of Gustafson's work. On the contrary, they are intended to point in directions that will enhance and strengthen it. I am as committed as Gustafson, I think, to a theocentric perspective on human life, and I share with him, therefore, a deep interest in seeing it adequately and effectively articulated. I believe Gustafson has gone a long way toward achieving such articulation, particularly with respect to the ethical importance of theocentrism, but also in his pointing out the excessive anthropocentrism of the Christian tradition. What remains is to develop, in more nuanced fashion than he has thus far achieved, a view of God that can provide an adequate foundation for human self-understanding in today's world, and can thus become a central focus for our loyalty, our devotion, and our work. I hope Gustafson will continue to work at this important task that he has already carried so far.

Let me conclude with one last—unhappy, I fear—remark. I have been quite dismayed, as I have worked through the two volumes of Gustafson's important book, that, with all his concern for clearing up inadequate ways of thinking in the Christian tradition, he has made no effort to modify the persistently sexist language in which that tradition has expressed itself. It is surprising that one who is interested in the practical import of ethics for the ordering of life—and not simply in ethics as a body of theory—should fail to show in his own writing a sensitivity to and understanding of the degree to which the use of exclusive forms of language helps to perpetuate and reinforce significant injustice, exploitation, and repression. It is equally surprising that one who is so conscious of the distortions in piety and in understanding produced by overly anthropocentric and anthropomorphic ways of thinking, and who advocates a moral and religious stance in which we are always "to relate ourselves and all things in a manner appropriate to their relations to God,"[67] should contin- ually use male gender pronouns in referring to that same God, thus suggest- ing, falsely, that there is a special or peculiar connection between maleness and divinity. It is a puzzle to me, and a disappointment, that Gustafson has failed to apply to his writing on ethics and theology what, as it seems to me, are very clear implications of the theocentric perspective he is attempting to articulate. It is regrettable that a work as important as this one, with the like- lihood of considerable influence on future reflection and writing, should be flawed in this theologically and morally significant way as it goes forth into the world.

KAUFMAN DISCUSSION

<u>Paul Ramsey</u> (Princeton University): Distinguish between Gustafson's symbolization (massing of images and metaphors) and his conceptual statements. Your lecture seems to refer to structures and powers and patterns only in the sense of physical or biological nature. I should have thought that the structures and powers and patterns that bear down upon and sustain us are social and cultural. The tragedy of when we are broken by the powers is that the very human things about us in total cultural situations break us, and not just fires and earthquakes; and that it is the human in us that is sustained. I feel that you were overdoing the emphasis upon nature, of the natural sciences over against the human sciences and the human dimension.

<u>Kaufman:</u> I may certainly have overworked this, and I will be happy to be corrected by specific texts. The point you are making comes out most clearly in Gustafson's discussion of the family. He says clearly that the family is founded in biological struc- tures, but that social and interpersonal structures also have to be taken into account. If you look at his other three practical cases, however, there are very few places where God's activity in and through the social and historical order is developed. Instead of language about God's activity, we have language about human stewardship. It is sig- nificant that stewardship language comes out in the talk about our resources. I have nothing against that, but what God is doing simply seems to drop out of sight. There are ambiguities; there are times that Gustafson would like to interpret his notion of God as working through all these constraining and creative powers and forces. Where he actually works out the conception of God, however, these specifically human and

---

[67]Gustafson, *Ethics,* 1:327, 2:279, and passim.

historical kinds of features of the divine activity are thrown away as anthropomorphic. I do not know what to do with that.

Tod D. Swanson (graduate student, University of Chicago): Your claim that an impersonal understanding of divine agency is insufficient to evoke piety seems to be falsified by many religions that have a more impersonal understanding of deity and in which the understanding of the sacred is not directly anthropomorphic. How would you explain that?

Kaufman: I certainly did not mean to say that there can't be a kind of piety toward the natural order. Gustafson is correct to maintain that there is a kind of natural piety. The question is whether or not that kind of piety is adequate to sustain our humanity in its distinctively human and humane features. Not every conception of God is equal to every other conception of God, and not all conceptions of piety are equal. We need to develop criteria for discriminating between more and less adequate conceptions of that to which we give ourselves in full devotion. A notion of the ultimate object of devotion that is not able to articulate the way in which that reality is connected with the humane and distinctively human aspects of existence is deficient.

William W. Elkins (United Methodist minister; graduate student, Drew University): If you introduce the distinction between the Other (in terms of the natural) and the Wholly Other (in terms of revelation), how would that begin to change your idea of history as a corrective to Gustafson's position?

Kaufman: If I understand your question, I do not share Barth's theory of religious and theological language. The view I hold is that all our conceptions of God are put together out of various metaphors we draw from everyday experience. Gustafson is right in suggesting that the notion of otherness is rooted in experience of the otherness of persons and things over against us; we may then generalize to the notion of some kind of great or radical Wholly Otherness. On this point there is no problem between Gustafson and myself. Barth, of course, would not agree that the notion of the Wholly Other is built up metaphorically in the way I have just suggested. That is because Barth holds, rightly I think, that the logic of the notion of the Wholly Other requires a notion of revelation as the only basis on which it can be apprehended. I agree with Gustafson, however, that this kind of talk about revelation (which we heard much about thirty years ago) has some serious flaws, not the least of them logical flaws already exposed by Hegel. For this reason my view is that the notion of Wholly Otherness is not built up in an encounter in revelation, but rather from metaphors of otherness in our common experience. I am not trying to hang Barth's theory of revelation on Gustafson. I am saying, however, that if Gustafson wants to talk about Wholly Otherness as rooted directly in a kind of piety, then he also is tied to the kind of doctrine of revelation that Barth has.

<u>Mary Potter Engel</u> (United Theological Seminary of the Twin Cities): I would like to take issue with your claim that Gustafson has intensified the metaphysical dualism of the Reformed tradition. I do not read the Reformed tradition as having a metaphysical dualism. I can give two examples, because Gustafson's book is in line with Calvin and Schleiermacher on this point. Calvin says there is a pious way to say that nature is God. He builds his whole doctrine of Providence on the regularity of order that one finds in the natural world. The miracles are only there to assure that we pay attention to the regularity of nature and God's ways of being present and active in the world. He puts that conception together with his notion of God as Other. Schleiermacher does something similar. He says that God is coextensive with the universe, yet distinctive in that God is related to the entire universe as the Almighty Eternal. I see Gustafson's book as being in line with those two Reformed theologians, as trying to put together these two notions of God—as Other and as being somehow coextensive with the order we see in nature.

<u>Kaufman</u>: Gustafson is closer to Schleiermacher than to Calvin. Depending on which way you want to read it, Schleiermacher's ultimate notion of God is the "Whence" from which everything comes (which is open and vague), or is absolute causality. Neither of these is a personalistic conception. I think the position that Gustafson is working out can be made to cohere with Schleiermacher's version of Reformed theology. With Calvin, though we have that one little passage where God and nature are connected, there is no reluctance to use personalistic and anthropomorphic metaphors. I think we have a much greater sense of otherness between human existence and God in the schemes of Gustafson and Schleiermacher than we do in Calvin.

FARLEY

Edward

Theocentric Ethics
as a Genetic Argument

A review essay of another person's work tends to follow symphonic form. There is the initial praise of the author. Then the Andante movement offers a quiet summary of the work. Things begin to heat up in the Allegro movement in which the reviewer mounts a vigorous assault, only to move to a short fourth movement that repeats how important the work is. This essay will not totally avoid some of these moves, but I hope it is closer to the messier beauty of the symphonic poem.

James Gustafson's theocentric ethics is a comprehensive, theologically originated vision of the moral life. This comprehensive vision is both a corrective and an exploration. The corrective is twofold. First, it corrects any theological ethics that retains precritical elements in its guiding convictions and methods. The criticism is ranged not simply against precritical ways of appealing to revelation and Scripture but also against the use of the Christian doctrinal tradition as a given, an unassessable authority. Gustafson refuses to posit the doctrinal accomplishments of Christianity as the a priori ground for theological ethics. He brandishes an Occam's razor (his critics see it as a Troeltschian ax) towards the classical loci. Because of Gustafson's corrective, his critics do not damn him by faint praise but praise him with shouted damns. This corrective indicates not only what Van Harvey calls the "morality of knowledge" born in the European Enlightenment and promoted so fiercely by Ernst Troeltsch but the empiricism and neo-naturalism of the Chicago school. When I enter the world of Gustafson's writings, I hear strains of John Dewey's *Quest for Certainty* and Henry Nelson Wieman's *The Source of Human Good*. There has been tension and small-scale bickering between this kind of theology and the more widespread contemporary heirs of European neoorthodoxy, and the *Aussaenandersetzung* between them is still a future event.

Unfortunately, many critics are so stunned by this corrective that they focus on it instead of the corrective that is the very center of theocentric ethics, the correction of pervasive anthropocentrism. Anthropocentrism means more than one thing in Gustafson's polemics: the idolatry of utilitarian religion, the human-centered premodern cosmology and soteriology of classical Christianity, the turn to the subject to the exclusion of nature and world in modern theology and ethics. It is not sufficient, however, to characterize Gustafson's work simply as a corrective. From *Can Ethics Be Christian?* to *Theocentric Ethics,* we have a series of explorations of the grounds, contours, warrants, norms, and contexts of moral life. The crown of this effort, which is the occasion of this gathering, is still a group of explorations. The explorations are, of course, guided by a large number of hard-won, firm convictions. There is a reason why Gustafson's comprehensive vision emerges by means of explorations. Explorations of this sort indicate a persistent and intensive sense of reality. In Gustafson's writing, this sense of reality finds expression in a principle, the primacy of experience. And what is reality, the concrete, actual matters that impinge on us? Whatever our simplifications of it are, its impingements present us with states of affairs that are always complex, and as complex, multidimensional, everchanging, ever interrelational. It is this complexity that gets Gustafson's attention and evokes his reflection. This sensed complexity of reality is the reason for Gustafson's impatience with all dichotomies and dualisms. And this is why his work does not fall into either teleological or deontological ethics, or into either the subjective turn or objectivism, or into a focus on individual or society, or into liberation ethics rather than traditional ethics, or into hermeneutics rather than metaphysics. Sensing the complexity, Gustafson invariably pushes the reality beneath and beyond these alternatives, combining, relating, sifting. This is, I think, why his vision is exploratory and not system-building. We now turn to that vision itself.

The Framework of a Commonsense Ontology

Gustafson's overall agenda is the exploration of a nonanthropocentric theological interpretation of moral life. Although many convictions guide the exploration, one of them is so fundamental and so pervasive as to have the status of a dominant interpretive grid or framework. This framework is the general ontology of reality Gustafson draws on when he deals with anything that is real or actual. Gustafson does not isolate this ontology for discrete treatment, nor does he press very far the concepts that bear it. I suspect he regards this ontology as sufficient partly because his primary agenda is something else; hence, he does philosophy as he needs it, and partly because it carries with it a certain self-evidence. I am calling this framework a *commonsense* ontology because of its relatively nontechnical language and its presumed self-evidence. When we gather together the concepts of this ontology, we recognize its general family, which is the neo-naturalist movements of the 1940s and 1950s whose primary terms were events, processes, and relations.[1] In many respects the ontology resembles process philosophy. Accordingly, Gustafson is sympathetic to Whiteheadian philosophy but declines the step to speculative philosophy and, therefore, to speculative description of the *res verae* of things, actual entities. What we have without this step is a more general and more commonsense ontology.

I hope it is not too oversimplified or oversystematized to say that this commonsense ontology finds expression in five basic concepts: individuals, contexts (wholes), interaction (participation), change, and patterns (conditions). There are throughout nature and history *individuals* that can be both the initiators and the recipients of influences. But reality is not simply a set of aggregates of types of individuals but is comprised of various spheres or *wholes*. The total ecological system of this planet is such a sphere, and so is a nation-state and even a hospital in a city. All real things, be they individuals or wholes, interact with other things. The most general thing that can be said about *interaction,* according to Gustafson, is that it involves reciprocal influencing; hence, the being of the interacting realities is constantly being influenced and is constantly influencing. Influencing and being influenced involve change; hence, *change* is intrinsic to any real thing and characterizes whatever is the totality of things, for instance, nature. Change, though not progress, does mean development of some sort. Change or development is both inter-

---

[1] If there was a single manifesto of that movement, it was probably Y. A. Krikorian, ed., *Naturalism and the Human Spirit* (New York: Columbia University Press, 1944), with contributions from John Dewey, Herbert Schneider, John Herman Randall, and others. See especially Randall's epilogue on the nature of naturalism. This collection was part of a larger movement especially associated with the University of Chicago. Religious philosophers such as Henry Nelson Wieman and Bernard Meland described their program as a "new naturalism."

nally generated in individuals and a feature of the reciprocity between individuals. Finally, real things have a certain *duration* or persistence over time. Gustafson would avoid any formulation of this continuity that appeals to timeless essences, but he does see sufficient continuity of features of real things to support discourse that classifies, typologizes, and even lists distinctive features. Gustafson's most detailed account of continuity occurs with respect to the *conditions* any real thing requires for its existence, survival, and well-being. Every real thing has requisite conditions for its being. Gustafson calls these conditions *patterns,* and in the course of interacting and change, new conditions are constantly emerging and with them the real things that are correlatively dependent on them. Gustafson calls this emergence of conditions or patterns *ordering.*

All of these concepts are available to the commonsense experience of the human being whose very survival depends on knowledge of the individuals, the participated spheres, the types of relations and interactions, the continuities to rely on, and the conditions of well-being. But rigorous study of this ever-changing network of individuals, spheres, and conditions is the work of the natural and social sciences. Needless to say, all these concepts together describe ways in which any real thing is *limited* in its autonomy, its isolation, and its self-determination.

Two features of Gustafson's commonsense ontology are crucial. The first is the stratification of reality. This does not mean hierarchical ordering but the presence of distinctive types of reality that then have their own distinctive ways of interacting, initiating influences, and continuity. Thus, "participation" names the distinctive way human beings exist in and toward larger contexts. "Traditioning" names a distinctive way human communities retain the past. The second feature is the all-pervasiveness of these concepts, which is why it is a general and not just regional ontology. The concepts, therefore, apply as much to history, society, culture, and human individuals as they do to nature and world processes.

This commonsense ontology is of critical importance to Gustafson's comprehensive vision for two reasons. First, everything he takes up is assumed to be part of this flowing network of interacting realities: the cosmos, nature, the human species, history, all events in history including disclosive and revelatory events, all human beings including Jesus of Nazareth, the church and its tradition, even Gustafson's own work. Therefore, the ontology is not only an interpretive grid but a criterion for assessing whatever theologies and ethics present themselves for interpretation. Second, the ontology serves as the conceptual apparatus for Gustafson's exploration and argument for a theocentric ethic. The meaning of God, God's relationship to the world, and human beings' relationships to God are all set forth through this conceptuality.

Landmarks of a Theocentric Journey

I have made reference to Gustafson's comprehensive theocentric vision, the exploration of which is his agenda and program. We turn now to the exploration itself. It would be misleading to say that the exploration has a starting point in any traditional sense of the phrase. The reason is that Gustafson does not proceed by a series of deductions, so there is no single *principium* that serves as his launching pad. No single epistemological commitment, set of warrants, or even discipline serves as the basis. Oriented toward the complexity of reality as Gustafson is, his "beginning" is the concatenation of a great number of elements in the situation of moral experiences and choice.

When we look at Gustafson's exploration as he reads it from the inside of the situation, we find him reflecting on human beings and societies that are in fact engaged in all sorts of valuings, respondings, and choosings. This is a situation of being and doing, and of both dispositions and virtues, and principles and criteria. This situation is as old as human history itself, and most would agree that this history is tragically marred. The being and doing of human beings is perpetually characterized by rapacious economics, unjust wars, oppressive societies, xenophobic cultures. Gustafson as theologian draws on the mythos of a religious tradition to interpret the "fault" of being and doing, and he concludes that moral life is skewed due to a false centrality human beings give themselves. So deeply rooted and so pervasive is this false, anthropocentric centrality that it is not correctable simply by the natural participations of human beings in larger spheres. The only real correction is a new orientation and discernment guided by the one thing that de-centers not just human beings but all the participating wholes, the one thing that can press considerations beyond any of them, and that is God. In other words, none of the spheres can redeem, and the only thing that can is that which is the condition for the existence and well-being of all spheres.

This is Gustafson's general reading of the situation, and this reading sets the tasks of his exploration. The *question* that presides over and guides the exploration is this: "How does it happen that God is so apprehended that there could be this corrective (redemptive) enlargement of perspective able then to shape the discernments of moral life?" Gustafson's response to this question is a genetics of theocentric piety. And this genetics constitutes his argument, his case. What do we mean by calling it a genetics? In the philosophical sense of the word, a genetics is the making of a case by an indication of the ordered strata that are the conditions of something. Genetics is neither a series of logical deductions from a single premise nor a description of elements of a structure. Gustafson resists both of these methods. Nevertheless, he does see a great number of spheres, processes, and patterns operative in theocentrical moral life. The reason his exploration is a genetics is that instead of simply listing conditions, he shows certain relations of dependence between them. Thus, what he means by piety presupposes the agential character of human being. Nor would piety occur without the historical mediation of a specific religious community. Gustafson's genetic exploration is, therefore, a kind of tracking, a journey. It moves from one place to another, and each place on the journey illumines the origin and basis of theocentric piety. When the exploration is finished, what we have are the "conditions of possibility" of theocentric piety. I hope I do not offend Gustafson by suggesting that this genetic method prevents him from totally departing from the Kantian tradition. True, he is nervous about philosophies and theologies that do a transcendental genetics, that seek conditions of possibilities in transcendental structures. In place of this Gustafson proposes a much wider genetic method that combines general ontology, philosophy of agency, sociology of communities, and many other things. He explores, one might say, a historical transcendental.

What follows is a very abbreviated version of Gustafson's genetics of theocentric piety. Gustafson may well view my version as turning the reader away from the actual course of his analysis, which goes from God to the human being's relation to God to the being and doing of moral life, but any other order would distort the theocentric intention of the exploration. It is clear that Gustafson does not simply start with *God*. As I previously argued, he starts with a situation and a concatenation of realities. Further, he proposes to us a multistep analysis as to how God is known. Hence, his genetics of theocentric piety is a genetics of the knowledge of God, not simply something that posits God as starting point. The ground or basis of theocentric being and doing is uncovered by Gustafson in four moves or explorations, which are an ontology of human historical being, a description of natural piety, a retrieval of the mythos of fault and redemption from a specific religious tradition, and the utilization of the commonsense ontology as confirmatory of theistic piety. All four of these spheres of experience constitute conditions of theocentric piety and ground the discernments and orientations that correct the xenophobic pieties that are so pervasive of human history. Needless to say, all four presuppose and constantly draw on Gustafson's general commonsense ontology of reality.

Gustafson's Ontology of Human Historical Being. Gustafson's ontology of human historical being is distributed throughout his works. Nevertheless, it has a place at the beginning because all the other explorations presuppose it. The first thing to be said about Gustafson's picture of human being is that it occurs in the framework of his commonsense ontology. Accordingly, a human being is an individual but like all real things occurs as part of the patterns and processes of nature. Human beings are an evolving species with a mammalian past and a biologically unforeseeable future. As part of nature the human being is vulnerable to the perils and limitations of nature. If we restricted ourselves to certain passages in Gustafson's work, we might get the impression that Gustafson virtually reduces the human being to the features of his common-sense ontology. This is, of course, not the case. Gustafson's version of moral experience calls for a highly developed account of human agency, a term he prefers to person and personhood. The agency of the individual has been so emphasized and exploited by anthropocentrisms, ancient and modern, that Gustafson is reticent to make too much of it. He does not, therefore, conduct philosophical inquiry into what gives human being an agential character, into imagination, time-consciousness, decisionality, and so forth. Agency is self-evident to him, and he is content to let the human being's experience of its own accountability and capacity for intervention suffice.

Nevertheless, human agency or self-transcending personhood is presupposed in Gustafson's interpretation of a number of things that distinguish the human being as a participating historical being. Thus, when Gustafson considers the power (faculties) of the individual human being, he gives a certain primacy to extrarational features: to desire (Augustine), affections (Edwards), disposition (Edwards), and valuation. These things do not occur in dichotomy with intelligence since they occur in various modes of reflection and self-consciousness. When Gustafson considers the human being's sociality, his retention of human agency enables him to voice the distinctiveness of human being-together, of institutionality, social memory, and traditioning. In fact it is in connection with this distinctive sociality that Gustafson offers a typology of "arenas" of human participation that amounts to what philosophers in one tradition call regional ontologies. The five proposed arenas amount to a typology of human experience of spheres of human participation. The anthropology of human agency in its distinctiveness and continuity with nature and the ontology of spheres of experience provide important grounds for Gustafson's subsequent descriptions. They constitute the initial step in his genetics.

Human Religiousness. The second step of Gustafson's genetic exploration carries him closer to actual historical human life than the more formal descriptions of agency, sociality, and limitation. Gustafson here looks at the human being immersed in everyday social life, and he sees certain very fundamental dispositions that preside over the way human beings relate to things. While these dispositions are primarily manifest as affections, they are not simply emotions like anger or joy because they are directional in character. They are "senses of." I am somewhat unclear as to whether these "senses of " have their location in the interrelations among the human being, the world, and the human other as such or in the more determinate social world of religion. Gustafson's examples of them come from the expressions of religion; however, on the other hand, he claims they are not unique to religion.[2] What yields these "senses of " to Gustafson? Is it a phenomenology of the social world, of human being-in-the-world, or is it the study of the affectional aspect of actual religions?

If the query were addressed to Schleiermacher, the answer would have to be both. Schleiermacher discovers piety in the dependent reciprocity the human being has with the world and in the social embodiment of such in actual religions. I suspect that Gustafson does too. The issue itself may not be very important to Gustafson. What is important is that in the everyday social world and experience of human historical being we find these senses of dependence, gratitude, obligation, remorse, and hope. There is, in other words, a religious dimension to human, historical life.

But Gustafson's analysis of piety does not stop here. He argues that human beings dispose these "senses of " not just toward their specified objects but in conjunction with the arenas or spheres of human experience. Thus nature, one of the arenas, can and does evoke senses of dependence, gratitude, obligation, and so forth. But the sense of human dependence is not restricted to nature, for society and culture also serve as matrices of our being. The reason for this is an important step in that it is in just this interaction with or participation in these arenas that certain strange sorts of questionings arise. We would miss these questions if we considered only the formal dependence or sense of dependence of human being or the isolated phenomenon of gratitude. But in the sphere of society the human being becomes aware of both the resources and the contingencies of society and is prompted to ask, what is really reliable? The same questions can be evoked by the human being's relation to nature or to the self. For reasons he does not state, Gustafson calls these strange questionings "religious questions." His justification presumably is that these are the questions we find persisting in the cultus of all actual religions. The outcome of this step is what Gustafson calls piety. Piety is not something one needs to establish speculatively. We simply find it pervasive of human historical existence. It arises from interworld and interhistorical relations of the human being that paradoxically combine both fulfillments and disappointments and thus prompt questionings that do not find their answers in the spheres themselves. Gustafson does not say this, but he implies that piety by its very nature is directed through and beyond the spheres that occasion it. It has, one might say, an open horizon.

The Traditioning Religious Community. With the third step, Gustafson draws into his considerations the specific religious community and its tradition. This

---

[2]James M. Gustafson, *Theology and Ethics,* vol. 1 of *Ethics from a Theocentric Perspective* (Chicago: University of Chicago Press, 1981) 199.

is the step one misses in the religious philosophy of Henry Nelson Wieman, and the reason for it in Gustafson's work is clear. One whole dimension of Gustafson's perceptiveness is created by social and historical science, by Ernst Troeltsch, Max Weber, and George Herbert Mead. And while it is unthinkable to him that any historical tradition could have a priori authority, he nevertheless turns to it as a potential source of wisdom, a heritage deserving a serious response. Accordingly, Gustafson is not an Enlightenment neologist, a trasher of positive religion. His sociological realism makes it impossible for him to think of piety or religion as anything else than embodied in tradition and institutions. It is inconceivable to him that the actual redemptive transformation of human beings occurs at some general level over and above the reciprocities of an actual community and the powerful mediation of its symbolism.

Two important things occur in this turn to the religious community. First, piety itself takes on the historical embodiment of a historically located tradition. Since Gustafson's turn is to the Christian tradition, piety becomes monotheistic piety. For Schleiermacher, piety itself has a kind of entelechy toward monotheism. Gustafson is silent on this issue. With the exception of certain negations, he is also silent about how piety would take a monotheistic turn. His negations are directed against attempts to establish this turn by some rational theology operating over and above all historical determinancy and also against any appeal to direct experience of God. Beyond these negations, Gustafson simply tells us that monotheistic piety occurs this way, a sociological and historical observation.

Second, Gustafson's turn to the specific Christian community yields something that is a persisting part of the mythos of that community and that he can appropriate, namely, the theme of human fault and its correction. Gustafson's appropriation of this theme finally turns up in the metaphor of contraction and expansion, or narrowing and enlarging. If there is any one unity of the various facets of fault, it seems to be that they all effect a narrowing of the human being. Whether fault is misplaced confidence or distorted reason, it has the character of false centering of the human being itself, an incapacity to habituate its dispositions, set its agendas, formulate its obligations beyond certain narrowed boundaries. This being the case, the correction of fault or redemption is a real transformation of the human being throughout its many dimensions of agency, inclinations, and communities so that its narrowness is enlarged. Needless to say, piety itself becomes determinate and embodied when it occurs in a community focused on the fault and its redemption. Hence, in Gustafson's interpretation, piety is stratified and thus is not reducible to simply the natural piety of the so-called "natural man."

The Indirect Mediation of Divine Purpose through World Processes. Gustafson's analysis of the origin of theocentric piety does not stop with a description of piety formed in the traditioning of a specific religious community. The religious community and its tradition is the specific historical matrix of the knowledge of God and the source of such primary symbols for God as Sustainer, Judge, and Redeemer. But God is not just a meaning correlate of the problems and interrelations of a specific community. God has something to do with world process, and apart from a certain reflectiveness about the way world process works, the question of God does not even arise.

Reflection and Response to the way things are is not the invention of modern science. Something of the sort has always been part of specific religions, a classic expression of which is Genesis 1. There is, in other words, a sense of being sustained by whatever brings life into being that characterizes the religious cultus. So far, Gustafson is still talking about human experience, piety, and tradition. He takes a step beyond this when he observes the many and varied efforts in history to determine just what nature itself is. The latest and most successful of these efforts is carried out in the sciences. The result is a view of nature that can be distinguished from earlier views. This view arises from the enormous success of the sciences in grasping very specific and delicate conditions of things. And this has led to an evolutionary understanding of nature in which nature is a succession of constantly changing, ever adapting states of affairs that obtain persisting and stable patterns only to undergo eventual destabilization and transformation. Gustafson's term for this succession that produces stabilities and conditions of stabilities is "ordering process."

Now if the very meaning of God has something to do with world processes, then piety will be impelled to reflect on God's relation to this ordering process. It will fill in the meaning of such symbols as God the Sustainer by drawing on the description of how nature works. Gustafson assures us that this "filling in" is not a natural theology. He perceives no deductive route from the studies of the sciences or from more general depictions of nature to piety's deity. On the other hand, piety has no deity if it cannot in any sense relate the deity to the way things are, to world processes, to ordering processes. This relating is, therefore, an important theological task. The outcome of the task is modest. It does not deliver a "knowledge of God." First, it shows that piety's primary symbols for God have plausibility in the universe as we experience it and know it. From piety's point of view, the various conditions of existence and well-being so minutely studied by the natural and social sciences are not demonstrations of God's existence but signs of God's activity. Second, the reflective appropriation of these signs assists piety in specifying the meaning of God and the nature of God's activity, namely as Sustainer, which seems to mean serving as the condition of the conditions studied by science; as Judge, which means the condition of the consequences visited on destructive movements in world process; and as Redeemer, which means the condition of certain renewals when processes become fated or oppressive.

What we have just traversed is one person's version of Gustafson's genetics of theocentric piety, his argument expressed as a series of moves from one grounding condition to another. Conducted in the overall framework is a commonsense ontology of world process and history. Gustafson's genetics proceeds from a specific ontology of human historical being and arenas of human experience to an interpretation of human religiousness or piety, to the specific traditioning of the religious community, to a confirmatory reflection drawing on pertinent sources for world processes, for the way things are. This is Gustafson's route *to* God, his grounds for theocentrism. Once he is at this place, he is ready for another journey, from theocentric piety to an approach to human being and doing. I shall not attempt to reproduce the checkpoints of this journey. The journey itself constitutes another argument, namely that God, God's purposes, or God's "enabling and requiring" are sufficiently manifest to provide clues for what we should be and do, in other words, for moral life.

Breaks in the Theocentric Trail

The tone of this exposition should make it clear how deeply sympathetic I am with this theocentric program. Accordingly, my critical comments are intended more to assist than undermine that program. Some of Gustafson's critics are offended by what Gustafson does not say at the point of classic Christian doctrines. My focus here is also on what Gustafson does not say, but the omissions I shall be concerned with are what look like lacunae in the argument, breaks in Gustafson's theocentric trail. I call attention to them in three questions: (1) What are Gustafson's reasons for affirming God at all? (2) What does Gustafson mean by God, especially as a power functioning in world process? (3) How does God or the knowledge of God provide clues to *value-oriented* being and doing, being and doing in the pursuit of worthy ends?

The Knowledge of God. Few would question a description of Gustafson's program as a "radical monotheism." Theocentric piety is a monotheistic piety. But how does Gustafson take the step to monotheistic conviction? In posing this question we must keep in mind that Gustafson's intent is objectivist, that he is critical of any merely symbolic monotheism, any mere historicism that eschews the truth question. The truth about God appears to be his passion. We should also keep in mind his determination to pursue a trail between the rock of natural theology and the hard place of fideism. Accordingly, he cannot take the cognitive step to monotheism by means of the arguments of a theological metaphysics or appeals to the authority of tradition and its texts. Does Gustafson's journey from the general grid of commonsense ontology and its application to a philosophy of human being, piety, tradition, and finally reflection on world process constitute an answer to this question? The genetics tells us something about how theocentric piety originates. Does it give us this piety's own warrant, its own grounds, for an affirmation of a power that is "the ultimate power [for] the conditions for human (and other) possibilities"? The final step of the genetics of piety clearly does not. Its contribution is a statement of the *congruity* and *plausibility* of piety's God with the world as we know it. The first two steps clearly do not. They articulate certain natural and agential features of human beings, and the "senses of " and "religious questions" of human piety. The most that can be said about the referent of these "senses of " is that it is an open horizon.

Does the third step, the move to the specific religious community and its tradition, provide the grounds for affirming God? Gustafson is surely right when he argues that piety, belief in God, and the affectional habituation toward God all occur in the concrete context of a religious community. But the correctness is of a historical, sociological description. It does not in this form provide us with piety's actual grounds, even the possibility for granting objective existence to a power that is the very condition of all conditions. The reason this third step to the specific religious community does not amount to a warrant for belief is that for Gustafson the traditioning of the religious community does not have a priori cognitive status. All of tradition's claims, including presumably its claim about God, must be assessed and critically established. But this assessing or critical establishing does not occur toward piety's monotheistic claim in either the steps that precede or the steps that succeed Gustafson's move to tradition. Accordingly, there seems to be a break on the trail, something unstated in the journey to theocentric piety, that is grounded in God as an objective reality. I do not raise this question in order to press Gustafson back into either natural theology or fideism. Other theologians have proposed ways between these alternatives. But in its present form, a description of tradition's forming of the conviction about God, it looks like a fideistic appeal.

The Meaning of God. What does Gustafson mean by God? Several things are clear at the outset. He does not regard God as a categorical entity that then can be the object of some discrete, and locating, act of meaning. He has, in other words, a developed sense of the mystery and transcendence of God that constantly strains and breaks the language directed to God. Second, Gustafson is aggressively opposed to anthropomorphic depictions of God, which, more specifically, means the viewing of God on the model of human agency. He does, however, appropriate some anthropomorphic symbolic language in the tradition, hence God as Sustainer, Judge, and Redeemer. The way this language is given content is by specifying the world functions of God. Further, there is one world function that is definitional, that articulates what we are talking about when we say the word *God* and that is the functioning of ordering. God names whatever it is that orders the world processes on which not only human beings but all things depend. What is not quite clear is the content of this language.

Let me develop the question in three steps. First, Gustafson does affirm what looks like a distinction between God the Orderer and the ordering processes constituting nature that are studied so closely by the sciences. Is there any difference in content in this distinction? Is there any difference between saying that the world is constituted by a variety of ordering processes and saying that the world is ordered by God? If there is a difference, it does not appear to be cognitively establishable. What is cognitively accessible are the orderings, that is, the conditions of possibilities of nature and history. Now Gustafson does say that these orderings are *signs* or indicators of God's ordering. Are they, we must ask, signs of an ordering that has any different content than the orderings we know directly? Even if they are, it is an unknowable content. What has happened is that Gustafson has offered us a functional definition of God, but its content is not differentiable from the perceivable orderings of world process.

There is a certain language in Gustafson's interpretation of God that might suggest a content that is distinguishable from the manifestation of the way things are. This is the teleological element in Gustafson's view of God. Thus, Gustafson can talk about God's "purposes." He can say that God is the "determiner of the ultimate destiny of things."[3] He can speak of God's "governance" and even of God's "enabling and requiring." In my judgment this is an anthropomorphic discourse. Whether it is or not, it surely is a teleological discourse. I cannot imagine any governing occurring that has no aims whatsoever. This teleological or purposing element may then be how Gustafson distinguishes the content of divine ordering from the perceived ordering of world processes. The difference then would be that all specific world processes or orderings have as *their* conditions a larger activity that arranges them in some way in relation to each other under certain aims. But if this is the case, it pushes us to a third question.

Why does Gustafson define God by means of the *ordering* aspect of world process, by which he means the setting of conditions of possibility? The world of Gustafson's own commonsense ontology is a world in which conditions and continuities are perpetually being destroyed, or transformed, giving way to other states of affairs. If God names simply the conditions-establishing power, then the nisus or creativity that is constantly pressing the conditions to some-

---

[3]James M. Gustafson, *Ethics and Theology,* vol. 2 of *Ethics from a Theocentric Perspective* (Chicago: University of Chicago Press, 1984) 293.

thing else must be the anti-God, the demonic element in things. I think it is clear that this is not Gustafson's position, and in fact he has some passages where he assigns to God both ordering of stabilities and destruction and de-stabilizing.[4] But this returns us to our initial question about a differentiable content in the meaning of God. If God names the ordering-destroying power of world process, how is God in content any different from whatever simply happens in world process? This, too, appears to be a break on the theocentric trail. And it brings us to our final question.

The Goodness of God. How does God provide clues to a value-oriented being and doing? Or put another way, how does Gustafson get from God the Or-derer indicated by patterns and processes of the world to criteria for what is *worthy* and to what may assist the discernments of moral life? It goes without saying that one can discern conditions of something else's existence, survival, and even well-being in a value-neutral way. One can come to know, with the help of the biologist, that certain species of South American frogs will not sur-vive their predators if they lose the toxic secretions of their skin. Presumably, the frogs themselves value their toxicity, but the knowledge of that condition tells us nothing about what is or is not a worthy aim. According to Gustafson, it is possible to grasp God's enabling and requiring, and this provides us as-sistance in moral choice. In his formulation, we do not perceive God's pur-posing and ordering directly; instead, we must study actual patterns and processes as signs of such.

Again I have three questions. First, are the signs of God's requiring re-stricted to the conditions or patterns of stability? Although the definition of God as Orderer of such conditions may imply otherwise, I think Gustafson's answer is negative. If the existing conditions of things were the only signs of

---

[4]For instance, Gustafson criticizes the anthropocentric view that sees catastrophic natural events (earthquakes, floods) as simply judgments on sinful human beings. Gustafson quite properly argues that these are "natural aspects of nature and not or-dered toward the survival or well-being of one planetary species" (*Ethics,* 1:209). The implication is that these natural aspects are destructive not just of human life but of various stabilities, species, in nature itself. Given such a view, why would Gustafson see these "destructive" aspects of nature as signs of God's *absence* or of the nondivine? And if God is defined as ordering process, surely he must see disordering, destabiliz-ing aspects of nature that way. Gustafson's use of the symbol Judge does in some way attribute disordering events to God (ibid., 1:246). A consistent position would argue that piety senses its dependence on God in both positive and negative forms, on the sustaining conditions of life, and on the destroying of those, which continues con-stantly in nature. If that is the case, why is God defined as *ordering* process?

requiring, it would totally exclude any element of creativity that presses for the transformation of those conditions. It would render whatever set of conditions that exists at a time, the nation-state, the human species, tennis clubs, into things merely to be preserved forever. We conclude then that the signs of God's requirements cannot be limited simply to conditions of stability.

Second, are *all* conditions and creativities signs of God's enabling and requiring? If they are, then whatever has happened and is happening should have happened. The evolutionary development of the human species is as desirable as the atomic holocaust that ends it, creating new conditions for a planet to heal itself. I think Gustafson's answer to this question is also negative. In one passage he says that the ordering of life in the world *can* be indications of the divine orderings.[5] I conclude that for Gustafson, not all but some conditions (patterns) and creativities are signs of the divine ordering.

Third, how are those conditions that are the indicators of divine ordering identified? Even if we acknowledge that there are divine purposes and that some patterns and processes indicate them, how do we identify which ones? It is just at this point that there appears to be another break in the trail. In one passage Gustafson seems to grant a kind of self-evidence to certain fundamental values, for instance, to life and respect for persons.[6] One could argue that such self-evident worthy things are clues to what God is enabling and requiring. But such an argument undercuts itself since intrinsically evident value makes the grasp of divine enabling and requiring superfluous. The dilemma this set of questions poses for us is that the divine enabling and requiring is either read off of any and all conditions of possibility we are able to discern, in which case there is no specific clue to what is worthy and to be chosen, or is read off of some selected set of conditions, which requires some basis of identification other than the processes themselves.

Breaks in Gustafson's Method

The breaks, that is, obscurities, undeveloped points, in Gustafson's argument, or case, for theocentric piety are not mere oversights. They are outcomes of the way method shapes the whole program. The breaks on the theocentric trail are themselves accounted for by certain methodological turns. And this presses our analysis beneath Gustafson's genetics to some of the principles of its operation. This step does not indicate disagreement but agreement with Gustafson's own principle of the primacy of subject matter to

---

[5]Gustafson, *Ethics,* 2:283.

[6]Ibid., 2:300.

method. It explores whether or not Gustafson consistently carries out this principle.

Let us restate, in the form of a thesis, the dilemma with which Gustafson's route to theocentric piety leaves us. If divine activity is simply identical to perceived world processes, with whatever happens, it cannot provide a basis for *moral* content. If divine activity is to be a contentful guide to moral life, then some locus of its manifestation that itself provides a principle for discovering divine activity in world processes is required. This thesis does not exclude divine activity from world processes, but it does argue that world processes as such do not manifest it as morally pertinent content. The thesis pushes us to the experience of God at a more determinate level than the reflective interpretation of world processes. In my view both Jewish and Christian faiths are created by and centered in an experience of divine activity that is more determinate than world processes as such and that has a moral content, namely the experience of redemption. Now it is clear that Gustafson's genetics of theocentric piety does in fact describe a determinate locus of the experience of God, namely piety and tradition. In principle he has a source that is not merely coincident with world processes. But for some reason redemption, or correction as he calls it, plays only a marginal role in his formulation of the knowledge, nature, and goodness of God. This is, in my judgment, the major reason for the breaks in his way of establishing the meaning of God and the clues to moral discernment. Furthermore, there are reasons for the marginality of redemption in the argument, having to do with the way tradition and truth are treated. We launch, then, an analysis of Gustafson's method as it concerns these three themes, all of which shape each other: redemption, tradition, and truth.

The Marginality of Redemption. It is clear that Gustafson does not see redemption as marginal to theocentric ethics. It does, however, appear to be marginal to his genetics, his journey and account of how God is apprehended. Because fault is a contracting or narrowing, redemption is an enlargement of the human being, and in three areas of reason or world-construal, the heart and affections, and responsibility and action. It occurs in the matrix and with the assistance of the first-order language of the religious community. And it grounds the discernments of the moral life.

What actually happens in the redemptive correcting of human fault? At a formal level, Gustafson draws on his philosophy of human agency and sociality to say that certain faculties are affected, that dispositions and a readiness to participate are created, and that all of this occurs in the reciprocities of a specific community. As to the content of the transformation of fault, it is an enlarging of perspective. In other words, Gustafson's theology of redemption focuses on the problem of the *scope* of human responsibility. Thus the redemption of reason is an expansion of reason's vision of things. The redemption of desires is an expansion of the narrowed desires of inordinate self-love pursing the self's power. Fault, then, as Gustafson says, is a "shrinking of the self and community."

There is nothing in what I am about to say that Gustafson's own framework or convictions could not say. It is, however, a different emphasis. When the problem of scope is the focus of a theology of redemption, what is omitted is redemption's normative content. To put the issue in the language of one of Gustafson's favorite theologians, "consent to being" does express the enlarged scope of true virtue. But for Edwards, what is being consented to is beauty or loveliness, the highest example of which is the unqualified exercise of benevolence. Gustafson's logic of redemption is a move from A to B, from contraction of fault, A, to its redemptive enlargement, B. When scope is not so emphasized, we have a three-step logic. Thus, certain fundamental human desires, faculties, capacities, interrelations, dispositions, and the like (A) undergo distortion and corruption (B), which in turn are transformed (C). But the transformation is not simply a return to A, the desires, nor are they simply expanded. Under the effect of the divine benevolence, these corrupted desires, even fundamental, biologically rooted desires, occur in a perspective or affection of benevolence to things. If the redemption of reason is our example, the basic human eros or desire to understand, experience, and know evoked by the mystery of things (A) becomes the idolatrous, self-securing desire to know absolutely, to be secured by that knowledge (B) only under the conditions of redemption to become a desire informed by benevolence, a benevolent and empathetic interest in the autonomies, mysteries, of all other things.

This focus on scope at the expense of moral content of redemption is one of the things responsible for the marginality of redemption in Gustafson's understanding of the basis for affirming God, the way God is known. As a theme, redemption comes into the picture after the genetics of theocentric piety and the account of the knowledge of God are in place. Thus Gustafson goes directly from the observation that monotheistic piety is formed in the determinancy of the religious community to the indicators or signs of God's ordering. But he does this without specifying how the correction of fault experienced in that community grounds that monotheistic piety. It is just this step I miss in his method. Without that step, namely redemption, and redemption in the sense of a moral content, that which is apperceived in the religious community is more or less coincident with world processes as such. In other words, Gustafson has left redemption out of his genetics of theocentric piety, at least out of the steps in the apprehension of God. It enters later as something that creates the ground of discerning what God is enabling and requiring, but by this time, the very meaning of God in distinction from world processes is elusive.

Gustafson's Sociology of Tradition. The general reason Gustafson is reticent to explore redemption in connection with his explication of the knowledge of God is evident. He fears such a step would endanger the theocentric character of his argument, the grounding of redemption in God and not vice versa. But redemption is marginal to the argument for other reasons, among which is the way tradition and traditioning are handled. It is important not to permit Gustafson's critical and selective use of Christian doctrines to obscure the important, even central, place tradition has for him. In his view the specific religious community, its traditioned past, and its ongoing traditioning are an inescapable part of human historicity. Tradition is a past inheritance that has present meaning in acts of consent, operates primarily in a first-order language, is available in selective retrieval, and functions to bestow values and to shape and guide present responses. Gustafson's own sifting and selecting from that heritage has yielded fault and redemption in a theocentric perspective. Yet, for some reason he does not draw on that retrieval in formulating the bases of monotheistic piety. Thus, while he can acknowledge that monotheistic piety does arise in connection with the community and its tradition, he does not draw on the content of tradition in determining the meaning of God. He does use the tradition's language (Sustainer, Judge, Redeemer), but the meaning of the language appears to be determined more by analyses of world processes than by the redemption that is funding that language.

Since tradition and the matrix of the community are part of the genetics, why does not Gustafson explore how redemption itself grounds monotheistic piety? Note the difference between Gustafson's way of handling tradition and his way of handling the question of God in world process. In the latter he works as a theologian, pressing a definition and defending it in terms of the way things are. In the former he works as a social scientist, and the way things are is the way traditioning works. In Gustafson's view, it is important to retrieve aspects of tradition critically, but at this point he does not retrieve. The reason is only in part his strong criticism of precritical and unhistorical usages of tradition. It may also be the assumption that tradition itself has little or no cognitive status. Tradition offers a matrix and framework for knowing, but it mediates no realities. Thus, Gustafson's answer to why we consent to tradition, especially at the point of belief in God, is simply descriptive: "They come to construe the world theocentrically."[7] A more theological and truth-oriented answer would be that human beings consent to tradition because it illumines and mediates the way things are. Thus the mythos of human fault and redemption does more than preserve a past conviction; it uncovers a perdur-

---

[7]Ibid., 1:234.

able though, of course, ever-changing reality. And this is what grounds the conviction of monotheistic piety.

Gustafson's Philosophy of Truth. There is nothing dogmatic or absolute about Gustafson's sociological and historical way of handling tradition. It is more an emphasis than an exclusion since he is convinced at a general level that tradition is a source of insight. How do we account for that emphasis? As I have already suggested, Gustafson's repudiation of the precritical handling of religion makes him reticent to make what may look like authoritative appeals to it. In addition, the emphasis has something to do with certain obscurities, perhaps even tensions, in Gustafson's philosophy of truth, which means also his way of understanding the relation between particularity and universality. This comment is meant more as a query to Gustafson than a direct criticism. First, it is clear that Gustafson's program is guided by the following truth-question: Do religious claims attest to "the way things are"? It is also clear that he sees all these claims as occurring historically, contextually, and perspectively, therefore not in the form of timeless ideas.

What does it mean, then, to establish the truth of something? Gustafson's criticism of narrative theology shows us it means more than simply showing something's coherent meaning.[8] Truth-claims apparently express some enduring character of the way things are, and to grasp this requires surpassing particularity to whatever larger whole is able to render the claim intelligible. I would raise two questions. First, if the pertinent passages are those concerning the way the sciences test religious claims, thus rendering a certain plausibility, this seems to be a version of coherence theory. This is because the norm for the testing is congruence between claimed things. But while incongruity may falsify a truth-claim, does congruity establish it? The elusiveness here is a kind of unresolved tension between an idealist, coherence theory and a realist one. Second, how do particularity and universality constitute the situation of the truth-question? According to Gustafson, particularity must be transcended toward what is in some sense universal in the truth undertaking. In what sense then is universality present in Gustafson's claims, if at all? He offers a number of accounts of human being, regions of being, fault, and redemption that are not simply descriptions of particular space-time events or even epochs. How is this trans-particularity related to truth? At every point Gustafson wants to assure us that we cannot transcend our particularity to the timeless. Toward what then do we transcend it? I suspect that an irresolution at this point prevents Gustafson from making too much of the universalizable character of tradition in its particularity. Thus, when he takes up tradition,

---

[8]Ibid., 1:29-30.

he remains a social scientist of particularity and tradition and not a theologian exploring its truth.

Our messy symphonic poem calls for a very brief coda that summarizes the major themes. I have argued that certain themes of Gustafson's method (redemption, tradition, truth) help account for what I have called breaks or lacunae in his genetics of theocentric ethics. The major step in my argument was that what makes Gustafson's project *theo*centric, namely God, is sufficiently coincident with all world processes so as not to be able to provide very specific clues as to what is worthy or valuable. Further, the reason for this elusiveness of the meaning of God was a method that acknowledged but rushed on by the cognitive function of tradition and the redemption that occurs there. This in turn has something to do with certain assumptions about tradition as a source and mediator of truth and the sense in which truth transcends particularity. If this is right, we have God as the condition of an enlarging scope of human moral life but not so much the condition of its moral content.

FARLEY DISCUSSION

Robert Audi: At one point you said that self-evident worthy things, like respect for persons, make arguments about divine enabling and requiring look superfluous. Your point is that if something is self-evidently valuable, we don't need divine assurance, and we don't need any theological ground to perceive its value. It occurs to me that there is motivational relevance in discerning God's will, as well as epistemological relevance for justifying a warranted decision. Also, when we think about how broad the ideal of respect for persons is, even if it is self-evident, it is far from clear what that really comes to in concrete cases. Gustafson's ethics seems to show us a way for a theocentric vision to guide us in concrete situations of decisions.

Farley: The problem I was raising had to do with the meaning of God. The text I was referring to is the passage where Gustafson speaks of discerning God's activity in the world. By discerning it, then, one can presumably determine what God means in content. As I recall Gustafson's language, God is the ultimate source of the conditions of possibilities of all actions. Now, does that source have any content distinguishable from what the sciences tell us about the world's operations and processes? That is the question. Then I speculated about a possible answer, namely, that there are certain self-evident values. The only point is that if these values are self-evident, one cannot argue that we need to discern what God is doing in the world to grasp them. That is what I mean by their superfluity.

Audi: I understand what you are saying, but it looks to me as if two points are at stake. I believe what I said in response to your point about self-evident values is at least prima facie reasonable. A value of a general kind could be self-evidently a value, yet we could still derive considerable guidance in realizing the value from a theocentric ethic. But you are now pointing out, given the conception of God, that there is no reason to take as normative a discernment of what the ultimate power is enabling us to do. That is a rather different point. I have one question about that. You have characterized Gustafson's conception of God rather unqualifiedly as functionalist. God names whatever it is that orders the world processes on which all things depend. It looks to me as though Gustafson is saying that any satisfactory conception of God must account for that aspect of the divine nature. I don't think he has committed himself to defining God functionally so that no intrinsic characterization is involved. You, yourself, point to teleological elements in his thought that seem to add something to the characterization of God. Why must we take him to be exhaustively characterizing God in functionalist terms, so that God turns out to be just anything that could conceivably order the universe?

Farley: Two things prompt me to take him that way, although I don't really take his intention that way. I think he is up to something else; that is why I call it a break in the trail. One thing is his language. His language about God is functional almost throughout. Wherever one discovers a definition, God is what it is that enables and requires, God is the determiner of destiny, God is the source of conditions of possibilities, and so forth. That is the main reason I take him that way. The other reason, which is a little more substantial, has to do with what Gustafson means by ordering. His world view, as reconstructed from his ontology, is an evolutionary one. You have a series of successions in which things are ordered, transformed, retransformed, and so forth. It is a flow of disordered order. Now, if God is the source of the conditions of the possibility of that, God is as much the source of the conditions of the possibility of the destruction of this galaxy, or of the holocaust, as of the rise of the Roman Empire. All that is ordering. If that is the case, given his method, on what grounds do we propose something that is morally more selective, or more discriminate, or more determinate? That is the problem I am raising. I think there are materials in his work to make a proposal, and I think he probably intends it. I just don't see it in the way his argument is made as a genetic argument.

Harlan R. Beckley (Washington and Lee University): In respect to your claim that redemption comes later and is not part of the genetic argument, what about the sense of possibilities evoked in the five arenas? Would that provide some explanation and justification for what Gustafson says later about redemption? Doesn't redemption come earlier than you suggest?

Farley: I see that material as part of the genetics I called an analysis of human agency. The content, including the arenas, looks like a rather general or formal analysis of agency; the human being is in reciprocal relations to nature, history, and the other arenas. In other words, the level of analysis looks parallel to what we find in Schlei- ermacher's *Reden*. There is some cultural determinancy, but it doesn't specifically draw on a theology of sin and redemption. It looks like a kind of historically determined fundamental ontology of human piety more than the explication of the radical cor- ruption of the human being and its possible correction and redemption in the sense of the mythos of the Jewish or Christian community. If that material is in there, I have not read the text carefully. If it is there, then of course redemption occurs earlier.

John P. Reeder, Jr.: Could you expand a bit on your distinction between scope and moral content? If you intend to distinguish between the enlargement of responsibility and concepts such as respect for persons, I think I understand. But I would have thought that the enlargement of scope involved concern for the whole. Yet you seem to dis- tinguish between the enlargement of scope and benevolence. I am not clear exactly how scope and moral content are related.

Farley: It is possible that my reading of Gustafson at this point is fostering a distinc- tion he will not accept. It may be that I am reacting to the formal character of the language of narrowness and enlargement, and that if one went further one might dis- cover a kind of philosophy or phenomenology of moral life. But if one pressed theo- logically for the structure and dynamics of human sin, let's say, and for what it means to break the power of idolatry, I think a whole lot more would be disclosed than just the provincialism of the human perspective and its expansion. There is a kind of de- provincializing that occurs to human beings when they move from a small town, let us say, to world experience. However, that may not be necessarily a moral develop- ment; it may be developing in the opposite direction. Deprovincialization does not itself look to me like a sufficient account of redemption, although it is important, and I don't want to play it down.

William Schweiker (University of Iowa): If I understand your question and argument, it runs something like this. What are the warrants for the move from piety to a con- strual of God so that we have differentiations to distinguish the divine from ordering processes? If we do not have the warrant to make that move, the position is difficult theologically; it can't distinguish God from ordering processes and is deficient mor- ally. Your own argument seems to agree with Gustafson that appeal to precritical un- derstandings of tradition or revelation are problematic, but Gustafson's construal seems problematic to you. You turn to the experience of redemption within a particular community, understood as the experience of benevolence to the good. You see be- nevolence as the warrant for moving to a distinction between the divine and ordering processes. From a theocentric perspective the question then becomes, benevolent for whom? Within a relational understanding, the good for whom? I think Gustafson has a way of making this distinction that also argues within the tradition and within a particular community's claim about redemption, and that has to do with the experience of harmony that demands certain sacrifices as seen in the life of Jesus of Nazareth. I think he operates within a particular tradition and makes some distinctions between the ordering processes and the divine.

Farley: I see that material there, but I don't see him drawing on it in the way he grounds his discourse about the meaning of God. I don't see anything in principle that would forbid that, I just don't see him doing it. In some places the discourse sounds to me very much like the set of definitions we find in the works of Henry Nelson Weiman. It could be that one could fill that in in the way you are suggesting. The closest Gustafson comes to filling it in is with his metaphors of Judge, Sustainer, and so forth. But when he moves on to say what he means by those metaphors, he moves to cosmological or quasi-metaphysical concepts. So I am not sure what the warrants are that would say that God is a certain sort of being, that God's judgment responds to certain sorts of things.

Ian McPherson (Covenant Presbyterian Church, Phoenix): You have suggested that world process equals God for Gustafson. Kaufman suggested that nature equals God in Gustafson. One of the burdens of being a thinking, modern person is that supernaturalism is not part of the package. The only thing you have is world process or nature. It seems to me that Gustafson has a subjective pole that goes along with confronting world process and nature. Through piety, and as part of an affectional approach to life, one makes discernments, construals, and responses. In some ways that seems like an alternative to a supernaturalistic scheme. What does Gustafson have to work with other than the world process and the nature of things and how we construe and respond?

Farley: I don't quite agree with Kaufman that Gustafson's view is that God is more or less coincident with nature. I wouldn't agree that in Gustafson's view God is identical with or coincident with world processes. His language differentiates them clearly. I am raising a slightly different question. Given the way his argument emerges, I am only saying that there is difficulty giving content to the intended distinction. Supernaturalism raises another area of discussion. In the past it has had cosmological connotations, for example, a two-story cosmos or a two-story understanding of reality with certain views of miracles, and so forth. But if one means by supernaturalism any theological or philosophical-theological tradition that makes a distinction between God and the world order, then I think Gustafson intends to be a supernaturalist, though not in certain cosmological senses of the word. I guess I do not see Jim Gustafson as a Spinozist. What I am raising is a break of clarity in the argument.

Edgar A. Towne (Christian Theological Seminary, Indianapolis): Both you and Kaufman have in one sense complimented Gustafson on this piety; you have said there are redemptive or personal themes lurking in his piety that don't find expression in the theology. Might it be possible that the way he construes the world has already taken its toll within the piety, so that it is not possible for him to use certain metaphors in theology and it is not possible for him to claim that God can be distinguished cognitively from the world? Maybe his position does not permit the kind of corrections you are asking for. I think the nub of it is the distinction between piety and theology.

Farley: My criticism comes from within the program or the intent of theocentric ethics. Let's go back and distinguish as Schleiermacher did between generic piety as the religiousness that simply attends the human spirit and the embodied, historical form that piety takes in a religious cultus. I think something like that distinction operates in Gustafson. On his route to warrants and grounds for the meaning of God, Gustafson analyzes piety in the arenas and spheres in the formal and general sense. But he does not really move to the embodied form of piety in a historical community whose redemption was determined in some way through the experience of the breaking of the power of sin; that is not very operative in his genetics. Both pieties are obviously operating in the theologian, but I think one was bracketed or suspended in the genetic argument.

Theological Revision
and the Burden
of Particular Identity

F or the purposes of this symposium it will be appropriate to identify those particular themes to which I do not choose to give prominence, so as to locate the fragment of the wider debate that I think I should be taking on in this particular context. I thus attempt to identify my specific stewardship, rather than to pursue all possible rewarding lines of analysis. This is not to deny that other themes might be equally promising or rewarding.

First, I do not speak in behalf of myself, John H. Yoder. My writings are cited by James Gustafson in volume one of his *Ethics from a Theocentric Perspective* as representing a significant alternative position, which he says he respects, although he does not choose to converse with it. Gustafson sees my thought as exemplifying a problem stated by Alasdair MacIntyre, which MacIntyre exaggerates. The reference to my thought has an odd function not only in that, as said, it is cited but not conversed with directly. The description of what my writings represent in Gustafson's mind does not correspond with my understanding of what I am doing. My function for James Gustafson is not that of a straw man, sketched to represent a position too easily rejected. Neither am I an authentic interlocutor whose work would be read carefully enough and interpreted fully enough that the reader of the Gustafson volume would know what I am saying. I rather represent a landmark visible farther down a road that Gustafson has already chosen not to take. For that reason, although it might be personally interesting, it would not be functional for the present symposium for me to pursue the specific questions that allusion would evoke.

Second, I do not propose to speak in favor of any particular alternative interpretations of specific practical ethical issues, like the four themes that are chosen for specimen treatment in the second volume. Gustafson's earlier books enriched us all by looking at case issues from the perspectives of first-order abstraction, like his Protestant/Catholic typology. Those metaethical tools threw light on issues of substantial moral decision. In these two books, on the other hand, the abstractness moves one level higher, and thereby sets aside for some other book or some other conference conversations that might be called for about either general substantive norms or specific casuistic quandaries that people in the ethical field generally try to use to test how their systems are working.

Third, I do not propose, except marginally, to cross-reference the earlier corpus of Gustafson's writings. Stanley Hauerwas has suggested that to some people these two volumes will represent a change from the earlier work and for others they will not; I shall not pursue that question.

Fourth, I choose rather for the purposes of this conversation to seek to represent the classical mainstream of Western Protestant moral thought, which is not otherwise represented by the participants on our panel. We have here no heirs of Jonathan Edwards. We have no one like Visser't Hooft, Hendrik Kraemer, or Arendt von Leeuwen to represent the perspectives of world mission and Christian unity. There is no Emil Brunner or Carl F. H. Henry to represent the neoconservative apologetic forms of the Reformed tradition. There is no one from the radical neo-Reformation tradition represented in Europe by the "Theology of Crisis" of the 1920s or since then by Karl Barth. Nor is there any Jewish position represented in the composition of our group, an omission that in the last decades has increasingly come to be seen as of constitutive importance. There is no one like Krister Stendahl, Marcus Barth, or Paul van Buren who feels that it is important to have learned from conversation with Jews. There is no hard Niebuhrian.

What all of the above-named positions have in common is that taken together they could be found in the institutional and demographic mainstream of Protestantism that Gustafson purports to represent. I would call this the "classical Reformed" (CR) position. It differs from the post-Reformation Roman Catholic view (a) with regard to the place of the abiding normative quantity of the earliest Christian tradition, as represented in canonical Scripture, (b) with regard to the place of the contemporary reading of the Scriptures in the assembled congregations as an indispensable element of their valid interpretation, (c) with regard to the critical leverage provided by the Scriptures and the congregation to question the perceptions of "the nature of things" that are enshrined in the ethos of establishment, and (d) with regard to the adequacy of the existing ecclesiastical hierarchy to implement either the unity of the body of Christ or that body's permanent self-criticism.

The symposium would be crippled if there were no voice for the mainstream ecumenical Protestant establishment from which James Gustafson comes and to which he speaks. With his mentor H. Richard Niebuhr in the middle, with Moltmann and Barth to his left, and Ramsey and Reinhold Niebuhr on his right, Gustafson takes for granted a middle-American, middle-Protestant culture's implicit theology. His many unfootnoted references to what others think, to standard arguments on all his major themes, allude to that mental world. It is, therefore, that world whose advocate I should attempt to be, discerning the fundamental points at which Gustafson takes his distance from it. That distance from his own baseline is more pertinent than the ways both he and his mainline reformed matrix would differ from high Catholicism or Anglicanism, from Fundamentalism, from early Christianity, or from Quakerism. If Gustafson's claim were to maximize ecumenical breadth by actually conversing with other faith communities, different questions would take priority.[1] Since, however, the structure of *Ethics from a Theocentric Perspective* sets itself to an understanding of generalizability that downgrades those questions, I shall not seek to use them as criteria.

This CR position differs as well from the numerous revisionist projects that have been developed in theology and theological ethics since the Enlightenment, in the fact that it accepts identification with a particular religious community, so that said community can provide its language and story as the context for binding moral discourse.[2] The just mentioned revisionist projects, strongly represented here, include the contemporary, most respectable

---

[1]Oral comments at Lexington indicated a greater level of motivation than the books seem to with regard to making sense to persons of other faith communities (or persons of natural virtues and piety in no faith community). Such an alternative audience would ask different questions.

[2]James M. Gustafson, in *Theology and Ethics,* vol. 1 of *Ethics from a Theocentric Perspective* (Chicago: University of Chicago Press, 1981) 317. Gustafson himself seems to accept this view.

achievements of Kaufman, Tracy, and Farley, all of whom affirm in principle some kind of community, yet without the historical bond's being able to hold them down.[3]

I am leaving even farther outside my perspective other orientations, for which I personally have considerable sympathy, and whose proponents would have something to say about the book: (a) post-post-critical neobiblicists for whom the modes of prophecy and apocalyptic are more pertinent and really more universal than the enlightenment access to generalizable truth: here I would see among others Brueggemann, Gottwald, and Walter Wink; (b) ethicists working in the same mode: Ellul and Stringfellow; (c) innovators in concrete pastoral methods of Christian community and social critical involvement "from below," like the *communidades de base,* or Sojourners; (d) the various theologies and moral theologians of liberation, which represent a systematization and domestication of all of the above. As far as I can tell, all of these people are closer to the real world, to the real church, and to the Scriptures than is the set of interlocutors chosen by Gustafson's two volumes. But for that reason, it would be hard to seek to stand in for them in the debate. From all of these perspectives, which I do not represent here, what Gustafson is doing represents very much the business as usual of the academic ethical discipline as they challenge it. Yet Gustafson claims to be innovating. I must, therefore, attempt to take, in order to read him, the baseline of the community he addresses.

The absence of a classical Reformed stance in the composition of our present panel does not represent a fortuitous slip or a fluke in the conference planning. The lacuna faithfully reflects a blind spot in Gustafson's magnum opus itself, and to my mind a way in which it differs from the earlier corpus. A blind spot does not designate a choice someone might make to ignore or set aside a certain body of information. It is rather due to the optical and nervous composition of the eyeball that there exists one point on the retina that, because it is central for organizing all the rest of the channels of visual impulses, is not itself able to perceive. The blind spot of the retina does not perceive a blank space in the world: it perceives nothing at a certain point. For each eye the data field of the real world has one point to which it cannot attend directly.

---

[3]A more appropriate title for the entire work might well have been *The God Problem from an Ethics Perspective.* Gustafson is more concerned with reconceptualizing our God language than with throwing new substantive light on what we are enabled and required to be and do. It does not become clear that ethics is or should be the best lever for the revision of theology. The revision of theology is important for its own reasons, not because of a difference it makes for ethics or vice versa.

This explains the peculiar challenge *Ethics from a Theocentric Perspective* puts to the reader coming from a classically Reformed perspective.[4] Since with regard to a few specific matters Gustafson directly affirms his allegiance to the Reformed tradition as he understands it, he does not prepare either himself or the reader to sharpen dialogue on the crucial points where he challenges or forsakes that community's tradition. Most of the time the classical Reformed reader will find herself saying, "yes, but . . . " (a) Yes, what Gustafson says makes good sense, but he presupposes something that would have to be demonstrated rather than simply taken for granted; or (b) obviously I can agree with this as far as it goes, but then it poses a further set of challenges that would need to be faced before we know what it really means. These "yes, but" foci are not lifted up by the author for critical attention; they are handled in asides or parentheses. It is, therefore, by the nature of the case, hard to be fair when I pull them out to look at them.

I quite agree with Gustafson in the use of a model of moral discernment that Professor Johann calls "deliberative," with multiple components at work, whereby a final decision will not be merely deductive but also intuitive, esthetic; but then I still must ask for reasons to believe that the decision will not be shortsighted, erratic, or whimsical.[5] I quite agree with Gustafson in the picture of moral process described by Professor Farley as a "commonsense

---

[4]The point being made here is not the "strong" claim that James Gustafson has committed himself to doing Reformed theology and, therefore, he is accountable for fidelity to a confessional tradition. His multiple references to his freedom from all traditions would undercut any such ascribed accountability. The point made here is rather the "thin" one, that in asking from which perspective it is most appropriate to ask "what needed to be demonstrated" when an author would summon us to follow him, it is most appropriate to begin with the stance the author defines as his own point of departure. The way remains open for any kind of variance from that base (there is thus nothing intrinsically conservative about this approach), but not without offering warrants.

[5]In my "Hermeneutics of Peoplehood" in *The Priestly Kingdom* (Notre Dame: University of Notre Dame Press, 1984) 15ff. (Which James Gustafson cites in *Ethics and Theology,* vol. 2 of *Ethics from a Theocentric Perspective* [Chicago: University of Chicago Press, 1984] 316), I make much of an accountable social form, with defined complementary roles and deliberative rules of order. Gustafson has written elsewhere about the Christian community as decision maker, but in *Ethics* it is hard to project the possible concrete feedback from this general affirmation in volume 2 (316-20) to the four big issues.

epistemology,"[6] but that heightens rather than diverts my call for assumptions and commonplaces to be named and tested.

When I observe that when he is read from the "classical Reformed" perspective James Gustafson seems to be elaborating the obvious and leapfrogging over the debatable, I am not accusing him of the intentional debater's tactic of locating the overt argument at points where I do not disagree with him. It is rather that in his prior choice of a different set of interlocutors and what he takes to be their questions he has left the CR conversation behind. This makes him a little like the Yahweh of Exodus 33: Moses could only see his back after he had passed.

Barriers to Interpretation

One of the ways in which Gustafson's style makes his writing difficult to critique fairly is the way historical figures are abstracted out of their real time and place in order to be used in the 1980s as "benchmark." Augustine becomes a timeless and placeless type, with no reference to his past connections with Manichaeanism or his current ones with the Pelagians, to whom actually Gustafson might be just as close. Thomas, too, is read timelessly and placelessly, without asking which of his myriad "objections" and "it might seem" considerations represent real persons or movements with truth claims and which are purely Thomas's own gymnastics. Even recent figures, like Kant or Barth, are thus distilled into formal positions.

The specific Barthian statement with which Gustafson converses,[7] for instance, has a specific meaning when seen over against the Harnackians of 1910–1930, or against the German Christians and (from another angle) the traditional Lutherans and Emil Brunner in the 1930s. For all my gratitude as an ethics teacher for the pedagogical value of Gustafson's typologizing approach and his skill at discerning deep logical structures, I must as a historical theologian protest that (probably more for Barth and Augustine than for Thomas and Kant) this dehistoricizing method undercuts the attention to concrete communities and (real, historical) larger wholes that Gustafson has taken seriously elsewhere in his opus. In principle, Gustafson is fully aware of the limits and dangers of typological grids. Yet when using a particular historical figure as a foil to make one particular point (I think just now of what he does

---

[6]Cf. below my finding no fault with long stretches of dense phenomenological description. This is why I saw no point in introducing my response with an andante section rephrasing what *Ethics* as a whole had said.

[7]Gustafson, *Ethics*, 2:26ff.

with what Karl Barth meant by saying that one way of approaching ethics may be "sin"), his sensitivity to historical density takes second place. The pastoral, systematic, *and political* reasons that it had to be said in 1934 that Jesus Christ is the only Word of God have been filtered out.

The limitations of this ahistorical use of historical figures are evident when John Calvin is called the "one decisive generating source" of Reformed thought. The John Calvin of history did not generate anything. He was an enormously gifted and fortunate synthesizer, moderator, mediator, and consolidator of what had been initiated by his predecessors, such as Zwingli, Oecolampadius, and even Luther, but especially by his direct mentors and colleagues, Bucer and Capito. To lift a few phrases from the *Institutes* without asking whether the adversary was Sadoletus, Servetus, or (even) Luther exemplifies the dubiousness of the method; with regard to Christology, Gustafson would seem to stand closer to Calvin's victim, Servetus, than to the Reformer.

A second characteristic of Gustafson's style of presentation that makes conversation more difficult is the way later passages in the opus build upon earlier ones, assuming a point to be stronger, when a later passage alludes to it, than when it was first touched upon. Thus he imparts a sense of growing momentum, of confidence in the way his project is building up, which the reader attempting to follow step-by-step cannot share. I say "style of presentation" because I am not sure that what puzzles me here has anything to do with the *substance* of ethics. An example: In the context of a discussion of the goodness of God's intentions, Gustafson says that traditionally "eternal life" has been part of the answer.[8] He does not discuss that conception in its own right. He does not give a hearing to either the more Hebraic ways of affirming the resurrection of the body or the more Hellenistic ways of trusting in the immortality of the soul. He does not review the varied functions that such beliefs may have in a religious world vision, not all of which were linked to his present concern for theodicy. His questioning is limited to two conditional clauses: "If one is agnostic about eternal life, or indeed believes that there is not evidence from our bodily structures to sustain it . . . " and also a citation from C.S. Lewis condemning as not really religious the idea that eternal rewards are a reason for morality. None of this constitutes even the outline of an argument. None of it attends to what the Reformed tradition called "glorifying God and enjoying Him forever." Then on the edge of his later conversation concerning Thomas Aquinas, Gustafson notes that in that earlier passage he had "brought into question" the "traditional Christian

---

[8]Ibid., 1:182ff.

conviction about human immortality."[9] The argument proceeds as if the matter had not been "brought into question" (which would call for argument) but as if it had been closed, negatively. The "traditional conviction" has been noted. It has not been the theme of argument, yet the reader is expected to acquiesce in its abandonment without being given further reasons.

A third frustrating methodological trait is the thinness of substantial argumentative advocacy. Only in the broadest and gentlest way is the warrant for the author's own view spelled out, usually on the rebound from a critical comment on one of the other so-called benchmark views. The author's own views are *located,* by being compared and contrasted to all the others, more than they are either argued for or exposited from the inside. Most of what *Ethics from a Theocentric Perspective* exposits from the inside is in the long passages of unexceptionable phenomenology describing all the diverse elements of a process of moral discernment, as in the chapters dedicated to "our circumstances," "nonreligious experiences," "Man," "Profile," and "Conclusions." In these the description is full and careful, so nuanced as to be unassailable (except perhaps by "prophetic" enemies of nuance), rich in documented and undocumented allusion to the entire discipline, and fuller than necessary to make the points it makes.

This indirectness of exposition means that the reader who is attempting to be fair can never be sure of having found all the fragments of argument on a theme that the two books do not argue at length. This difficulty is more pertinent for the perspective of which I speak, namely from that of the mainstream Reformation heritage with which—*at the points where he diverges from it*—he converses the least, than for some others represented in the symposium.

The very skill that made the earlier works of Gustafson especially valuable as teaching tools makes his normative project difficult to interpret and, therefore, difficult to evaluate fairly. Any of us would put high on the list of those virtues his ability to interpret a variety of positions on any question typologically, letting their strengths and weaknesses show through inductively, so to speak, by virtue of the juxtaposition.

This approach does not work as well when it replaces elucidation of one's own position and responsible advocacy. To have seen in volume one the pro and con sparks from glancing encounters with Rahner, Tillich, Moltmann, G. Ernest Wright, H. Richard Niebuhr, liberation theology, and process thought does not even support *clearly* the modest summary of "bearings" provided.[10] Yet as we go on we find that Gustafson assumes we are sharing in a

---

[9]Ibid., 2:55.

[10]Ibid., 1:31ff., 61.

certain sense of momentum that should thrust us into the following sections with some trust in where we are going. On the third reading even more than on the first, I found myself unable to say why I should come along. The warrants the author considers conclusive are often tacit and when stated are often not argued, for example, "Whether nature can be historicized is a matter of scientific, not theological, investigation."[11] Often the reader cannot tell what Gustafson would consider a pertinent argument against his conclusions.

I do not choose to make this avoidance of the directly confrontable an issue for its own sake, but it does point to one set of questions, namely the doubts *Ethics from a Theocentric Perspective* raises about the place of methodological self-consciousness within the believing community. Is such self-consciousness an autonomous value or must it serve a community?

Christology, Incarnation, and Truth

The classical confession of Jesus as Lord is pertinent for our purposes in more than one way. It formally calls into question the utility of such a simple slogan as "I take it to be unassailable that man is not God."[12] The classical confession of the Incarnation affirms a breach in that categorical wall. Not that there is by definition an overlap between the set of entities named "God" and the set of entities named "man," thereby positing prior definition of the two substantives, and not because "man" as a class has some intrinsic divine dignity. It is rather that YHWH of Hosts, in his sovereign freedom from his creatures' history, elected by pure grace to associate his cause particularly with one thread of human experience and with the meaning of those events (mythic and historical) from Noah through Abraham, Moses, David, Jeremiah, and all the others, culminating in Jesus. When the early theologians said "the Word became flesh and tabernacled among us" or when the early poets sang, "He did not cling to equality with God / but humbled himself / and became as men are . . . ," they were not interested in an ontological paradox or puzzle. They were announcing the public priority of those events as the measures—chosen not by men but by God—of what God enables and requires.

Of course all reflection must proceed from experience, but all experiences are not equal. Of course, in the order of knowing, man is the measurer, but the yardsticks we use are not equally valid.[13] The Christian doctrines of election and incarnation confess that God has sovereignly chosen *certain* public

---

[11]Ibid., 1:47.

[12]Ibid., 1:16.

[13]Ibid., 1:115ff., 33.

events to clarify what He enables and requires. Man is not God, but God has graciously chosen to be knowable to men and women in a way that He has not made himself knowable to events such as tornadoes. From the confessional perspective, it is a *less* anthropocentric procedure when one thus lets God set the terms of our knowledge of Him than when man the measurer claims for himself the authority to set those terms. Classically speaking, a vision that lets God set the terms of our knowledge of God is more theocentric than one that entrusts this knowing to the contemporary marketplace. *Ethics from a Theocentric Perspective* gives no reason to grant that the presumptuous adjective *theocentric* should be claimed as favoring this particular reconstruction. The adjective would more appropriately be claimed by other views that do not at the same time redefine *God.* [14]

One of the disconcerting dimensions of the (in principle unexceptionable) projection of larger wholes is the trusting simplicity with which science is invoked. Phrases abound of the following sort:

"What we know about the development of the universe";[15]

"well established data and explanatory principles established by relevant sciences";[16]

"well established data and explanations from the sciences";[17]

"material from the sciences. . . . what we know about nature";[18]

"evidences and explanation of the origins and possible end of the universe";[19]

"some modern ways of interpreting nature and its relations to the ultimate power and powers";[20]

---

[14]I do not deprecate or fear the reconstructive task. I have alluded above to my respect for the contemporary work of Tracy, Farley, and Kaufman, and recognized above (note 2) that Gustafson worthily joins their ranks. My *general* objection is that the rules distinguishing valid from invalid reconstruction need to be more clear. My objection here is that invoking the name of God specifically in favor of one's own project over against the others may be petitionary, self-contradictory, and impious.

[15]Gustafson, *Ethics,* 1:90.

[16]Ibid., 1:257.

[17]Ibid., 1:264.

[18]Ibid., 1:266.

[19]Ibid., 2:15.

[20]Ibid., 2:54.

"what we know about nature";[21]

"We know too much about how our species developed";[22]

"well established explanations and data from various sciences."[23]

The allusions to information drawn from the sciences are always brief, simple, and in laymen's terms. In addition, Gustafson rarely cites his sources. A distinction of level between the firm conclusions of specific empirical disciplines, on one hand, and the cosmological and philosophical superstructures extrapolated from the practice of the sciences, on the other hand, though visible in Gustafson's vocabulary, is not taken account of when it comes to drawing conclusions about God, yet it is only the former that have relatively clear results and only the latter that offer pertinent theological alternatives. This seems to me to abuse rather than respect the methods, the warrants, and the conclusions of the natural sciences. There is no procession of alternative benchmark syntheses from the field, from Haeckel to Monod or from Eddington and Jeans to Carl Sagan. In one two-page passage there is reference to Burhoe, Wilson, and Jaki, from which far less clarity comes than is taken for granted in the rest of the confident allusions cited above. Gustafson is aware that knowledge in the sciences is also changing and community-bound,[24] but when it comes to weighing what we know from the sciences against the experience and piety to which the canon testifies, the levels of readiness to define, to test, and to doubt are quite unequal.

I, and the mainstream CR theologians I am seeking to speak for, have no investment in a science-versus-religion debate. Gustafson misleads us by suggesting occasionally that that is the issue or by claiming that his openness to data from the sciences is his originality. What is at stake is his lack of attention to clarifying the ground rules for cross-disciplinary conversation, so that appeals to sciences enjoy a simpler authority than do appeals to the traditional language of piety.

Whether the practitioners or the philosophers of the natural sciences recognize this use of their conclusions is not for me to say. What does fall to me to say is that such data are of only very indirect relevance to determining what

---

[21]Ibid., 2:108.

[22]Ibid., 1:305.

[23]Ibid., 1:310. At this point space constraints dictated the excision of further examples of the same kind of reference.

[24]Ibid., 1:124-25.

constitutes the fulfillment of the promise made to Abraham or on what grounds YHWH will be gracious to sinners. The debate is not about whether the natural scientists have evidence on the questions with which they deal. It is about whether those questions are dealing with the God and Father of our Lord Jesus Christ or with some other "God" so defined, a priori on petitionary grounds, that this kind of argument would seem pertinent. The question is not *whether* God is central; it is which God is central. Is it the participant in the stories of Abraham and Moses, Jeremiah and Jesus, Augustine and Edwards, all of whom sought to let His grace dictate the terms of His knowability, or is it one whose credentials need clearance not only from our anthropocentric readings but also from our unhistorical readings on species and planets? I am not uninterested in the scientists' results. The scientists whose evidence and explanations I used to read about were less univocal than Gustafson portrays them to be, but again that is not my assignment. My question is how, without any attention having been given to the matter, the meaning of the confession of election and incarnation for the question of God's knowability was not argued, somehow disposed of, or redefined, but simply bypassed. I cannot evaluate carefully an argument that is not presented; I can only note its absence and wonder whether there is some link between that absence and this so uncritical cosmological argument for a different God.

If I were seeking to respond to *Ethics from a Theocentric Perspective* from an antiestablishment angle rather than that of the mainline CR, I should point out that Gustafson shortchanges both history and science with his tilt in favor of the metaphors of organism and order. Historically, collapse, catastrophe, and decay are as important as progress. Cosmologically one-time events like the big bangs, the meteor impact or volcanic cloud that may have starved the dinosaurs, or the change in ocean level that might lie behind the flood cosmogonies and deluge legends common to so many cultures are just as "scientific" as are the regularities. The preference for integration over turbulence, organism over conflict, the uniform over the catastrophic, not only correlates with a certain cultural and social orientation that a theocentric ethic in the Hebraic mode would need to question, but it also represents *within* the realm of the natural sciences a challengeable narrowing of the data base.

The conversation between historical and cosmological conceptions of deity is ancient. I do not intend to take the opposite side from Gustafson; I do not think his way of outlining the sides advances any authentically theocentric concern. I would not, and the theologians of classical Christianity would not, accept a fundamental disjunction between the two realms, or the two kinds of evidence; but there would need to be more direct work on how they connect. Simply to subordinate the complexities of the historical deposit to the screening of a modern cosmology is not the way to make the dialogue manageable.

Incarnation as Universal

Gustafson identifies as the central issue of theological method the fact "that Christianity has always claimed its historic particularity . . . to have universal significance and import." If he did tackle that central issue, Gustafson says that the way to do it would be to "generate options" and "provide a set of ideal types by which all theologians . . . could be illumined."[25] This descriptive-pluralistic approach to varieties, by assuming that this method question, while interesting, need not be pursued, implies an agnostic answer to the truth question; yet the agnostic answer is given only by default. From then on, the several assumptions Gustafson makes—(a) the attitudes to "natural" and "reasonable" knowledge developed in dialogue with Catholic approaches; (b) the especially high level of confidence placed both in the contribution of the natural sciences and in the phenomenology of religion and of anthropology;[26] and (c) the assumed freedom of any contemporary intellectual to "develop" or "generate" his own set of selections from the treasures of tradition—all add up to a specifically focused relativizing of what for the Reformed tradition was the center of theology, namely the unique dignity of Jesus of Nazareth as prophet, priest, and king.

One of the differences between scholastic Protestantism (generated out of the anti-Catholic polemics of the age after Trent) and the classical Reformed vision is the relationship between Scripture and Jesus. The former believes in Jesus because of the Bible; the latter is guided by the Bible because of Jesus. The former seems to be the silent interlocutor behind Gustafson's occasional indirect argument. I shall come back to it. The latter is the more important and seems not to surface.

Universality is for Gustafson a goal or an "aspiration" to be approached by "striving" and by "overcoming the boundaries of our communities."[27] While saying elsewhere that all truth is particularly perceived and formulated, he seems here to believe that there are procedures for moving toward universality through some process of dilution, sifting, or abstraction. Such procedures seem to decrease both the substance that can be known and the clarity of what can be known about what God enables and requires. The hope seems to be that there is in the wider public arena a set of reasonable people who will agree to a departicularized set of affirmations. I would hold that assumption to be philosophically confusing and empirically false, but that is not my bailiwick.

---

[25]Ibid., 2:68.

[26]Ibid., 1:16ff., 281ff.

[27]Ibid., 1:127, 151.

It is within my responsibility to report that the empirical history of religious communities yields a different set of options. What to do about particularity is not a *logical* trilemma whose only solutions would be to renounce interest in the universal, to claim an achieved universality, or to revitalize one's parochialism by seeking an approximation to the goal of universality by way of selection or dilution.

What to do about particularity is a concrete *historical* challenge posited by the (quite varied) interrelations between real communities, to which different communities have found various answers. One answer is to accept ghetto status, to acknowledge that one's identity is provincial and that one's view of reality will not make sense to others. This may take the withdrawn-tolerant form of saying that all provincialisms are equal but that there is no reason that they should meet one another. Or it may take the racist form of denying that other peoples are as fully human as we are; the denial may be expressed in intertribal warfare or in apartheid supremacy.

Another response, while granting that it is prima facie only perceptible as true for those who are acquainted with it, is to claim that one's truth could be understandable and convincing to others if they heard it. Thus to be *particular* and to be *public* are not alternatives. One's own view, though particular in its origins, is information that others could receive: that is, it is news. Further, it may even be claimed that it is the kind of news that others, if they received it, might for their own good consent to: that is, it is *good* news. This evangelical option is absent from Gustafson's palette. Perhaps it is absent because he does not distinguish it from coercively imposing an alien view on others, or from ghetto defensiveness, or from claiming that the reason others should receive it is that by nature or reason they know it already. He lists numerous responses to boundedness, and three ideal types, but this is not among them.[28]

The reason Gustafson seems to have no category for "good news" may be that he has little space for history. Although he does identify being-in-history as one of the marks of our humanness, his statement is a reasonable anthropological generalization that does not impinge on the universality question. He does draw from past thought some paradigms of moral thought with which to compare his views. None of those points of comparison is older than Augustine, and none is from missionary or minority Christianity. Despite these fragments of historical awareness, his own synthesis is so modern and individual that the lived experience of centuries of missionary faith does not register as an alternative model. To be "missionary," as the cultural historian

---

[28]Ibid., 1:126-27, 153-54.

would call it, or "evangelical," as I prefer to say, is not to claim universality as achieved either on the grounds of a revelatory privilege or because one can apologetically subject it to everyone else's concepts of natural reason. It is to discover approximations to universality in the lived experience of transtribal communication and reconciliation.

Such transtribal communication and reconciliation is not served by jettisoning as useless baggage those elements of prior identity that the host or target culture of the other tribe does not understand. The reconciliation event is only authentic if changes take place in the host language to enable it to carry the good news.[29] This has in fact happened repeatedly over the centuries. Judaism has done it effectively since Jeremiah, Christianity has done it since Pentecost, and Mohammed did it in the early years. Each of these communities has since fallen away into coerciveness or isolation, but such falling away can be denounced as a mistake from within its own frame of reference. Such falling away from announcing good news to coercion does not refute either the "news" quality or the "good" quality of the message.

Christ as Prophet
and the Place of Scripture

What the classical Reformed view meant by the doctrine of the perspicuity of the Scriptures was that the canonical texts as a whole, when read by the discerning community as a whole, in a context guaranteeing the proper interrelatedness of the numerous pertinent kinds of data, expertise, and perspectives, can by God's grace lead to a morally adequate knowledge of what God enables and requires believers to be and to do. "Morally adequate" means good enough to work with, sufficient to enable the community process of discernment. It did not mean absolutely clear, immutable, or without exceptions. It means that my brother or sister within the discerning community has a basis for counting on me, blaming or praising me, correcting or commending me as we together proceed through the discernment process in the midst of our being and doing.

The classical Reformed view differs from its High Protestant Scholastic children, and from its fundamentalist grandchildren, in not making the claim that this morally adequate guidance is univocal, systematic, immutable, without variations over time and place, without exceptions or tragic choices. High Scholastic Protestantism, like its Tridentine manualist contemporaries,

---

[29]For a specimen of how the news creates new vehicles within the host culture's language, compare my *Priestly Kingdom* (Notre Dame: University of Notre Dame Press, 1985) 50-54.

did make such claims. Like its fundamentalist heirs, it sought to found scriptural authority in a rationalistic argument about the unique revelatory status of the propositions enclosed in Scripture, which status in turn was thought to be defensible only if the whole of the Scripture formed one logically coherent system.

The silent presence behind *Ethics from a Theocentric Perspective,* the absent interlocutor, seems to be the Scholastic or Fundamentalist heritage. *Ethics* is constantly telling us that absolute knowledge and immutable principles are not available. We are repeatedly told that about the facts of any case needing an ethical decision, about the network of underlying values in any situation, and about the data of Scripture and tradition. We are repeatedly reminded that we must live with uncertainty, that every decision is risky. This is, of course, all true.

I thought I knew that already, on other grounds. I suspect that every reader of *Ethics from a Theocentric Perspective* thinks the same thing. Gustafson's argument on this matter is what the German idiom calls taking a battering ram to an open door. The first fundamental orientation needing interpretation is his assumption that the interlocutor most powerful in setting the terms of the debate should be an absent advocate of immutable and exceptionless certainty.

His warrants for accentuating uncertainty are numerous and obvious: (a) there are many strands of "backing" in the traditions and in the Scriptures;[30] (b) the empirical data underlying moral choices are increasingly complex; (c) the simplicity of a coherent universe of moral discourse, which was experienced at some times and places in the past, is gone; (d) no one but God knows enough to value aright. This fragment from Milton, echoing as a litany with shifting accents in the conclusion, is the only point specific to Gustafson's argument, but it does not necessarily prove what he uses it for. First, historically, what Milton meant in his context was not to reject perspicuity in the interest of relativism. Milton meant to save perspicuity from prelacy and censorship, by arguing that the context in which the Scriptures provide morally adequate guidance is one of free preaching, free assembly, free press, open debate, and congregational decision making. Milton was furthermore reasoning from axioms regarding God's personlike purposiveness and mindlike omniscience that sustained a biblical reverence before the Almighty. I will defend, maybe more than Milton would have, Gustafson's freedom to redefine God as he thinks he should, but it is not a fair argument after such a redefinition to cite the Puritan poetry as if it were a warrant for a quite different thesis. Second, logically, if God be truly God, then a principled agnosticism that says

---

[30]Passim, for example, Gustafson, *Ethics,* 1:152, 245, 339; 2:34.

"I know for sure what the limits of valid knowledge are" is no less presumptuous than the tradition that says "I bow to what it seems to have pleased God
to say." Substantially, the former statement sounds more modest. Epistemologically, it is more presumptuous, since it denies that God can have made
known in morally adequate ways what it pleases Him to enable and to require.

The extent of Gustafson's attention to the place of the Bible as a landmark
for theology is his repeated but always cryptic accent on the diversity of the
strands of biblical witness. That constitutes an argument against Protestant
Scholasticism and Fundamentalism. It does not warrant silence regarding the
various intellectually and ecumenically responsible ways in which the post-
critical disciplines of scripture scholarship have been working *within* the full
awareness of the diversity within the canon to elaborate major themes: some
of them distilling as commonalities behind the diversities; some of them set-
tling out when one observes the trajectory of a theme through the coming into
existence of the canonical corpus; some of them through attention to the later
churches' selectivity in closing the canon and in discriminating among canonical themes in terms of relative importance and pertinence; some of them
by letting prophetic and pastoral challenges of the present evoke sensitivity
to themes previously forgotten. Some of these biblical/theological disciplines
are classical belonging to the way any literate community reads its literature
respectfully; some are new but quite credible. *Ethics* pays them no heed. This
is one of the ways in which the *Ethics* differs from the mainline Reformed tradition. The only explanation given for that heedlessness is that there is diversity within Scripture. Yet the only subschools of Reformed thought for which
that would constitute an argument are the scholastic and fundamentalist forms.

The one exception to what I have called heedlessness is the passage where
the theme is not the substance of ethics or of theology but Christology.[31] There
the argument is that since everybody else is selective too, *Ethics* will be free to
choose those particular strands that are most compatible with its beginning
bias. The fullest explanation for this is the image of resonance borrowed from
H. Richard Niebuhr.[32] Just as each pipe of an organ picks out of the white
noise of the wind that frequency for which it is tuned, so we are free to select
from the canonical corpus the themes and accents to which we are attuned.
"Everybody else is selective too" seems to make of diversity a warrant for
normless, intuitionistic selectivity on one's own part.

Having thus justified selectivity in principle because everyone else does it
and having explained his own selectivity with the metaphor of resonance,

---

[31]Ibid., 1:275.

[32]Ibid., 1:277.

Gustafson claims the freedom to set aside the Hebrew heritage, the experience of the missionary churches, everything apocalyptic, everything trinitarian, everything substantially ethical, and to settle for a Jesus much like the Jesus of Harnack's *Essence of Christianity*.

This strikes me as the least respectful of all ways to use a tradition. First, it eliminates far more than it receives from the tradition. Second, even within the Gospel narrative that is favored, it denies the pertinence of the purposeful and personalistic path of Jesus through the events of the passion, paring Jesus down to a Harnackian rabbi whose main distinction was the subjective certainty he seems to have evoked in his hearers. Third, it is biased against the tradition's ever being able to tell me with authority something I need to hear but do not want to hear. Fourth, the "German Christian" reading of the Gospels would have been authorized formally though not substantially by this approach. Fifth, since the theme is Christology in a formal sense, this approach is empty of specifiable ethical guidance. This passage is thus an exception to what I said about not drawing on biblical substance, but it is an exception that proves the rule.[33] Analyzing it substantiates the reading from the rest of *Ethics from a Theocentric Perspective*.

The view that freedom of unaccountable selectivity should follow from the existence of a diversity of strands within a literary corpus (or within any body of data) does not obtain in any other discipline. The literary disciplines of reading bodies of literature carefully, developed in the West since the Renaissance, have ways to be less selective and arbitrary in letting a body of texts, in its natural variety, speak its own message. There are ways to find coherence within a variety of texts by dating and locating the original statements with regard to their adversaries and the challenges they met (a part of the hermeneutic concern whose absence I already noted with reference to other figures like Augustine and Calvin). There are tools of lexicographical analysis, redactional anaylsis of the trajectories of specific themes, structuralist analyses of how in different contexts quite different forms of words had the same moral impact, whereby unity demands diversity in order to be faithful to its message. Such studies of unity within diversity would not short-circuit the freedom or the responsibility of justifying one's own selectivity in the appropriation of tradition, but they make it harder for the selection to be arbitrary and for the result to support one's own predilections.

Not only since the Renaissance and Enlightenment have there been usages of Scripture independent of the Scholastic Protestant criterion of uniformity. From the patristic period through the first generation of the Reformation there

---

[33]Ibid., 1:275ff.

were other ways to live under the authority of canonical literature without being either crippled or let loose into arbitrariness by the diversities within the canon. Theories of the fuller sense of Scripture, theories of the attestation of the Holy Spirit, theories of the guidance provided by bishops and councils, and familiarity with the texts due to the use of some of them in worship and education all combined to enable confident commerce with the thought world of the Bible. None of these resources can do for us what they did then, but for the historically oriented understanding of what counts as a fundamental problem they are not negligible. Both pre-Renaissance and post-Enlightenment hermeneutical experience demonstrate how little reason there is to let ourselves be boxed into a formulation of how Scripture functions that was dictated by Scholastic Protestantism and its executor Fundamentalism.

Christ as Priest and the Need for Redemption

Christ as prophet represents the issues we have been pursuing. Christ as priest points to another realm *Ethics* evacuates. What Augustine and Calvin called "sin" and saw as needing a divine cure has become for Gustafson "the human fault," a complex of finitude and miscalculation that leaves persons with a sense of the need for forgiveness, though much of it is not blameworthy. God's being redeemer is projected independent of reference to Hebrew sacrificial cult and the Cross of Jesus; it is an extrapolation into "the powers that sustain us" from our human experiences of forgiveness. In more than one way this reduction jettisons essentials.

The first impact of the human fault for ethics is, classically, epistemological. What Protestants called "the noetic effect of sin" poisons not only the ability to will and to do the good, but even the ability to know what it is. What we know does not all become false. Yet what we know naturally is warped, blurred, inadequate. That is one aspect of the need for revelation. *Ethics* notes sketchily and dismisses summarily the notion of a flaw in human cognition.[34] This view is congruent with the generally high level of trust in our own capacity for moral knowledge that pervades the rest of the book.

A second aspect of human sinfulness is, however, more than ethical. The wherewithal for renewing both the knowing and the willing of the good has been spoken of as regeneration, or as sanctification, that is, as power for change in the orientation and composition of the human person, in the light of faith, under the power of the Holy Spirit, with resources of the believing community. That these new possibilities can be caricatured and cheapened by "born-again" and "holiness" movements does not refute their real roots in Scripture

---

[34]Ibid., 1:302.

and experience. That an act of God or an act of faith could change persons-in-community significantly, in ways that modify their potential for moral behavior, cannot be denied on the grounds of Gustafson's evidence; but neither can that possibility be given any importance. The maximum promise is that piety might favor some growth in insight, some openness to alternative construals. The change we may most properly hope for in persons will be the result of self-interest or coercion.[35]

The central impact of human sinfulness for classical Reformed theocentric ethics is the meaning it gives the Cross of Jesus Christ, relating to both past human moral failure and future possible obedience in indispensable ways. That the death of Jesus had to be, that it was part of a plan, necessary, was at the heart of the earliest confessions. No serious theology since then has sought to avoid the task of explicating that saving necessity. *Ethics* offers only one paragraph on the subject. The fact of crucifixion is circumlocuted into "the events that the Christian community remembers and relives in Holy Week."[36] Whatever happened then is described as an event of human fidelity, yet with no interest in why fidelity required what it did. The event itself is less important in explaining its power over us than is the dramatic form in which it is recounted. Information about the subjective side of Jesus' finding his way is provided for which there is no basis in the narrative. The result is said to be the insight that what appears as a human good may need to be sacrificed for God's purpose. Every line of this reformulation of what might be done with the passion narrative has some truth in it, and every line flattens the particular and historical to a point where some other pedagogical drama, some other Christ-figure, could probably make the point better, less subject to the errors of overinterpretation.

Christ as King and the Civil Order

The third dimension of the classic confession, Christ's kingship, is similarly hard to find in *Ethics*. In the earliest documents, the issue of whether or not Jesus would be a zealot king is privileged above the other dimensions of ethical instruction and modeling. Jesus' answer to that question was more weighty, more original when related to the traditions of the time, more specific to his vocation, than were many other ethical teachings found in those same sources. The notion that biblical faith is concerned with the political realm and with change in that realm heightens the weight of the particularity

---

[35]Ibid., 1:307ff.

[36]Ibid., 1:279.

of the Jewish and Christian traditions. In Protestantism, it has been the Reformed strands, from Zwingli to Cromwell and New England, that have most carefully kept the political realm within the scope of theological concern, whereas the other traditions have more easily excised it through various kinds of dualism.

Gustafson does not ignore the political realm. Moltmann, Lehmann, and the Catholic political theologians are taken note of and passing references to issues of social justice are frequent; yet our author seems to have a stake in *relatively* depoliticizing the field.[37] The four major theme areas chosen for attention in volume 2 do not include any points at which the state as such might be challenged. He commends the United States Roman Catholic Bishops' pastoral letter on peace as a serious process of discernment but does not discuss the substance of the arms race, nor nuclear proliferation, nor superpower neocolonialism. The national state is the only unit of community Gustafson identifies that is larger than the family, ignoring the importance of many other kinds of nonstate organizations (currently given much attention by neoconservatives) and the many larger-than-national values that one would have thought his interest in larger wholes would have drawn attention to. The population/nutrition theme is intrinsically worldwide; yet its analysis is also uncritical of the function of government and commercial elites in managing the development of the issues.

Description and Prescription

There was an intended ambivalence in the assignment made to the authors of papers for this symposium. At one end of the scale, the task was to be evaluative with regard to the adequacy of the landmark work *Ethics from a Theocentric Perspective*. Participants have been invited to offer their more fundamental criticism of Jim's project. That I have been trying to do, from an "evangelical and reformed" perspective. At the other end of the scale, we were asked what we have *learned* from the encounter with Jim's theological ethics, as a benchmark for our own ethics. My first statement in response to this part of the invitation is essayed here in conclusion, intentionally without benefit of reference to the other critics and commentators.

What I have learned thus far concerns first of all the limits of the comparative-descriptive method of pursuing any normative discipline, whether theological or not, whether ethics or something else. There is an ecumenical a priori at work in the preference for beginning with description rather than prescription. It says, of the person who holds a view different from my own,

---

[37]Ibid., 1:43ff.

that I begin by affirming her or his right to begin at that position, even though it differs from my own. This respect for the other's standpoint is heightened when, by attention to cultural setting and logical types, I exercise my capacity to understand cross-culturally how that other person's position makes sense within its own location. The third level of ecumenical a priori is still more optimistic; it is the hope that through the dialogical process I (or both of us) may be changed, whether in a modest organic form that might be called "growth" or "learning" or in a stronger way that might be called "conversion" or "reconciliation." On the second level, learning may occur. On the third level, it will preeminently be expected that the interlocutor's difference comes to be seen more as complementary and less as contradictory, at best as saying in that context something similar to what I am saying in mine. It is in this context that the earlier corpus of Gustafson's writing has been especially helpful. His most learned capacity to interpret other people's views, as it were, from the inside, watching how their logic makes sense in its own terms, has been a means of learning I trust to many of us, and I know to many of our students.

The threefold ecumenical a priori stated above is true in principle. My conclusion from reading *Ethics* is, however, that in the present case it has not led to greater agreement, or even to much greater clarity, in the ways in which Gustafson wants to lead us beyond the Reformed place where he began. His detailed and nuanced awareness of where other people stand, especially of the benchmark positions he uses in each major block of the work, does not drive him to state his views in a way that might convince them that they had missed something.

The meaning of a benchmark, in the profession of the surveyor from which it comes, is congruent with this low expectancy with regard to dialogue. The surveyor's benchmark is not supposed to move; it is part of the already solid lay of the land. One uses it for orientation precisely because one does not expect it to move, or even to listen. If Paul Ramsey or Jürgen Moltmann (to speak of the living) were to hear, and to be convinced of something, were they to change, they would be less usable as specimens of a type on which to base our comparisons.

Gustafson has transcended his teacher, H. Richard Niebuhr, in the use of higher-order methodological analysis to illuminate ethical dialogue. The five-fold typology of *Christ/Culture* has for decades been helping students sort out alternative moral styles and make sense of variety. It raised people's sights from casuistic debates about telling lies, or sexuality, or taking lives, to second-order or third-order metadecisions about nature and grace, revelation and reason, univerality and particularity, and the like.

What H. Richard Niebuhr did not do was to offer an open (debatable, verifiable) account of what this comparative structural analysis of varied views assumed or affirmed as to the nature of moral truth. *Sometimes* Niebuhr seemed to make a positively relativistic statement, saying that all the views have their element of truth, each in its place; the error would be to choose just one. At other times, the structure of analysis constitutes a visible, though not avowed, claim for the superiority of the fifth "transformationist" type, which most dialectically included the valid elements in all the others. Why such a formal claim to include all the others should be a mark of truth was assumed, not argued. All the while, the power of the grid reinforced the untested (and from my perspective wrong) prior definitions of *Christ* and *Culture* upon which the entire system was built. Seldom did the second- and third-order abstractions came back to earth by indicating how one line of behavior, one kind of decision, or one set of virtues could be more right than any other.

I make these (already well-recognized) observations about H. Richard Niebuhr because it seems important to recognize that the mode of analysis that *Ethics* raises to a higher power is part of a tradition. Yet Gustafson does raise it to a higher power and thereby weakens its verifiability. The attention to varieties of modes and models becomes a new kind of autonomous truth claim, as if the act of having passed in review the many options, having been fair to them and typologized them, somehow itself validated the momentum with which he then moves on to his own answers. After four readings of both books I can still not honestly tell whether Gustafson really thinks his major moves *ought* to convince me that they are in some way true, in the classical sense that I should follow him in them, or whether he wants only to be recognized as projecting, within the polite pluralism of the university, one more possible coherent type. If the latter is intended, I have no argument. If the former is meant, I must report that I find no warrant given for his major moves: (a) why Reformed should be better than Catholic or "Wesleyan"; (b) why in the dialectic of the particular and the universal we should move from the epistemological priority of the particular as it was affirmed in *Can Ethics Be Christian?* or *The Church as Moral Decision-Maker* to the reverse of *Ethics;* (c) why suicide is a more appropriate test case than war; (d) why in the tension between more consequential and more deontic readings of any issue, the less stringent option should regularly be preferred.

If, on the other hand, the intent of Gustafson is really less normative than this, if he would rather I remain representative of an alternative view that he respects and can use as a foil than that I should agree with him, then I do not know why he wrote *Ethics.* I have said this in the first person, but it is more than a personal statement. The validation of the ministry of the teacher, the scribe, the moderator, according to the Pauline vision of the Church as a community of discernment, is not the metalogical consistency of the thought system in its own interior coherence, so much as it is the servanthood and the dialogical vulnerability with which the ethicist remains accountable to the community, whose logic and language it is not his or her vocation to replace with his or her own. Awareness of issues of structural coherence is an important ancillary ministry; it is not an autonomous or a sufficient norm. But then when anyone, even someone so erudite and understanding as H. Richard Niebuhr or James Gustafson, demonstrates understanding of many positions and of the structures of their variations, that does not count at all to show that his own view is more right than other views.

When Niebuhr assumes tacitly that his own grid is validated by the fact that he has used it on everyone else first, the claim is made understandable (though, to me, unconvincing) by the architectonic way in which the other types he surveys seem to exhaust the available options, by the way his own vision arises dialectically above the others as their synthesis, and by the ability to convince the reader that "how do Christ and culture relate?" is really the basic question. Gustafson's raising this mode to a higher power loses these strengths: (a) the other benchmark positions do not exhaust the available options, (b) it is not argued that the questions they are tested by are basic ones, or are always the same, and (c) it is not argued that his view transcends and includes theirs, only that they provide a basis for comparison and contrast. The same close reading of another person's view that deems the other view worthy of note, as a benchmark, may also assure me that I know all it has to teach me, that I need no longer listen to any claims it might have on me. The same pluralism that lets each view be understood in its own terms may lash back (as we have seen it doing in Gustafson's interpretation of the Christology of the Bible) in skepticism about whether one view can be more adequate than another, so that one's own choice needs no warrants that could call others to hear and to change. At this point description has become a substitute for prescription, instead of its preamble.

I am not sure how to take the places where it is said most openly, "I recognize that some people will not recognize this as Christian, or as ethics." Is this attitude defiance, warning us that we have no hold on Gustafson, since he has chosen to cut himself loose from the common discipline? Or is it modesty, recognizing that since making the moves he has made, he has little hold on us? Whichever virtue it is, it correlates with the low level of dialogical expectancy I have seen indicated in other ways.

Values beyond the Human

The other point where I had hoped to learn something was the critique of anthropocentrism expressed in the book's title and recurrently alluded to throughout the work. When we take our signals from the general shape of the book's argument, we expect the most significant new guidance to come at the point of the larger wholes to which individual values need to be subordinated. Yet that expectation is disappointed.

Sometimes the larger whole that does come into view is a human community, such as ethical concern has classically known under such headings as "the common good," "posterity," "civilization," "nation," or "church." In these reminders there is much that is very true, and little that is very new. They do not transcend anthropocentrism at all.

And yet there are references that allude to larger wholes that are more than human: the animal world, the vegetable world, or even the mineral world. On the strictly formal level, the projection is stated more than once, perhaps most clearly at the beginning of volume two, "that there are occasions or circumstances in which a course of action that is apparently beneficial to the well-being of individuals or communities is not necessarily the right thing to be done."[38] Yet the only solid specimens of such a claim that are proffered are where a larger or more important (human) community is to be benefited; anthropocentrism is not overcome after all.

There is *after all* no *firm* affirmation of a specific larger-than-human whole to which primary human values should be sacrificed. Each time Gustafson approaches this possibility he pulls back. Phrases such as "the human race and the rest of nature" abound; yet I have not found any specification of a case where "the rest of nature" or any larger whole would demand the sacrifice of otherwise imperative human values.

"If things could speak they would complain,"[39] but it is not specified what that complaint would be or what weight we should assign it.

Food for the human species is not the only end to be realized by interventions into nature; yet just what "the rest of nature"[40] wants us to do for it is not said.

Kant's denying that we have duties to animals except as animals are humanly useful is noted as a question, but not refuted.[41]

To alter the primacy of the anthropocentric focus does not necessarily lead to equating the significance of man with the significance of animals, plants, and trees.[42]

----

[38]Ibid., 2:5.

[39]Ibid., 2:284.

[40]Ibid., 2:243.

[41]Ibid., 2:134.

[42]Ibid., 1:109.

My unsureness about what to think at this point has no sectarian intent, no axe to grind. I would not mind if it were possible to claim a set of duties and dispositions called for in favor of larger wholes. I see no reason to expect a priori that if such claims could be concretized they would design an ethic more Reformed or more Catholic, more bourgeois or more biblical, than we would otherwise have known within the limits of our more human-oriented traditions. My share in the confession of Christ as Lord has nothing to fear or to lose from the discovery that another compartment of the cosmos also has claims upon me. It would be fun to learn that a monsoon or a jungle needed me.

So the question I am pursuing here is a sincerely open one. I just want to know what is being said that can be known and what different dispositions and decisions it enables and requires. The explanation, as far as I can understand, for this empty set where the structure of the opus had led us to expect a new chapter, is not neglect or inattention. It is a double problem in the very logic of the larger wholes whose interests we might be called to weigh against human values. When the larger whole that has a claim on me is human—be that the clan, the common good, the people of China, posterity, or the unborn—there exist instruments and mechanisms of empathy, imagination, extrapolation, and representation whereby I can acquire some serious notion of what those larger-than-myself claims are. There are also ways to make me aware of my failings. When I fall short of fulfilling those claims, someone may tell me. These instruments of empathy or reprimand cannot be extrapolated in the same way to larger-than-human wholes. We have no way—nor does Gustafson suggest any—to say with regard to a water table, a cold front, or a vegetable species what it wants or how we could sin against it.

Animal species might be closer to our capacity to extrapolate collective survival claims empathetically. I could understand it—though I might not agree—if Gustafson had taken up Peter Singer's plea for the animals, but he does not. The multiple references in volume one to Mary Midgley's *Beast and Man* laid the groundwork for such affirmations, but nothing is built thereon. I could understand a review of Lynn White's criticism of our domineering abuse of the ecosphere; yet in that debate the stake of humans in the health of nature puts our deepest real interest on nature's side, not against it.

So the lacuna is first of all defined formally. There is no way to *know* what dispositions and choices are enabled and required by God on behalf of larger-than-human wholes. I can try to understand the Mayan piety that built pyramids on which to kill children—if that is really what they did—so that the sun would come up. But I cannot assent to the thesis that the sunrise needs the child's blood. Might it not be constitutively the case that any larger-than-human whole, because it cannot be encompassed in human categories, cannot be specified as obligations in terms of history and ethics?

But the other half of the logical problem is probably deeper. Gustafson's definition of God has itself been deprived of the standard of personlike metaphors that fit with requiring: (a) it would be incongruous to speak of God as "just,"[43] (b) God's final end for all things is unknowable,[44] (c) to speak of "interacting" with the natural world is metaphorical,[45] and (d) to speak of God in terms of will, agency, as characterized by intelligence or purpose, would be excessive.[46] Once the personlike methaphors have been systematically evacuated, in order to stay within the parameters of what is called a scientific world view, the context for ethical discourse has been undercut. I remain unconvinced that we can have it both ways. By revising one dimension of the heritage at a time without starting at the beginning, discussing the metaissues without attending to their roots in particular communities stuck with particular decisions, Gustafson has avoided testing whether the language of requirement can still have a *moral* sense at all if the powers that bear down upon us are best described impersonally.

God so defined cannot be manipulated, cannot be ignored or denied. The last words of *Ethics from a Theocentric Perspective* are true by any constuction. But the price has been high. To say of God so defined that "He" can be "glorified" or "obeyed" has become an excessive and substantively empty metaphor.

YODER DISCUSSION

John P. Reeder, Jr.: I think I could understand if it were said, "For me and mine, we have been spoken to in an authoritative way mediated through a tradition and its Scriptures." But you seem to say something else as well, that if one understands the nature of historical communities and their traditions, then Gustafson's way of working, and the relative degree of freedom he has in regard to tradition, is somehow dubious. I am not clear about the latter. How does one criticize the relative degree of freedom he has vis-à-vis the classical Reformed tradition by drawing attention to the realities of life in community and the inheritances these people have from particular traditions?

---

[43]Ibid., 2:292.

[44]Ibid., 2:112.

[45]Ibid., 2:12.

[46]Ibid., 1:270.

Yoder: The claims on someone who is heir to a community's story are stronger than a statement, "As for me and mine, we will do it this way." Gustafson's references to Jonathan Edwards and the Reformed family seem to claim that his was the right thing to do with that tradition. We have to ask about the nuts and bolts of the tradition rather than leaping away from its central categories. If the claim had not been made about expositing the Christian tradition, and the Reformed tradition specifically, these questions would still be intrinsically important, but I wouldn't have felt the same mandate to have them noticed in this symposium. The reason I have asked these questions is that they are the questions that are raised by the claim to be expositing anything in some recognizable solidarity with the tradition.

Reeder: I suppose the issue might come down to what constitutes recognizable solidarity.

Yoder: Yes, there would have to be a conversation in which these subjects would show up in the text.

Reeder: Right, I didn't mean to say that one is just confessing, "It's me and mine." I understood you to say that from where one stands, one has been spoken to authoritatively. I take that to be a very strong point. But in addition to that theological claim, you would ask of Gustafson's claim to stand in continuity with that tradition, "Does it satisfy certain criteria of historical continuity that we could all agree upon if we discussed it?" That would be a kind of agreement we could have independently of theological disagreement, but he really is too free in that sense too?

Yoder: I am not sure he would have to be judged too free in that sense, but we would have to look at the particular lines of tradition that have been left aside without being looked at.

Reeder: So to settle the question, we would discuss the criteria of continuity.

Martin L. Cook (University of Santa Clara): I am confused about the general argument. You seem to say, "The Reformed tradition has central features that Gustafson does not take up. Therefore, any claim on his part to be the legitimate successor to the Reformed tradition in the modern period is misguided because it fails to attend to those features." If that is the argument, I am puzzled because I understand Gustafson to be saying, "This is what I think is true on various grounds, largely scientific. There are features of the Reformed tradition that I can affirm, and there are features that I cannot, including a strong doctrine of historical revelation, a high Christology, a strong doctrine of redemption, and so forth. If someone chooses to rule me out of the Reformed or Christian tradition on grounds I don't affirm, so be it. The claim is simply true and I continue to use the language in certain ways." Now, one could argue that he didn't defend adequately or sufficiently the affirmations and retrievals that he made. But I don't think he argues that he is a legitimate successor of the Reformed tradition and that anyone who thinks otherwise is false.

Yoder: I stated the puzzlement that the text gives me. There are places that say, "Maybe you don't even think this is Christian." But he still wrote five hundred pages he wants us to read, and apparently we did and we came. So there is something of a flippant disregard for the questions inherent in the tradition. Even if one is going to say, "My retrieval is selective, and take it or leave it acording to my criteria," it would be helpful to know whether he wants to retrieve all the fundamental structural perceptions of human reality that we have in the classic Reformed tradition, or whether he thinks they are false and silly. Their neglect is not simply a matter of my saying, "You can't claim to be an executor of the tradition if you deny too much of it." Until they are actually looked at, I don't know in what sense this reformulation or selective retrieval is something that I ought to listen to.

Cook: That is a personal matter, I take it.

Yoder: It is a community matter.

Gordon D. Kaufman: I think it may be that the issue that John Yoder has been trying to call to our attention is the question of the vocation and task of the theologian and theological ethicist. Most of the points he makes presuppose a notion of the theologian as having the articulation of a tradition as a fundamental part of his or her task. Presupposed in that task is a certain loyalty to the main claims that the tradition has made in its previous articulations. So John finds himself somewhat at a loss when Gustafson simply points out that he is related to the tradition in this way, and disconnected from it in that way, but doesn't go on to argue the points. The loyalty to the tradition that John is looking for seems to be absent. It seems to me that is a very important question to be raising—whether and to what extent this matter of loyalty to a tradition is part or maybe even the center of the theologian's task. Certainly for a long time, Christian theologians have understood themselves in that way, and that does seem to be missing. John is asking, "What are we to make of that?"

What I see in Gustafson's book is a rather different concept of the theologian's task. It is a task of what I like to call imaginative construction—of a way of seeing the world and human life that draws on traditional resources but also takes into account different kinds of sources of insight and understanding that either were not known or recognized in the tradition or were explicitly rejected. This imaginative construction can be done on different levels. It can be simply the presentation of a vision of how we ought to see ourselves in the world. I think that is part of what Jim Gustafson is doing—a vision that has some connections with the Reformed tradition, but as he acknowledges, is also disconnected in very important ways, particularly on the matter of Christology. I think Gustafson's work is not as closely argued as it might be. I think Gustafson is presenting a vision that he says Christians ought to take seriously. Some others might disagree. So part of the debate here is the question of what theologians are supposed to do today. What is their proper business?

If I may recur to a slightly different point, John Yoder talked about an evangelical approach to diversity. An evangelical approach was one of bringing news, not necessarily making arguments, but of bringing news to a situation or community that hadn't yet heard a message they need to hear. It seems to me that Gustafson is an evangelical in that sense. He is trying to bring some news to the Christian community in particular, but also to others who might be interested, which he thinks they haven't heard. So he is perhaps more of a preacher than a theologian in the traditional sense.

Yoder: Those flashes of light on the setting are all helpful and pertinent. I don't think it is the case that my questions apply only to someone who has a classical definition of the theologian's role, though that is one way to say why these questions need to be attended to. I need to do some disavowing so as not to be misunderstood. I have no qualms about imagination. I have no qualms about construction, and I have no qualms about the modern scientific world view. I am interested more than Gustafson seems to be in getting the information about what a water table wants from me. I would be quite interested if the conversation about the ethical meaning of larger wholes became concrete instead of purely abstract. So it isn't that any of the things that one can positively say Gustafson's book means to do are things that I don't want to see done.

I just need to be brought along with them. There need to be warrants for bringing me along. It is not that either I or the author should be in a chair where we are supposed to do theology in some classical sense. Rather, he has written a book with the thought that people ought to be convinced by it, and he has used the name *God* in ways he somehow has borrowed for the wider society, enough that we ought to listen to it. The invocation of God and the publication of the books are two reasons I have to ask these questions. If I weren't a theologian by profession, I would still have to ask these questions. The announcing of a certain body of convictions or insights as news and as good does not seem to me to mean that one just spouts the new ideas without giving reasons for them. Authentic evangelism and communication of good news is profoundly occupied with its being contextualized in a language that the recipients can understand. That's what Paul was doing writing in Greek instead of Aramaic. So I don't think that the fact that Jim wants to tell us to be more open to these things explains why he wouldn't need to give his reasons.

William Schweiker (Univesity of Iowa): You seem to understand the term *tradition* as handing on a particular confession about the central normative claims of a religious community within an ecclesial context of witnessing. That is certainly an understanding of the process of traditioning in the West. But I think we can also ask another question concerning the use of tradition to speak about God. It seems to me that Gustafson's particular concern is asking, "What is the normative center of a tradition and how does that normative center influence our interpretation of the confessions and other symbols of the tradition we hand on?" It is not only apologists who are concerned with this; it is a constant feature of the theological community's past. Are you suggesting that the Reformed tradition doesn't acknowledge this distinction between levels of tradition? Or are you acknowledging that separation? In the latter case, I would contend that Gustafson is wrestling with the problem of God and raising the major normative question a theologian must raise.

Yoder: I certainly wouldn't say that the Reformed tradition doesn't recognize that question. It can't recognize it in modern terms, but historical imagination enables us to find it through the centuries, at least since the Church broke into the Hellenistic world. I sense in your phrasing about how a tradition works something more rigid and more normative than I am actually interested in. Part of the reason I tried to use the Reformed base is that my own family doesn't have confessional documents, bishops, or synods; so it can't have the rigidity that you seem to think I am trying to impose on the question. But when we ask the question about how the central norm of the affirmation of God's caring, willing, disposing, bearing down—whatever is more appropiately predicated about God—wouldn't it help, in the process of elucidation and retrieval and redefinition, at least to touch base with the old language, in order to know which of the things we bring to the modern world has root in the story and history? I can't agree to your assumption, that those two concerns are somehow disjunctive, or that if you do more of the one you are doing less of the other. It would seem to me that the process of clarifying what we mean by using the word *God* could best be carried on by keeping in the discussion the peculiarities of the Hebrew and Jewish Jesus instead of starting after Constantine, with Augustine being the oldest father. The struggle for what it means for God to be the center of our discussion would belong with the incarnation rather than bypassing it as a warrant.

Mary Potter Engel (United Theological Seminary of the Twin Cities): I would like to follow up on what constitutes the Reformed tradition in reference to the concept of sin. You were saying that in the classical Reformed tradition, sin destroys the human capacity to read traces of God in the world, and that is why we need a special revelation of the Scriptures and Jesus Christ. I disagree with that because that is not exactly the way that Calvin presents revelation. What he says is that sin does not destroy but alters. There remains a sense of God and a sense of equity and conscience. Enough remains not only to render us all guilty and inexcusable, but enough remains to prevent the world from reverting to choas. In other words, God and God's providence have left to us this constitution of human nature. We can operate with at least a minimum of justice among ourselves, whether or not we have the special revelation of Jesus Christ. Jesus Christ is a superior revelation, but people who do not have that revelation are not destitute. Therefore, there is a kind of natural piety, and a natural sense of equity, and a sense of conscience. A lot of his efforts are built on the natural conscience.

Yoder: I don't disagree. I never said it was destroyed. It is marred, it is flawed, it is skewed. It is sufficiently twisted that we can't count on it for salvation or for full unity, so there does need to be a corrective. I don't deny anything of what you said positively. I think there would be differences in parts of the Reformed tradition as to how much trust is placed in those affirmations about what people know who don't know anything about special revelation. Those people weren't alive in the sixteenth century. There weren't many of them, really, to talk to. But conceptually, when we speak of people knowing they are guilty and that their conscience is bad, all of that presupposed what you are saying. But it calls for redemption, for a redemptive change—the same kind of thing Ed Farley was noticing in completely different categories, placing less trust in the unhelped human scene.

JOHANN
Robert O.

An Ethics
of Emergent Order

Much has been written already about the "revolutionary" character of Gustafson's *Ethics from a Theocentric Perspective.*[1] What is usually meant is his thoroughgoing unmasking and critique of the anthropocentrism of our Western philosophical and theological traditions. However, in my judgment, the real importance of his work—its true title to being called revolutionary—is the view it develops and exemplifies of moral reasoning. There is, I think, something genuinely novel in the concept of rationality that is operative here. Alasdair MacIntyre has suggested that moral philosophy can escape its present plight only by returning to some form of Aristotelianism.[2] Aristotle or Nietzsche is the choice he confronts us with. But Gustafson's *Ethics* works out

---

[1]See, for example, Stephen Toulmin's "Nature and Nature's God," *Journal of Religious Ethics* 13:1 (Spring 1985): 37-52, esp. 38.

[2]Cf. Alasdair MacIntyre, *After Virtue: A Study in Moral Theory* (Notre Dame: University of Notre Dame Press, 1981) esp. chs. 9 and 18.

and exibits a third alternative, one which, while having more affinities with Aristotle than with Nietzsche, nevertheless combines aspects of both and moves decisively beyond them. At least that is the contention of this paper. I shall try to show how Gustafson develops a notion of reason as primarily practical and deliberative and how only such a conception can resolve the crisis in moral thinking that MacIntyre has chronicled.

My paper is divided into three parts. In the first, borrowing a tactic from our author, I shall spell out the circumstances of today's world that have especially preoccupied me in my own reflective efforts and in relation to which I read the *Ethics*. These circumstances constitute what I shall call "The Problem of Radical Choice." Since this is the problem that I take Gustafson's thought to be especially helpful in resolving, a brief sketch of its outlines will not only explain my approach to his work but will also indirectly illumine the work itself. In the second and main section I shall indicate resources in the *Ethics* for meeting the problem. Central to these, I will argue, is the conjunction of reason and affectivity that is manifest not only in Gustafson's theory of moral discernment but throughout the argument of both volumes. This more than anything else is what allows the *Ethics* to move beyond the traditional objectivist-subjectivist debate. I shall entitle this section "Reason as Partial: Conscience and Conscientiousness." Finally, I shall develop what I take to be some of the philosophical and theological implications of this "new" conception, not the least of which have to do with the nature of those disciplines themselves. One of the questions I shall raise concerns the relation between theology and ethics. Is the relationship, for example, that Gustafson seems to envisage between them really consistent with his view of reason and experience? I shall call this section "Human Judgment and God's Will."

The Problem of Radical Choice

The problem of radical choice is the problem of choosing our principles, that is, our standards of choice. It is a problem because it is difficult to see how such a choice can be rational. Let me explain. That human life is problematic is a commonplace. It proceeds in the light of distinctions and alternatives: true/false, real/unreal, good/bad, right/wrong, and so forth, which is to say that life, as human, is not something automatic, a matter of course; choice is always at work. But in today's world this problematic character of our lives has deepened dramatically, and the choices confronting us have been radicalized. In the not too distant past, a person's fundamental choices had to do with whether or not to conform to accepted norms and principles. Despite the plurality of traditions and life forms on the national and world scene, it was still possible to grow up within homogeneous communities in which what was expected of everyone was quite clear. Within the group, everyone knew what was right, even if one did not always do it.

All that has changed. The question today is not simply whether or not to obey, but what the relevant rules are. Through the media explosion, the pluralism of the larger scene has forced its way into the individual's consciousness, and no one is immune to its influence. This influence, as Gustafson points out, is not only corrosive of past traditions; it can also be liberating.[3] But, be that as it may, from their earliest years and prior to being formed in any one tradition, persons are confronted in their own living rooms with an almost endless variety of life forms and with the radically different options they imply. As Alasdair MacIntyre has put it, "Each of us . . . has to choose both with whom we wish to be morally bound and by what ends, rules, virtues we wish to be guided."[4] This, for example, is what lies behind the up-until-now improbable phenomenon of "Selective Catholicism" noted by contemporary sociologists.[5] And it is a problem that even traditionalists must face, for church authorities no longer speak with a single voice. "Whom is one to follow?" a friend recently asked, referring to the different emphases of the American and French bishops in their respective letters on nuclear deterrence. Prior to conforming or not, one must choose the very principles to be acknowledged. Even within the Catholic Church, one must choose one's authorities.

Needless to say, this situation has engendered a measure of confusion. If we have to choose our standards and principles, what standards or principles will guide that choice? When it comes to forms of life with different norms and mind-sets, can a choice among them be other than arbitrary? Underlying these questions is a conception of rational choice that views it as the conclusion of a practical syllogism in which principles serve as premises. Hence, if our first premises must be chosen, they cannot be chosen rationally. Thus, the pervasive pluralism of our society both forces radical choices upon us and seems to deprive us of an objective basis for making them.[6] They are simply left to

---

[3]James M. Gustafson, *Theology and Ethics,* vol. 1 of *Ethics from a Theocentric Perspective* (Chicago: University of Chicago Press, 1981) 290.

[4]Alasdair MacIntyre, *A Short History of Ethics* (New York: Macmillan Publishing Co., 1966) 268.

[5]See, for example, Andrew M. Greeley, "Selective Catholicism: How They Get Away with It," *America* (30 April 1982): 333-36.

[6]See Alasdair MacIntyre's examples of the kinds of "radical choices" contemporary culture forces on us in his "Why Is the Search for the Foundations of Ethics So Frustrating?" *Hastings Center Report* 9:4 (August 1979): 16-22.

an individual's inclination, which, in view of the high office it is called on to fill, is often enough dubbed conscience. That is why we are hearing increasing appeals to individual conscience these days and also why the appeal to conscience is so often taken as final and indisputable. It is just another matter of taste about which there can be no argument.

I do not want to quarrel with the appeal to conscience as such. The circumstances I have alluded to make a resurrection of the notion, in some form, necessary. For the modern psyche is increasingly aware that any particular way of life is but one of many possibilities and, therefore, essentially a matter of selection. With no external norms to determine that selection, an internal and, in some sense, subjective one becomes inevitable.

However, I do want to insist that the interpretation of conscience as *merely* subjective, and as implicitly equal to individual liking,[7] is not inevitable but is the result of our intellectual history. That history has been dogged by the (I will argue, false) notion that the only alternative to an already existent and determinate moral order, an objective "system of laws or precepts . . . the content of which is ascertainable by human reason" (as Donagan puts it),[8] is out-and-out relativism and subjectivism. It is the prevalence of this conception that has kept philosophers from developing a theory of deliberative rationality. (Donagan describes the use of deliberation to determine norms as philosophically "fraudulent" and morally "lax."[9] MacIntyre says it is a metaphor "empty of application."[10] Gewirth complains that it allows persons to come up with "conflicting moral judgements even if they have made no logical or empirical errors."[11]) The consequent lack of understanding regarding deliberation proceeds then to pervert the contemporary idea of conscience.

---

[7]The following remarks of James Finn, a Catholic journalist, quoted in the *New York Times* (11 August, 1984, p. 7) are typical of what I mean: "Catholics have assimilated a great deal of the country in which we live. Individual conscience has been lifted up as the supreme judge. As soon as you do that, there is no basis for objection to abortion and a number of other things. When individual conscience makes religion a private matter, you don't have to consult with anybody else."

[8]Alan Donagan, *The Theory of Morality* (Chicago: University of Chicago Press, 1977) 7.

[9]Ibid., 23.

[10]MacIntyre, "Search for the Foundations," 17.

[11]Alan Gewirth, *Reason and Morality* (Chicago and London: University of Chicago Press, 1978) 4.

In other words conscience was viewed in the past as a kind of repository of general principles, and its exercise was limited to subsuming particular cases under those principles. Thus Frankena's example regarding Socrates' reasoning in the *Crito:*

General Principle: We ought never harm anyone.
Particular Case: If I escape from prison, I will do harm to society. Therefore . . . [12]

Or again, Donagan:

General Principle: It is impermissible not to respect every human being as a rational creature.
Particular Case: To kill another human being merely at will is not to respect every human being (in particular, the one killed) as a rational creature. Therefore . . . [13]

However, the growing awareness that traditional principles are really relative to particular forms of life leaves this kind of conscience up in the air. What an individual judges about particular moral matters is viewed as a function of the form of life to which he happens, either by habit or choice, to adhere. Thus MacIntyre has argued that the identification of value judgments with emotional reactions and attitudes that has characterized much moral philosophy in the last half-century simply reflects our cultural situation. It inevitably happens when the concept of good is emptied of the content it derived from the unquestioned acceptance of a particular form of life. Stripped of such content, the word *good,* he says, "has no distinctive use or function to distinguish it from a simple imperative or expression of approval."[14]

This, I think, is a mistake. And it is rooted in the same misunderstanding that pictures objectivism versus subjectivism as exhausting our alternatives. The dependence of conscience on principles *wholly* external to itself is the result of mistakenly interpreting reason as purely cognitive and separate from appetite. Reason was deprived of any inherent practical aims. Since, however, the end to be attained is the first principle of action, reason could become practical only by going beyond itself—to the purposes inscribed in human nature or society—for the needed directives. In this sense, reason's practical thrust was viewed as secondary. It was a matter of determining the effective means to already accepted ends, of discerning what it was rational to do given certain

---

[12]William Frankena, *Ethics* (Englewood Cliffs: Prentice-Hall, 1973) 2.

[13]Donagan, *The Theory of Morality,* 72.

[14]MacIntyre, *A Short History of Ethics,* 91.

ends derived from elsewhere. With no practical aim of its own, it had no standard or norm for appraising those ends. Appraisal was limited strictly to the means—objects and actions—of reaching them.

Thus, if conscience is identified, as it was traditionally, with practical reason, its present plight is understandable. It has nothing within itself to withstand the relativizing effects of pluralism. On the other hand, if the problem of radical choice is to be resolved, if our choice of life forms and the standards they imply can also be rational, then a different conception of rationality is required. As indicated earlier, I believe Gustafson's *Ethics* develops such a conception. To that we now turn.

Reason as Partial:
Conscience and Conscientiousness

The Piety of Reason. Gustafson is well aware that he is engaging in what I have called "radical choice."[15] Indeed the two volumes of the *Ethics* may be viewed not only as the product of such choices but as an extended model of how to go about making them. Thus, as the author indicates, a Christian theological ethics involves choices not only about what sources are relevant to its construction, but also about which ones are decisive when they conflict, what specific content is to be used from them, and how this chosen content is to be interpreted.[16] They are choices, in other words, that are determining the very conceptual framework within which future moral judgments are to be made.

Moreover, these choices are not taken to be mere discharges of pure will. They are products of practical reason,[17] which is to say they are *reasoned* choices or, what comes to the same thing, practical *judgments.* "I shall be as clear about the choices made as I can," the author writes, "and give as good reasons for them as can be developed in limited space."[18] And again: "Theology primarily is an activity of practical reason."[19] How does this practical reason function? First of all, not deductively. Gustafson's good reasons are not higher

---

[15]See, for example, Gustafson's description of the ideal type of purpose that, he says, motivates his theological work (*Ethics,* 1:154).

[16]James M. Gustafson, *Ethics and Theology,* vol. 2 of *Ethics from a Theocentric Perspective* (Chicago: University of Chicago Press, 1984) 143.

[17]Ibid., 1:158.

[18]Ibid., 1:153.

[19]Ibid., 1:158.

principles entailing the ones chosen. We have already seen that in the case of radical choices that is impossible. But Gustafson's conception of rationality is wider than the classic model. "To be rational is not simply to reason logically from certain abstract or general principles to their application to the particular 'facts' at hand."[20] Reason is viewed, rather, as an ordering process; it is our capacity for organizing our lives and experience. "Our rationality is exercised," he writes, "in determining what things are good for . . . ; how to order and govern . . . our conflicting motives and how to relate things to each other in the external world."[21] And he quotes Mary Midgley approvingly: "Reason is not the name of a character in a drama. It is a name for organizing oneself. . . . It is the process of choosing which [desires will be restrained] that is rightly called reasoning."[22] Reasoning is a matter of rightly weighing the alternatives confronting us. The theologian, for example, has to decide "the relative 'authority' to be given to various points of reference. . . . What weight will contemporary scientific accounts of nature . . . be given . . . ? What weight will be given to the test of confirmation by human experience? . . . How will ideas be recombined?"[23] In other words, MacIntyre's contention to the contrary notwithstanding (that the idea of weighing conflicting claims is a metaphor without application), practical rationality is deliberative rationality. To choose rightly is to assign the proper weight to alternative proposals for ordering and organizing experience. Let us look at this more closely.

The first thing to stress is that reasoning is a matter of organizing *experience*. Since experience is a central theme for Gustafson, how does he conceive it? First of all, experience, for him, is not just the initial phase of a purely cognitive affair, a matter of sense presentations from which intellect can abstract the forms and essences whose grasp and manipulation was often taken to be the very stuff of knowledge and the substance of rational life. Experience is more than cognitive. It is the interactive process itself in all its complexity and in all its dimensions in which the human organism is involved and participates. It is, therefore, more than something subjective. It involves others, indeed the whole range of the other. "Experience is social,"Gustafson writes, "it is a process of interactions between persons and natural events, and between persons and historical events. . . . It is experience of others, of 'things' objective to human persons."[24] Indeed distinc-

---

[20]Ibid., 1:286.

[21]Ibid., 1:287.

[22]Ibid.

[23]Ibid., 1:153.

[24]Ibid., 1:115.

tions like that between subject and object are distinctions we make reflectively within experience, and their value is something to be tested by experience. Experience is prior to these reflective distinctions and "resists, to some extent, our concepts and our analysis."[25]

As the context within which our reflective life arises and in relation to which it has its meaning, experience is thus not only primary but also ultimate. If reflection is to issue in knowledge, its results must in some way be validated by experience. "All our knowledge, including our knowledge of God, [has, Gustafson claims, an] experiential basis."[26] Indeed it is in order to make sense of experience, to have it in more meaningful ways, that we engage in reflective inquiry in the first place. "Theology," for example, "is an effort to make sense out of a very broad range of human experiences, to find some meaning in them and for them that enables persons to live and to act in coherent ways."[27]

This brings up the other point. Rational inquiry is a matter of *organizing* experience. It is a constructive, transformative enterprise, requiring not just logical analysis, but imagination and affectivity. This means that inquiry stands midway between two qualitatively different states of affairs, the relatively haphazard and disorganized and the relatively more directed and organized, and, provoked as a response to the first, its aim is to bring about the second. Judgment, therefore, in which inquiry terminates is not a simple beholding, a grasp of being or reality in its self-sufficing form. Judgment is essentially an answer to a question, the conclusion to a search, a quest. The real logic of inquiring is not demonstrative, the deductive unfolding and linking of concepts; it is inventive. Inquiry is a matter of *finding new* and more satisfactory ways of ordering and relating the elements of our experience. Writing about theological inquiry, but making it clear that what he says is not limited to theology,[28] Gustafson writes, "Even its more abstract forms are constructive; arguments are made that do not follow the strictest rules of formal logic, but which commend themselves as reasonable ways to deal with the realities of religious life."[29] So also with moral inquiry. "The final discernment is not the conclusion of a formally logical argument, a strict deduction from a single

---

[25]Ibid., 1:117.

[26]Ibid., 1:202.

[27]Ibid., 1:158.

[28]Ibid.

[29]Ibid., 1:229.

moral principle."[30] It is a matter of determining the most reasonable course, the most reasonable ordering of the inclusive situation. This reminds us of Charles Peirce's notion that the final end, in the sense of that end which is pursuable in all circumstances, is nothing other than "concrete reasonableness."[31]

This brings us to the heart of the matter. The crucial questions are: What constitutes a reasonable course and how does one go about determining it? If reasoning is a weighing, what is the scale? We have already made a beginning on these questions with the understanding of experience that has been presented. We have said that experience, whose elements reason is to organize appropriately, is a process of interaction and interrelationship in which everything is involved and on whose patterns and structures (which Gustafson insists are patterns of interdependence) all things depend for their existence and their possibilities. In other words, experience is never something without form or structure; it is always more or less organized. Hence, it is not reason's task to introduce order de novo. Rather its function is critical. Its aim is to reorganize, to reconstruct, to enhance what is there. For if the meaning and existence of things are a function of their interrelationships, they can be interrelated in ways that enrich their meaning and broaden their possibilities or in ways that diminish these. Some orders, in spite of what they make possible, are more limiting than they need be and can be improved. To bring about such improvement is, I suggest, the inherent aim of all our interventions. An action is irrational if its only effect is a limitation or reduction of possibilities. On the other hand, no deliberate action is possible that does not aim to make some kind of objective sense, that is, to fulfill some need, satisfy some desire, realize some capacity. Every deliberate action intends a situation that is newly whole at least in some respect.

This ties in with the classic formula according to which it is impossible to intend anything except under the formality of good. If it goes farther than the formula, it does so by identifying *good* with *what it makes sense to do,* and by interpreting *making sense* as effecting a whole of some sort with new meanings and new possibilities. Of course, intervening so as to maintain present possibilities that would otherwise diminish is a case of the same thing.

These ideas have important implications. They involve abandoning the idea of reason (that is, the human being qua rational) as an uninvolved, disinter-

---

[30]Ibid., 1:338.

[31]See, for example, Peirce's essay "Ideals of Conduct" (part of his Lowell Lectures of 1903) in *The Collected Papers of Charles Sanders Peirce* (Cambridge: Harvard University Press, Belknap Press, 1931-1935) 1:591-615.

ested spectator, which was the classic view.[32] Reason is itself an interest structure. Instead of having to borrow all aims from elsewhere, it is itself a dynamic orientation to a goal. Instead of being inherently indifferent to what goes on, it is itself partial to some possibilities over others. In Gustafson's terms, it has a kind of "natural piety" towards the possibilities for being inherent in experience.[33] Thus, "the radical distinction between 'reason' and 'emotion' creates a false dichotomy."[34] Reason is itself emotional, affective, valuing. Reason is itself bent and bias.

Implications for Morality. Now this natural bent of reason is, I want to argue, the natural root of morality, and its recognition is essential for a proper understanding of conscience. As a first step towards this understanding, let me remark that a partiality for sense would make no sense apart from the other interests and wants of the human species that "are to a great extent," both Midgley and Gustafson point out, "shared with other animals."[35] Where there are no needs or wants, no natural ends whose attainment requires the enlisting of forces external to the organism, there is no possibility of failure or fullfillment, no basis for intervening in the situation in one way more than another. We "can indeed only understand our values," Gustafson quotes Midgley as saying, "if we first grasp the given facts of our wants."[36] Thus our rationality is not something over against and "discontinuous" with our appetitive nature. Not only is it itself an appetite, but it is such a one as to require the presence of other appetites for its own functioning.[37] Together they constitute a working whole: reason gives order and form to our natural impulses and desires, while these in turn give content to reason's quest for sense.

Thus reason not only needs other interests if it is to have anything to do; reason's very presence transforms these other interests. They cease to be mere given biases and bents and become standards of appraisal, norms for determining right and wrong ways to proceed. To be partial to wholeness while at the same time involved in a situation of need and want is to experience oneself called (once one becomes aware of resources making it possible) to meet those needs and fulfill those wants. Both what things are and the consequences of

---

[32]Ibid., 2:145.

[33]Ibid., 1:158-59.

[34]Ibid., 1:287.

[35]Ibid., 1:285.

[36]Ibid.

[37]Ibid., 2:8.

reordering them in different ways cry out to be taken into account. Facts cease to be neutral; they put claims upon us. Thus, what Gustafson says of piety is to some extent true of this natural bent of reason, this natural piety. It provides "the hinge which joins the frame of the . . . natural ordering of life to the door of human duties and obligations."[38] Reason's partiality to being, its interest in enlarged possibilities, converts given relationships and connections into prima facie norms. They become factors that claim respect, reasons for specific behavior. Moreover, since the adequacy of the agent's interventions in behalf of greater sense is to some extent a function of the accuracy of his grasp of what is what and what is connected with what, reason's very interest becomes a motive for scientific, that is, disinterested, inquiry. Our interest in sense makes it important to find out how things really are, independent of our interests.

However, if reason converts the needs of the situation into norms of behavior, these norms often conflict with one another. They are indeed norms only with the proviso "everything else being equal." But "everything else" is rarely equal. That is why reason's task becomes one of "*sorting out* our motives and desires,"[39] including, I should add, reason's own desire for sense. Since an action cannot be intended except as effecting some kind of whole, the conflicting possibilities must be ordered in some way and one interest selected as overriding. The choice of a de facto dominant or final end, although often only implicit, is a necessity of deliberate action.[40] For sense can be made only from some standpoint or other, and the interest selected as standpoint becomes in effect the final standard of appraisal with regard to all others. Every deliberate act is the (at least) implicit adoption of a final end, and, it should be noted, it is the agent, by his action (and not nature), who constitutes the end as final.[41] Contrary to much traditional thought, there is no natural final end to which all others are subordinate. As Gustafson remarks about his own position, "The theology of this book and the ethics that follow from it do not warrant the formation of an immutable rank order of ends. . . . There is no automatic harmony of ideal ends. . . . [nor] a single substantive moral prin-

[38]Ibid., 1:167.

[39]Ibid., 1:285. Italics mine.

[40]See Joseph Margolis, *Values and Conduct* (New York: Oxford University Press, 1971) 8.

[41]See Robert Johann, "God and the Search for Meaning," in *God Knowable and Unknowable,* ed. Robert Roth, S. J. (New York: Fordham University Press, 1973) esp. 257-63.

ciple which always overrides all others."[42] And again, criticizing Thomistic ethics on this point: "A 'naturalistic' basis for ethics must be satisfied with a variety of ends of human activity that are not forged into an ultimate single end."[43]

With this last, I am in full agreement. But to deny the existence of a natural final end is not to deny the existence of an interest that deserves, because of its nature, to be made final. And with this we come to the ideas of conscience and conscientiousness that, although not explicitly highlighted in Gustafson's *Ethics,* are, I think, fundamental to what he does say.

Conscience, let me suggest, is practical reason judging our actions, not as a means to some chosen end, but as ends themselves (that is, as specific orderings of the inclusive situation, specific orderings of the agent and the environment in interrelation) in the light of its own interest in sense. The question is not whether the action accords with the agent's proposed goal (a technological question) nor whether the end proposed makes some kind of sense (we have already seen that "making some kind of sense" is a psychological condition for its being an action). The question is whether the end result is reasonable, whether the overall situation effected by the specific action is in accord with the inherent aim of any action, an achievement of concrete reasonableness. For it is often the case that the intended enhancement of the situation is at the expense of greater, more urgent possibilities to which the agent, under the pressure of the narrower interest, neglects or refuses to attend. One becomes aware that one's action makes sense only up to a point, that overall it makes no sense, that it is, in the court of reason, indefensible. One experiences oneself at odds with one's own being as rational and with the claims of objective reasonableness upon one. One has, in short, an uneasy conscience.

Here, it is clear, reason's essential interest in sense is functioning not only psychologically (to make deliberate action possible) but in a morally normative way.[44] And, it must be said, although it is by nature only one of many interests, it is suited by its nature to become the final norm. For since the interest in sense underlies any action as deliberate, it is reasonable to require that the overall result of a specific action be consistent with it and to regulate our choice of ends accordingly. The adoption of the interest in sense as the

---

[42]Gustafson, *Ethics,* 2:298-99.

[43]Ibid., 2:55.

[44]Cf. Donagan, *The Theory of Morality,* 81, where he misinterprets, I believe, Aquinas's first principle in practical reason (*bonum est faciendum*) as a matter of *aiming* at the good rather than as *effecting* the good.

final standard, since it alone insures the possibility of comprehensive sense, is itself an instance of "what it makes sense to do" and so puts a claim on our natural piety. Indeed, I would say it is the naturalness of having this interest serve as final norm that gives rise to judgments in its light even in a person who has chosen to act on another basis.[45] In this sense, having a conscience is natural, whereas being conscientious is strictly a matter of choice, the choice of a way of being.

What then is conscientiousness? In light of the above, conscientiousness results from a firm commitment to conscience. It is the disposition to act always and only on the basis of reason's judgments of what it makes overall sense to do. Conscientiousness enshrines reason's interest in sense as the final standard of appraisal and overall sense (or concrete reasonableness) as the final end of all endeavor. Making such a commitment presupposes the possibility of formulating for ourselves an appropriate first principle. It is, after all, a matter of self direction. Such a principle or directive might be: "Always do that which most contributes to the overall sense of the situation," or more simply "Always do what makes the most sense." It can even be formulated in the traditional way: "Do good and avoid evil," so long as good and evil are understood as the concrete situation so ordered as to evoke reason's approval or disapproval respectively and, just as important, so long as *do* is understood to mean not merely "aim at" but "effect," "bring about."

Such a formulation can, of course, provoke the objection that Gustafson does in fact raise with regard to the first principle of natural law: "it is . . . so general that it solves few particular dilemmas that occur in human life."[46] However, to make this objection to what is being argued for here is to misunderstand the function of the formulation. As I indicated above, the method of moral discernment is not one of demonstration but invention, not one of proving conclusions but of searching for and finding new and more reasonable ways of ordering experience ("more reasonable" meaning "more in accord with the natures and possibilities for being of the elements being organized"). Hence, the formulation is not that of a first premise in an argument, but of a directive for the agent, the formulation of the agent's quest, the specification of his search. By this directive, the agent constitutes himself a living question in relation to which he proceeds to reconstruct the situation and the answer to which he will know only when the situation is so organized that to one committed as he is it gives rise to no objections—or to put it succinctly, only when

---

[45]This ties in with the "accusing" function of conscience noted by Gustafson in connection with Aquinas's doctrine on conscience (*Ethics*, 2:64).

[46]Ibid., 1:29.

his quest is put to rest. This is an instance of what medieval thinkers called knowledge by connaturality. It is a matter, not of logical analysis, but of so reordering the situation that, precisely as one committed to overall sense, instead of experiencing himself at odds with it the agent finds himself newly at home with it. The process is not wholly unlike that of the artist's seeking to order and organize sensible materials into a satisfactory object for contemplation and who comes to know what that is in detail only when he has the finished product before him. Or again, because moral inquiry is not a free synthesis but is under the constraint of taking the actual orderings and connections of nature into account, we can use Gustafson's own example of the discerning biographer, trying to construct an interpretation of his subject's life "that is not only insightful but can be tested by others for its accuracy and explanatory power."[47]

Now, unless I have completely misunderstood him, something very much like what I am calling conscientiousness is at work in Gustafson's theory of moral discernment and indeed in the overall structure of his *Ethics*. Since a judgment of what it makes sense to do depends on an interpretation of what is going on, and since such an interpretation is itself a construct answering the question "what does it make sense to believe?" one cannot be serious about the former without being equally serious about the latter. I take Gustafson's two volumes to be, and to be a model for, a conscientious inquiry into these two questions, volume one seeking an answer to the question about belief, volume two to that about conduct. But more on this in the final part of this paper. What I want to do now is briefly to point out how by providing us with the elements of a theory of conscience and conscientiousness, and even more by conspicuously exemplifying the latter, Gustafson's work resolves the problem of radical choice outlined above.

Summary. The problem of the appeal to conscience that, we saw, the pluralism of contemporary culture makes inevitable stems from the view of conscience we have inherited. Conscience has been looked on as a repository of general principles of conduct to be applied in particular cases. With the growing realization that these principles are themselves a matter of choice, there appears no way for that choice to be a reasoned one (reasoning being interpreted as arguing from premises to a conclusion). The appeal to conscience then appears as nothing more than an appeal to individual likes and dislikes.

As we have seen, Gustafson rejects both horns of this dilemma. He refuses to reduce the choice of principles to arbitrary preference, insisting that we back such choices with sound reasons. On the other hand, he refuses to limit sound

---

[47]Ibid., 1:329.

reasons to "known propositions entailing others for which they are reasons."[48]
His principal move here is to overcome the traditional separation of reason from
affectivity and appetite and to see reason itself as an interest structure, an interest in making sense out of the experiential process. Reason ceases to be purely
cognitive; we are not just spectators. Reason is our capacity to order and shape
the world in a reasonable, responsible way, that is, a way responsive to the
natures and possibilities of the elements being organized. Having thus an end
of its own, what Peirce called "concrete reasonableness," reason now has a
standpoint from which it can appraise the adoption of other natural ends (for
the human being is a complex of wants and desires) as standards of appraising
alternative courses of action. In other words, in the absence of generally accepted norms, we are not bereft of guidance. We can, if we choose to, base
our choice of principles on their consistency with reason's inherent orientation
towards good order, its "natural piety" towards being and intelligibility. Since
the adoption of this orientation as the final standard enhances the possibilities
for reason in the world (the choice of anything else as final means subordinat-
ing concrete reasonableness to some other end), it is a reasonable choice to
make. On the other hand, only if we make it (and making it is the basis of
what I have called conscientiousness) can conscience be reliably invoked. For,
if practical judgments are not merely conclusions from premises, they are
nonetheless answers—and answers presuppose questions. The question to be
resolved determines what considerations are relevant and what can count as an
answer. The question is a quest which the answer, the judgment, fulfills. Thus,
right order can only be known as that which satisfies the quest for right order.
Without that quest, we are simply not asking the moral question and in no
position to recognize the moral answer.

Radical choice, the choice of standards and principles, can thus be a reasoned affair. The reasons backing such choices will be those characteristics of
the order they would, if adopted, institute that make the order a suitable can-
didate to fulfill our quest for good order. It is not the conformity of the proposed order to some antecedent model that validates it, but its qualities as an
order—for example, its relative comprehensiveness, balance, the respect for
being and its possibilities which it manifests, in comparison with possible alternatives. Moreover, these will be reasons for adopting the proposal only for
one who is conscientious, who has made reason's concern for right order the
supreme regulative principle. As Gustafson rightly notes, the role of dispo-

---

[48]This is Kurt Baier's formulation of how "reasons" have traditionally been conceived. See his Presidential Address to the A.P.A., "The Social Source of Reason,"
Proceedings and Addresses of the A.P.A. 51:6 (August 1978): 708.

sitions in the process of reaching sound judgments is, though often over-looked, absolutely crucial.[49]

Human Judgment and God's Will

In this part of my paper, I want to address the theocentric character of Gustafson's *Ethics*. So far in my reflective commentary on it the word *God* has not even been mentioned. Part of the reason for that has to do with the cen-trality of the problem of radical choice in my thinking as I read the *Ethics*. This means that ethics as I have been concerned with it is primarily what has come to be called metaethics. My focus has been on ethics as the theory of moral choice. Gustafson, while not neglecting metaethical questions, centers on normative issues. For him, ethics is the theory of right or proper order,[50] and a proper order turns out to be a God-centered one.

But the question can arise as to whether the theory of choice we have lined out is really consistent with Gustafson's metaethical views. For if there is a constant refrain in Gustafson's work, it is that man is not the measure of right and wrong. Man is the measurer, yes. The human being inevitably has to do all the discerning. But humanity and its welfare are not the standard or norm. Yet the burden of my own analysis has been that, in a very real sense, man is the norm, man is the measure. What I have argued is that the problem of rad-ical choice requires a conception of rationality as primarily deliberative and that what has chiefly blocked the development of such a conception is the tra-ditional separation of reason from desire and affectivity. But with the inter-pretation of reason as itself an interest structure and the recognition of that interest as having to do with the reorganization of experience in the direction of sense, the weighing of alternatives ceases to be a matter merely of consult-ing one's individual inclinations and becomes a reasoned affair. Deliberation, even on ultimate matters, becomes respectably cognitive. For we have now a scale with which to do the weighing. And that scale is our own rationality. Thus, in this view at least, man is the measure. Not only does man do the judging, the measuring, but man's practical reason is the final standard of judgment.

Now there may be, as we shall see, an important difference between Gustafson's views and my own, but I do not think it is here. What Gustafson is criticizing in his rejection of anthropocentrism and the notion of man as measure is not the notion of practical reason as norm but the idea that human

---

[49]Gustafson, *Ethics,* 2:12.

[50]Ibid., 2:6.

well-being is the norm. "That human judgment determines what is right," he says, ". . . is necessarily the case,"[51] and here we must remember that the interest underlying human judgment as an activity, that is, inquiry, is for Gustafson also our interest in making sense. After all, in Gustafson's view, religion itself is grounded in our natural affections, and not only our ethical theories, but also our theologies are human constructs. No, what Gustafson objects to is the view that "man's good is the principal consideration in determining what God wills" or that "man's good is the moral measure of all things."[52]

However, as should be clear from part two above, human well-being or happiness is not the final end or norm for us either. To make it so would be to subordinate the achievement of good order—concrete reasonableness—to a particular objective, to countenance overall disorder, entailing an overall lessening of the possibilities for being inherent in experience as inclusive process, for the sake of satisfying some particular interests. For the thing about reason as an interest, in comparison with other interests, is its universal and inclusive character. Anthropocentrism is wrong because it represents a kind of contraction of rationality (one of the main elements in Gustafson's view of the human fault).[53] Contrary to reason's unrestricted interest in wholeness, such an ordering subordinates the whole interactive process to one of its participants.

Again, even though for the reasons indicated above the word *God* did not figure in our theory of moral choice, the position outlined is not only consistent with a theocentric ordering but favors it. For, as we saw, the rightly ordered situation will be the one that, compared to possible alternatives, most fulfills the quest for right order. It will be the one that makes the most sense from the standpoint precisely of one committed to making overall sense. Such a commitment, as an abiding disposition, defines the conscientious person. But if *God* is the name for the ultimate source of possibilities for being inherent in experience, then God is the one who *by nature* is concerned with the whole, and the conscientious person may be interpreted as seeking to appraise the situation from the divine standpoint. For someone nurtured in a theistic tradition, the question "What ordering would make the most sense?" easily becomes "Lord, what will you have me do?"(Acts 9:6) Theocentrism is thus not only consistent with the inclusive character of the moral interest, but is suggested by it. Or to put it another way, reason's natural piety, in giving

---

[51]Ibid., 1:90.

[52]Ibid.

[53]Ibid., 1:300ff.

rise to conscientiousness as a reasonable stance, also gives rise to the idea of God as final focus.

But here I must confess to a difficulty with Gustafson's position. For while I agree that a proper moral theory is a theocentric one, I am not sure I concur with what Gustafson seems to think, judging from *some* of his remarks, that entails. The question has to do with what it means to discern God's purposes, or perhaps more precisely, with just what it is that justifies the moral judgments we make. In the view I have developed, the justification of a proposed ordering of the inclusive situation is *not* its conformity to some antecendent and independently known moral order. There is, to be sure, a knowable antecedent order that our judgments must take into account. But that order is not the moral order, it is the order of nature; and as Gustafson himself points out with regard to natural relations, while they "form the bases of ethics, they are not sufficient in themselves to determine the proper ordering."[54] Indeed, Gustafson rightly criticizes Thomistic natural law theory for assuming that the order of nature is already a moral order.[55]

What *does* justify a proposed ordering is precisely its qualities as an ordering and the measure in which, by reason of those qualities, it satisfies (as an answer satisfies a question) the unrestricted quest for sense that is the moral quest. In this light, as we saw, anthropocentrism is to be rejected because of its limitation as an ordering. And this certainly seems consistent with much that Gustafson says. Thus, for example, the radical choice of particular theological views will be justified in so far as they "commend themselves as *reasonable* ways to deal with the realities of religious life."[56] Or again, "Those who continue to give a measured consent to aspects of the tradition find that a heritage from the past provides a *worthy* way of understanding certain meanings of present human life and experience."[57] Finally, the tragic choice of suicide is viewed as acceptable in the measure that it is a conscientious one made in circumstances in which "there is no other reasonable choice."[58]

There is no question here of justifying these practical judgments by their conformity to a known antecedent order. Yet, unless I misunderstand him, that is what Gustafson seems to do when he rejects anthropocentrism. He does

---

[54]Ibid., 1:340; 2:293ff.

[55]Ibid., 1:78; 2:58.

[56]Ibid., 1:229. Italics mine.

[57]Ibid., 1:235. Italics mine.

[58]Ibid., 2:215.

not reject it only because of its lack as an ordering (its subordination of the whole to a part, its unresponsiveness to other parts, and so forth). He rejects it because God does not have human well-being at the center of His concerns, and we can infer that He does not because of man's late arrival in the universe and because, as science assures us, our planet and solar system are doomed.[59]

Here the procedure seems to be to try to determine God's purposes as matters of fact (that is, matters knowable independently of our interests) and to use these known purposes as the pattern for ours. Our purposes will be justified if they conform to the knowable (at least in some cases) moral order constituted by His purposes. The difficulty with this view is that it seems to fall into the very objectivism that Nietzsche attacked so effectively and that is at odds with the overall thrust of Gustafson's own work.

Conclusion

I entitled these reflections "An Ethics of Emergent Order." What I meant by that should now be clear. The moral order is an emergent order. It does not preexist in any knowable way its elaboration by human deliberation and judgment. But that does not leave us with arbitrary choice. Nietzsche's mistake, precisely because of his limited view of rationality, was to think that rejection of an antecedent order left us only with irrational will. I have tried to show that such is not the case—and I think Gustafson's own work massively confirms my point. Reason itself is an interest in sense, order, wholeness, concrete reasonableness. It is, we have seen, a kind of quest. This fact, when taken in conjunction with a knowledge of what things are and what their possibilities are (hence the importance of science in this regard), makes possible a process of rational (reasoned) radical choice. The moral order is a product of that process. It is a human invention, a construct of practical reason, and something known—and it is known—only in its elaboration. What is constructed is, moreover, an objective ordering, with objective qualities as an ordering that make it more or less acceptable as an answer to reason's quest. Again, as an answer to reason's quest, it is not something independent of that quest. It is not an independent matter of fact that can be ascertained scientifically. There is, as I said, no natural final end. The final end is constituted by choice. This puts the position beyond that of Aristotle. Since, however, it is a reasoned choice, since a case can be made for deliberately ordering our lives and our world in response to our natural interest in a world that makes sense, the Nietzschean alternative is also surpassed.

---

[59]Ibid., 1:97.

What then about God's will? I wrote earlier that *God* is the name for the ultimate source of the possibilities for being in experience. Let me say now that if it makes sense to construe human life as a response to our natural interest in sense, it also makes sense, because that interest is not our doing, to construe God as its source. God becomes a kind of transcendent interest in concrete reasonableness, and our own rationality is viewed as a participation in His. To be responsive to reason's quest is thus to be responsive to His will. And an effort to determine what is required to order well the inclusive situation in which we find ourselves is equivalently an effort to determine His will for that situation. In other words, we find out God's will by determining what it makes overall sense to do; we do not find out what it makes sense to do by first ascertaining His will. For we must remember, as Gustafson so often reminds us, theology no less than ethics is a work of practical reason, a human construct in the interest of greater sense. If ethics is our effort to reorder our ongoing world in a way that makes more sense, theology is our effort to make sense conceptually of our experience as a whole, including the ethical enterprise. God's will is not an ascertainable matter of fact. It is a matter of interpretation. It is not an objective norm for choice but a theological construal of reasoned choice. And, as I said at the outset, I think it is in explaining and concretely demonstrating how the radical choice of conceptual frameworks and moral principles can be a reasoned affair that Gustafson's monumental work makes its most significant, and indeed revolutionary, contribution.

JOHANN DISCUSSION

William C. Spohn (Jesuit School of Theology at Berkeley): Could you extend your comment on the contrast between Gustafson's notion of God and the notion of God that John Dewey has?

Johann: Dewey is trying to make sense of experience as itself a quest for sense. Theology interprets that quest—experience as a quest. I do have a bit of a problem with using the notion of ordering with God and then ruling out any type of intentional activity, as Gustafson seems to do. On the other hand, part of that is the result of his own conscientiousness. In his conception of theology, in saying something about what ultimately is the case, he does not want to affirm more of God than he thinks he has real warrant for. The idea of dependence on powers that bear down on us is clear from experience. He is reluctant to interpret those powers in personal ways, as if that would be saying something about God Himself. He is reluctant to make that move. I don't think it is a question of the conception of God as Wholly Other, as was suggested yesterday. For Gustafson, I think, otherness is within experience as our encounter with the Other. As I move to try to make sense of this, I try to construe a whole within which my own quest for sense makes sense. In following out this quest, I myself am being responsive to an intention. This inclines me to use a personal metaphor, but I recognize it for what it is. It is a way of conceiving. We are constructing this way of conceiving in the interest of making sense of our experience. The idea of transformation and reconstruction is at the heart of Dewey's thought, in the interest of the ideal. I think I have been more personalistically concerned and oriented than Dewey.

Martin Cook (University of Santa Clara): I think that Gustafson wants to stress a radical discontinuity between one's natural moral sense, which tends to be anthropocentric, and the kind of leap to theocentrism.

Johann: Where Gustafson sees the work of theology as an effort to make sense of experience, it is going to be sort of pious. It is not going to be based on theological premises, but on our own functioning, as experiencers and as agents. For him too, theology is a human work, a human invention. I do think there is a tension in Gustafson, which I alluded to at the end of my paper. I think a lot of what he says does not jibe with an already determinate society or order that we must conform to, though that seems to be the case when anthropocentrism is rejected in terms of what God's purposes seem to be. On the other hand, his own efforts presuppose a naturalistic orientation. It has its roots in human nature. This may stress the naturalness of the moral, the religious, and the philosophical enterprises more than he does, but all these are efforts to grasp and order experience in different ways. This is consistent with his own general idea of reflection as organizing experience, to see it rooted in our nature as rational agents.

Mary Midgley: It certainly looks odd when Gustafson says, "Since the physicists have now told us, we know what God's will is, as follows." He really seems to be saying that, and that cannot be right, can it? How about this analysis? Gustafson is denying the tremendous claims for human value that were associated with quasi-scientific stories meant to validate them. We had the Ptolemaic system in astronomy, and we had the Genesis-chronology or the story of this day when God arranged it so. Now, since modern science has broken up these quasi-scientific stories, it has made it harder for people to take these positions. Of course, two things are happening here. Modern science is saying, this did not happen in 4004 B.C. Second, the horizons are not what they used to be, and it gets less plausible to say that on a particular day God said as follows. Gustafson is saying that if the heavens opened and a chap came out with a trumpet at lunchtime, this would clearly seem to all of us to be some publicity stunt. I think Gustafson's procedure can be defended. It is a double negative. He has taken away certain quasi-scientific jobs [from religion] and ended by saying that what God actually wants isn't a question of fact; it's a question of interpretation. I am not sure that that antithesis can be quite right. To have a seriously religious position is to say that it is a question of fact what God wants or purposes. To find it out is terribly hard, so our interpretation comes into it. But the word *fact,* I think, is a bit ambiguous.

Johann: About Gustafson's idea of God's will as a matter of interpretation rather than a matter of fact, I have been trying to combine or synthesize the "conform" and the "transform" theories of knowledge. John E. Smith criticizes Dewey for being a "transform" theorist. I don't think that is altogether fair. It seems to me that Dewey is saying that our judgments are not grasps of essences, not grasps of the reality directly itself. They are ways of resolving problems by making more sense of them. They are transformative, but we grasp something of the real in knowing them as answers. Talking about it as a construct is not a purely personal or private question. It is a way of interpreting this inclusive process as a quest for sense. Experience itself is not seen as something wholly determinate. It involves the idea of a task, something to be achieved, and how to make sense out of it. It seems to me that theology is a way of making sense of experience as a quest for sense.

Robert N. Bellah: This question is based on my desire for a somewhat more socially interactive picture of moral reasoning than you give, though, of course, that wasn't a focus of your presentation. There is choice, of course, and we are very aware of the fact of how much we choose all of the time. But there is also the situation. The sense of being chosen is crucial in both ethics and religion—being chosen in a situation that from one's own perspective one would not have chosen. One may feel called to a choice involving sacrifice or renunciation against the whole grain of one's life. Yet sensing that, and sensing that as ethical and ultimately religious, one cannot simply consent or accept but through the grace of God. One affirms joyously something that absolutely breaks one's life in terms of what one has expected all along. There is a sense that one is not final in oneself. It is more than simply finding God as the context for the broadest interpretation of one's moral inquiry. Is there room in your perspective for that kind of aspect of moral and religious life?

Johann: Perhaps I don't give it proper emphasis. I did mention the experience of being called, and this calling can go against a lot of what one has been doing. Contrary to the liberal view, what I am trying to argue here is a notion of morality that is rooted in a full and comprehensive rationality. I try to make use of Gustafson's notion of contracted rationality. I don't want to have God simply as an overall framework. I am trying to see this intention-of-sense in terms of which I experience things as making claims upon me. That is why I agree so much with Gustafson in the combination of deontology and teleology. Both are aspects of this quest for sense. I get a sense of being intended in this experience of claims. That's why I am a bit wary of Gustafson's completely impersonal view. The kind of God that will make sense of this quest is precisely where I am called. "What will you have me do?" It seems to me that this sort of question becomes very real. It is a way of organizing our experience—not just that this becomes a kind of framework, but I am called and I may be called in ways that go contrary to all that I have been doing. This would leave room for and require a kind of conversion. We are never wholly committed to sense; there is a continual growth in this commitment to the more widely moral. This is the only fully rational quest.

Gordon D. Kaufman: There was a great deal of use in your paper of the metaphor of order and ordering, and I don't think that is anywhere examined but is a presupposition taken for granted. We need to look at that. You use the idea of emergent order. You and Gustafson both use notions of right order, good order, and so on. It seems to me in Gustafson's general treatment order is something to which we must conform—some kind of patterns or regularities to which we must conform. But as you pointed out in your paper, we are creating order in our moral activity. We are not simply replicating what is there. We are bringing into being an order and, in fact, superimposing the order we are creating on the order that is already there. What that is, of course, is the whole process of history superimposed on nature—bringing into being new orders that transform the orders that are in place before human beings come on the scene. To the extent we are creating this order (the order of history), we are generating the criteria. We ourselves determine what right order is. Our activity of generating these new orders is obviously anthropocentric; it is a completely human activity. Gustafson's theocentrism, on the other hand, seems to suggest that the right order is already there and it is God's order. If I hear him rightly, our task is largely a task of conforming ourselves to the already given. If it is not that, if he is more along the line of your point, then I think we still do not have it all clear. What kind of moral criteria are there that might guide us, or what kind might we create to guide us in this process of developing an emergent order? I think the whole question of order is very ambiguous in the way we have been using it. It tends to cover the central problem.

Johann: I had originally titled this paper "An Ethics of Emergent Form." A part of this whole process is where reality itself is understood as a movement toward integration, a movement toward form. I see order as integration. The notion of form is a principle of integrating plurality into a kind of whole, where the parts reinforce one another.

Now about the order already being there for Gustafson, he is quite clear that the order in nature is an order to be taken into account, but it is not finally decisive. You take the facts into account the way a biographer does. In moral discernment, it is a question of integrating the facts in a way that is insightful. Therefore, there is a kind of creative balance. It's not just imposing; you have got to take the scientific order into account. There are patterns that are there, forms if you like. This movement toward form has been operative throughout the evolutionary process; you can interpret it this way if you want. What is at question here is greater or lesser integration. We are continuing this process, and that is why I like to think of the moral life as rooted in nature, as in a sense continuous with the whole process of nature. If you take the notion of form, ordering is a direction. The thing I have in mind is Dewey's insistence that you don't have to move beyond experience. The basic mistake is to move to some sort of transcendent realm to provide justification for norms we find within experience. Experience can provide and develop its own norms. It is not an end in the sense of a particular state of affairs. There is a kind of quest involved—a formal object, if you like—and that form is the answer to that quest. I take form as basically integrative. You are going to have a plurality of different forms suggested, different orderings, but I want to suggest that one can critically look at those in terms of the measure of how integrative they are. The whole idea of form and ordering has to be filled out more than I have done here, but I want to get more than the idea that the order is any kind of ordering, or that what Gustafson is identifying as order is already there. He talks about the idea of discerning God's will. When you discern God's will you find out what is integrative in the situation. That seems to be Gustafson's own process.

Kaufman: You are creating God's will.

Johann: No, I wouldn't say I am creating . . .

Kaufman: I know you wouldn't say that.

Johann: All right. Create as specify, if you like. It is a process of further specification, maybe.

Gustafson: If Bob Johann has created God's will, Gordon Kaufman is creating God.

REEDER
John P., Jr.

The Dependence of Ethics

I n *Ethics from a Theocentric Perspective,* Professor Gustafson has provided a subtle and sophisticated view of moral experience in general, and theocentric ethics in particular. I want to identify some basic points about how he works and what he says, and then move off in directions I think are consistent with his thought. The dependence of ethics—the embedment of moral convictions in webs of belief—is Gustafson's keystone; I will begin by focusing on what this embedment means for him and try to show how it sets the context for other crucial themes in his ethics: the appropriation of tradition, the relation of philosophical and theological ethics, the distinctiveness of theocentric ethics, and the possibility of cross-traditional agreement.

The Dependence of Ethics

Central to Gustafson's enterprise is the thesis that moral traditions are shaped by a variety of assumptions about human existence. He shows how this is true in the thought of others and in his own constructive ethic. First, there are assumptions about the origins, nature, and future of the planet and the general place of humankind in the cosmic drama; second, there are views about the nature of self and society, for example, theories of human motivation and agency. It makes a difference, Gustafson argues, whether one assumes an anthropocentric creation or a dualistic view of the self that pits freedom against sensuous inclination.

I believe we should understand dependence in this sense as the thesis that beliefs about the general and specific contexts of human experience provide necessary but not sufficient building blocks in the construction of moral views. For example, Thomas Aquinas held a certain view of the self that is not merely consistent with his ethic but is part of the overall explanation and justification his theory provides. Aquinas's view of the self—the relation of desire and reason in particular—is a necessary presupposition, but it does not furnish the ethic all by itself; Gustafson is not saying that the ethic of Aquinas is simply a function of his theory of the self.

Taking the thesis in this way, it should be clear that the point applies not only to forms of theological ethics but to moral traditions where the rationale of morality is said to be independent of beliefs about transhuman reality. As Gustafson often remarks, moral views of this sort (let us call them for convenience "Enlightenment" views) rest on assumptions, for example, about the nature of freedom and the relation of selves to one another. Thus the dependence thesis is true of Rawls; it would hold for him just as it would for Barth.

Gustafson's own ethic, however, should be contrasted with an Enlightenment view. There are reasons rooted in Gustafson's beliefs that explain why he could not speak as Rawls does of the "independence" of ethics. For Gustafson, beliefs about transhuman reality figure in the construction of his moral view; they enter into the rationale. Evidence about the origin and fate of our solar system leads him to conclusions about God's purposes. Since the human species seems doomed, and an afterlife is implausible, God's basic purpose must not be the well-being of the species or the individual. Retaining the assumption that God is beneficent as well as powerful, Gustafson reasons then that the purpose of God is the well-being of sentient life and in some sense the well-being of the nonsentient creation as well. Since we have a duty to conform to God's purposes and we approve of them as well, we should seek the good of all creation. Thus Gustafson establishes one basic part of his moral framework, a duty to serve the good of the whole. While he acknowledges that others may arrive at this moral view without theological premises, his rationale requires them.

One could say, of course, that since the believer approves of God's purposes, it is the purposes that are crucial and not the fact that they are God's. And the duty to conform to God's purposes seems to rest on gratitude, the moral rightness of which seems to be taken for granted. But for Gustafson the rationale works as a composite; the rationale consists of beliefs about God's purposes as well as the notion of gratitude and the believer's approval of the purposes in themselves. What sets Gustafson off from an Enlightenment ethic is the role that premises about God play in the construction of at least one of the basic constituents of his moral view. This is not to say that he holds some form of a divine command ethic, as if the only alternative to an Enlightenment ethic were some form of the theory that a divine legislative act creates all moral requirement. But Gustafson would agree, I think, that such theories themselves assume normative content—it is usually a loving or a just God who does the creating. A divine command theory of this sort, therefore, not only refers to a divine act of legislation, but assumes the believer's approval of love or justice; love or justice is a reason for accepting God as the creator of specifically *moral* requirement. The fact that the believer approves of love or whatever other qualities of the Deity the theory picks out would not in the eyes of defenders of divine command theories signify that their views are not dependent on theological premises. Thus, if a divine command theory counts as a theory in which moral views are dependent on theological premises, then so does Gustafson's. In Gustafson's theory (where gratitude figures as a moral element *in* the rationale), as well as in a divine command theory (where no *moral* content is assumed independent of the divine will), the rationale is a composite of beliefs about God and normative considerations acknowledged by the believer. In this sense his rationale is also dependent on theological premises.

Thus let me venture a general observation: while the ethics of Rawls, Gustafson, and a Mahāyāna Buddhist, for example, all depend on assumptions, *which* assumptions are necessary will depend on other parts of the system, in particular assumptions about human good or other normative considerations. Rawls's neo-Kantian starting point, for example, requires, as he argues, some assumptions about human nature but not others.[1] Thus, while for Rawls as a neo-Kantian premises about God's relation to human beings are not necessary for the derivation of the moral framework, they are for Gustafson; similarly while a theory of personal identity is perhaps not necessary for Rawls's enterprise, it apparently is for forms of Mahāyāna Buddhism.[2]

There are then two important senses of the dependence of ethics in Gustafson's thought: first, the sense in which he claims that any moral tradition necessarily incorporates some assumptions about the general and specific contexts of human life; and second, the sense of dependence on theological premises that pertains to his own ethic, and sets it off from Enlightenment theories. As

---

[1]John Rawls, "The Independence of Moral Theory," Presidential Address to the A.P.A., *Proceedings and Addresses of the A.P.A.* 48 (1974–1975): 5-22.

[2]I speak here as if Rawls had a general theory of morality, but strictly speaking he has only proposed a theory of justice.

regards the first, Gustafson's thesis encompasses other moral theories, for example, Rawls's neo-Kantianism; as regards the second, Gustafson would from his own perspective distinguish himself from Rawls's notion of the independence of ethics. Gustafson cannot—from his own perspective—accept a morality whose rationale is independent of theological premises.

Pragmatism and Appropriation

Given his general view of how moral convictions are embedded in webs of belief, and his sense of how his own ethic must rest on theological premises, Gustafson begins the work of construction. How does he go about it? I think it is fair to cast him as a certain sort of pragmatist; he does not believe in an ahistorical, immutable foundation for scientific or moral knowledge (although some scientific beliefs are not likely to be revised), and theology is also a historical phenomenon. Nor does he believe that world views and moral traditions constitute hermetically sealed systems between which there can be no overlap or critical communication. It seems to me that his working epistemology is very similar to the emerging view that Richard Bernstein calls pragmatism (also called coherentism or holism), a view that Bernstein sees as a step "beyond" the false alternatives of "objectivism" and "relativism." Bernstein means by objectivism, "the basic conviction that there is or must be some permanent, ahistorical matrix or framework to which we can ultimately appeal in determining the nature of rationality, knowledge, truth, reality, goodness, or rightness."[3] And relativism claims that concepts of rationality, and so forth, are "relative to a specific conceptual scheme, theoretical framework, paradigm, form of life, society, culture . . . there is no substantive overarching framework or single metalanguage by which we can rationally adjudicate or univocally evaluate competing claims of alternative paradigms."[4] Along with this basic claim, the sort of relativism Bernstein wants to go beyond also holds that "there can be no rational comparison among the plurality of theories, paradigms and language games—that we are prisoners locked in our own framework and can't get out of it."[5]

I gather that, like Bernstein, Gustafson accepts the antiobjectivist thesis of relativism, but that also like Bernstein he would reject the idea that one is locked into traditions. What a pragmatist epistemology has to show is how

---

[3]Richard J. Bernstein, *Beyond Objectivism and Relativism: Science, Hermeneutics, and Praxis* (Philadelphia: University of Pennsylvania Press, 1983) 8.

[4]Ibid., 8; cf. 11-12.

[5]Ibid., 92.

we can understand others, compare, criticize and be criticized, offer reasons and arguments, convince and be convinced, all without supposing there is a neutral, ahistorical framework.[6] I think this is essentially what Gustafson endorses: "knowledge-conditions" are relative to particular communities.[7] But nonetheless, "To affirm that explorations and meanings are socially tested . . . is not to argue that there are no more objective references that transcend particular communities by which they can be tested. But even such tests develop as communities interact with each other, as they alter their received traditions and views, and as they evolve into new communities."[8]

Gustafson, then, works, and he believes we all work, from the perspective of particular cultures. One works out of traditions one appropriates by affirmative or critical reinterpretation. In fact, one may live in multiple traditions, connecting parts of these traditions in tighter or looser ways in one's web of belief. One assumes some part of one's web is true, even as one subjects another to criticism. In principle, no beliefs are immune to revision; one aims at coherence but not in the sense of mere consistency, for one tests, changes, adjusts in an ongoing process of explanation and justification.[9] Gustafson would endorse, I believe, this statement of Hilary Putnam's and extend it to theology and ethics: "I am assuming that verification in science is a holistic matter, that it is whole theoretical systems that meet the test of experience as a corporate body; and that the judgment of how well a whole system of beliefs meets the test of experience is ultimately somewhat of an intuitive matter which could not be formalized short of formalizing total human psychology."[10]

Thus, when Gustafson says he begins with experience, I think he means he begins with various strands of his own culture. He is interpreting interpretations when he connects the notion of God to the various "senses of" that for him are salient categories of experience. For Gustafson, all experience is in

---

[6]Ibid., 107-108, 167-69.

[7]James M. Gustafson, *Theology and Ethics,* vol. 1 of *Ethics from a Theocentric Perspective* (Chicago: University of Chicago Press, 1981) 340.

[8]Ibid., 1:124.

[9]For example, ibid., 1:178, 233-35. My interpretation of Gustafson here is similar to Jeffrey Stout's in *Ethics after Babel: The Languages of Morality and Their Discontents* (Boston: Beacon Press, 1988).

[10]Hilary Putnam, *Reason, Truth, and History* (Cambridge: Cambridge University Press, 1981) 133. Note that Putnam states that he is trying to overcome the objectivism-subjectivism dichotomy (iv-xii).

part interpretation, although it is prior to reflection. While he does want to claim that the "senses of" are types of experiences shared in some respects by believers and nonbelievers alike, I think he could admit that in strands of Western culture the meaning and significance of these particular categories are perhaps at least partly due to their historic connection to a broader theological framework.[11] As I read him, this is what he is claiming: in many if not all cultures one finds concepts that are similar to our notions of dependence, obligation, hope, and so forth, but such concepts do not necessarily refer to ultimate reality—for example, dependence on God. In his cultural tradition, however, these notions are extended to construe the relation of human beings to God.

When Gustafson says experience, therefore, he means cultural experience, that is, experience as interpretation, as a cultural system of meaning that shapes our physiological and psychological capacities and produces, in interaction with our environment, the felt story of our own particular lives. He does not intend to suggest that there is some ordinary or religious core that is not interpreted but can be expressed or construed in various ways; thus, it would be wrong to see him as advocating something like what George Lindbeck calls an experiential-expressive model.[12] Neither his view of experiences widely shared by theists and nontheists nor his own experiential, affective sense of the reality of God commits him to anything like the view that there are deep, core experiences that come to expression in various ways. Gustafson simply assumes that experience, including religious experience, is theory-laden.

Thus, as a pragmatist, Gustafson could accept *part* of the meaning of this statement by Rawls:[13] "The search for reasonable grounds for reaching agreement rooted in our conception of ourselves and in our relation to society replaces the search for moral truth interpreted as fixed by a prior and independent order of objects and relations, whether natural or divine, an order apart and distinct from how we conceive of ourselves."[14] What Gustafson could accept is Rawls's epistemology: what *justifies* a notion of justice is not its "being true to an order antecedent and given to us, but its congruence with our deeper

[11]Gustafson, *Ethics,* 1:228.

[12]George A. Lindbeck, *The Nature of Doctrine: Religion and Theology in a Postliberal Age* (Philadelphia: Westminster Press, 1984) 31-32.

[13]Gustafson, *Ethics,* 1:258.

[14]John Rawls, "Kantian Constructivism in Moral Theory," *Journal of Philosophy* 77 (September 1980): 519.

understanding of ourselves in light of our history and traditions."[15] What Gustafson could not accept is Rawls's rejection of the metaphysical belief in a divine order of objects and relations; Gustafson has not given up his belief in an order established by God. But with Rawls, Gustafson has turned from an epistemology that seeks a set of immutable beliefs about such an order. We never transcend our historical constructions.

Gustafson could also agree with David Wong in *Moral Relativity* that we cannot reach a final and true morality. But with Wong, Gustafson could hold that given one's own notion, in Wong's terminology, of an adequate moral system, one can say that moral statements are true or false relative to the system and that moral statements correspond to facts about the system. Within one's own system, many of the so-called objective features of moral belief and discourse can be accounted for.[16] Thus Gustafson can, on the one hand, hold that there is no immutable starting point and at the same time claim that in light of certain beliefs about God and the world it makes sense to say that one believes in a framework constituted by God's purposes, aspects of human and nonhuman well-being, and the functional requisites of human society (themes to which I will devote more attention later). One seeks coherence within and among all three parts of the framework. In Wong's terminology, these reference points are Gustafson's "standards" for an adequate moral system. Various cultural systems could meet these standards depending on circumstances, and indeed for Gustafson, even for individuals or groups within cultures, various combinations of values and priniciples could meet these standards. Even within the history of an individual or group, the combinations could differ as conditions change.

Taking Gustafson as a pragmatist also helps us understand the role of historical interpretation in his thought. His view can be seen, I think, as a middle way between W. K. Frankena's distinction between intellectual history and philosophical argument, and the historicism sometimes identified—I think wrongly—with Alasdair MacIntyre. Gustafson would not be satisfied with either alternative. He would not want to say that one gets views from the past and then subjects them to considerations pro and con that are entirely independent of their historical context. Nor would he want to suggest that philosophical argument really is just a mode of historical understanding. He would claim, I think, that interpreting and appropriating are distinct, but intimately related. One interprets out of issues and tentative answers in the

---

[15]Ibid., 568-69.

[16]Gustafson, *Ethics,* 1:340; cf. Rawls, "Kantian Constructivism in Moral Theory," 568-69.

present, and what one interprets shapes one's formulation of issues and answers. One walks around the raft looking for a spare piece of wood with what one wants to fix in mind; what one finds will determine what one wants to fix as well as how one can fix it. Thus one's account of one's own preferred alternative is a theory that gives the best explanation and justification one can find; it does not merely take specimens from the past and then subject them to independent scrutiny. One arranges what one knows of past and present in the best theory. To arrange, one must understand, but arrangement is more than understanding, it is argument. [17]

Philosophical and Theological Ethics

How does Gustafson think of the relation between philosophical and theological ethics? He takes philosophical ethics, at least in the "modern world," to advance proposals whose rationale does not rest on theological premises. Philosophical ethics in this sense is independent of theology;[18] it is Enlightenment ethics. Thus while a theological ethic may incorporate Kantian elements, Kant himself was not a theologian doing theological ethics. This difference aside, systems of philosophical ethics also arise from moral traditions that are carried by communities and cultures. Philosophical systems of ethics have functional surrogates for the missing theological premises, and thus they exhibit as well the general sense of dependence.[19] They are dependent on certain beliefs as necessary presuppositions of the moral structures they erect. Even if these traditions claim a foundationalist epistemology, Gustafson, I believe, would argue that they show signs of their historical roots and change as other traditions do. As to method, they use metaphor, interpretative analysis, and argumentation just as theological ethics does. In a word, both theological and philosophical ethics are attempts to offer the best explanatory and justificatory theories possible given the knowledge available in particular times and places.

The nub then of the distinction for Gustafson is the separation of the rationale from theological premises. On all other counts, there simply are moral

---

[17]Gustafson, *Ethics,* 1:253-54; cf. W. K. Frankena, "MacIntyre and Modern Morality," *Ethics* 93:3 (April 1983): 579-87, and Alasdair MacIntyre, *After Virtue: A Study in Moral Theory,* 2d ed. (Notre Dame: University of Notre Dame Press, 1984) 270-71.

[18]James M. Gustafson, *Ethics and Theology,* vol. 2 of *Ethics from a Theocentric Perspective* (Chicago: University of Chicago Press, 1984) 97.

[19]Ibid., 2:97-98.

traditions and ethical reflection about them; in particular, Gustafson clearly admits that there are functional surrogates in Enlightenment systems. If we adopt a concept of religion similar to Clifford Geertz's—which does not tie religion to a notion of God or even to a distinct sacred reality or object over against the profane, but locates its function as an orientation to the ultimately real, to basic elements and causes that influence human life for weal or woe— then we can say that both theological and philosophical ethics can be religious.[20] In this concept of religion, moral traditions, in so far as they build on certain assumptions, are religious; the functional surrogates have to do with "how some things really and ultimately are."[21] I think there is clear evidence in the two volumes that Gustafson should be sympathetic to a Geertzian concept of religion. Not only in his own religious view, which involves a specific notion of dependence on a purposeful power that creates and governs the cosmos, but in general, he sees human beings trying to relate themselves to the realities and powers that influence their existence, that create their limits and possibilities.

Thus, in Gustafson's view, and mine as well, the distinction between Enlightenment moral philosophy and theological ethics is only a distinction between groups of traditions that rest on different sorts of religious beliefs. Gustafson catches the matter correctly when he says that there are "ethical implications of theological beliefs which must be developed philosophically by the theologian."[22] This statement makes it clear that the Enlightenment thinker and the theologian both work philosophically in a methodological sense, that is, they use metaphor, argument, or whatever, to construct and apply theories.

In this view, then, it would also follow that forms of Judaic, Hindu, or Buddhist tradition, for example, can be construed as moral systems that rest on religious premises. Indeed, there are traditions within traditions. Gustafson himself, of course, rejects some versions of theological ethics in the West, and it may be that other forms of theism are closer to his view than certain Christian traditions. Indeed, it was a sense of the fact that religious beliefs shape moral traditions in contexts beyond Christian theology, as well in some cases a personal loss of theistic belief, that led a number of us to use the phrase "religious ethics" to designate the descriptive and constructive work we do.

---

[20]Clifford Geertz, "Religion as a Cultural System," in *The Interpretation of Cultures* (New York: Basic Books, Inc., 1973) 87-125.

[21]Gustafson, *Ethics,* 2:98.

[22]Ibid., 2:99 n. 6.

It seems to me that a person interested in ethical reflection should be free to stand in one tradition or to link more than one, to attempt the dialogical process of understanding, criticism, and construction that Gustafson endorses and exhibits as he engages in selective retrieval from several Western traditions.

The real problem with the notion of religious ethics is that it may suggest to some a dividing line between the religious and the philosophical; indeed, some people who have wanted to use the category have employed a notion of religion that, while broader than theism, still focuses on the idea of a religious object or sacred reality over against the profane. Such a notion of religion would clearly exclude systems whose assumptions make no reference to such an entity. The use of such a concept of religion has been correlated with current institutional arrangements; Enlightenment ethics is assigned to philosophy departments and religious ethics to religious studies. Thus, I share Gustafson's dissatisfaction with the phrase "religious ethics." In my view, it is better to say that many moral traditions rest on assumptions about "how some things really and ultimately are";[23] for these traditions ethics is both religious and philosophical. Even now, there are Kantians in religious studies and divine command theorists in philosophy.

The Distinctiveness
of Theocentric Ethics

Theological ethics then is distinctive in that its rationale rests in part on theological premises; theocentric ethics is distinctive in that it presents a particular sort of theology. How does Gustafson specifically see the relation of his views to other systems? He sees himself as a particular sort of theologian, who offers reasons for moral views that others may hold on different grounds. In general, he sees overlap in content, divergence in rationale.

I think this is basically correct, but it might be better to say that there can be overlap and divergence also within the rationale. One dimension of Gustafson's ethic is shaped by both theological and nontheological premises; the rationale is a composite of elements that produce a principle to the effect that the good of the whole creation should be attended to. Part of the rationale for this principle can be shared with others, namely, beliefs about the solar system, gratitude, the value of the whole. Keeping some of Gustafson's views and adding others, Mary Midgley or Mahāyāna Buddhists, for example, could come up with a similar first principle, the welfare of all sentient beings or of the whole cosmos. Thus, there is partial overlap in rationale.

---

[23]Ibid., 2:98.

Another dimension of Gustafson's ethic is his notion of functional requisites. Here, I believe, he intends to say that both content and rationale can be shared with anyone with certain beliefs about the evolution and nature of human communities. Arguments as to the meaning of these requisites can be conducted without reference to theological premises, although the theocentric ethic will take the requirements as signs of God's ordering.

In the middle, as it were, of Gustafson's ethic are substantive notions that determine how the good of the whole and the good of parts within the whole are to be pursued, taking into account what we know about the requisites. Beyond the requisites per se (for example, *some* form of child rearing), we also know something of what is required for mutual well-being or flourishing (interdependence), and on this basis we work out duties and obligations.[24]

I will say more about this middle dimension in the next section, but let us note now that neither the warrants nor the content here seem distinctively theological. I believe that Gustafson fills in the middle of his ethic with a notion of duties or obligations based on the good. Health and self-determination, for example, are presented as values or goods, as elements in human flourishing or fulfillment. We are to consider as well and try to include the good of the rest of sentient and nonsentient creation.[25] But these goods or values, or at least some of them, are incommensurate; there is no common measure by which they can be weighed. Not only are there incommensurable values or goods, there is no metavalue or principle by which these goods can be ranked; there is no principled way of adjudicating a conflict. Furthermore, there is no single value or principle to be discovered or invented that can direct how the goods (however ranked) are to be distributed between human individuals or between humans and other parts of creation. Painful, tragic choices are to be made. The good of all should be considered, but which principles of distribution we should adopt is neither revealed by God directly nor known through human resources. "Discernment" involves a discrimination of the values involved in a case, and then an "intuition," which, I believe, means a decision to rank and distribute goods in a certain way in certain circumstances. There is no metareason, I gather, for choosing one ranking or pattern of distribution over another.

Thus, Rawls's insistence that there is an inviolability based on justice that the good of the whole cannot override is rejected. The value of the liberty and the well-being of the individual is not established ab initio as distributively protected. At most, Gustafson would say that we have a prima facie obligation

---

[24]Ibid., 2:133.

[25]For example, ibid., 1:271, 309, 319.

to protect the well-being or liberty of an individual. How the well-being and freedom of one agent is to be normatively related to the well-being and freedom of another is to be decided in relation to particular circumstances. On the other hand, Gustafson also rejects a utilitarianism that treats values as commensurate and imposes one favored distributive pattern (greatest good, counting each as one).

The middle space then is filled by the category of well-being or flourishing, but some of the goods that make it up are not commensurate, and there is no way to establish choices either between values or between the good of one and the good of others; there are only decisions. The content and rationale of this notion of flourishing do not seem to involve any distinctive theological premises, although it can also be interpreted in terms of the categories of gift and task, stewardship, or participation.

Thus, to catch the distinctiveness of Gustafson's theocentrism, one must look at different dimensions of his ethic. Only in one part of his framework—the good of the whole creation—does it seem to me that theological premises play an essential role. In light of how God and the cosmos are interpreted, Gustafson reasons that the good we seek should include the good of the rest of creation, sentient and insentient. The requisites and the middle space stand alone, although one can add a layer of theological meaning. To borrow some other terms from Geertz, theocentric theology enters one dimension synthetically, the other two stratigraphically.[26]

The Prospect of Moral Agreement

I have suggested that Gustafson's substantive ethic moves between a commitment to the good of the whole and the functional requisites. What prospect of agreement is there between Gustafson and other traditions and theories?

We should look first at how the commitment to the good of the whole is established. It is built, as I have interpreted it, on a composite rationale that

---

[26]Clifford Geertz, "The Impact of the Concept of Culture on the Concept of Man," in *The Interpretation of Cultures*, 37, 44. When Gustafson says, "relate ourselves and all things in a manner appropriate to their relations to God," I think he means (1) seek the good of the whole as and because God does and (2) inquire into the requisites and possibilities for good that God has established (*Ethics*, 1:319). "The human capacity to be participants in the patterns and processes of interdependence of life grounds our vocation to discern what God is enabling us to be and to do" (ibid., 1:321). The search for and weighing of goods is interpreted by the believer as a "vocation" because the believer sees the cosmos as a "divine ordering"; the believer adds this layer of meaning to the process of judging "what ends ought to be sought" (ibid., 1:319).

appeals to an assumed duty to honor God's purpose (apprehended through scientific knowledge) and a correlated endorsement of those purposes. The latter is best seen as a valuation, as a judgment of God's purpose. I value what God values, namely, the good of the creation as such. In this sense, the good is more than the sum of the parts; I value as God does the whole qua whole. Thus there is a basic desire or love for the whole. In this dimension of his ethic, Gustafson relies, it seems to me, on the sort of neo-Aristotelian good that is at the heart of Alasdair MacIntyre's ethic.

> For what education in the virtues teaches me is that my good as a man is one and the same as the good of those others with whom I am bound up in human community. There is no way of my pursuing my good which is necessarily antagonistic to you pursuing yours because the good is neither mine peculiarly nor yours peculiarly—goods are not private property. Hence, Aristotle's definition of friendship, the fundamental form of human relationship, is in terms of shared goods. The egoist is thus, in the ancient and medieval worlds, always someone who has made a fundamental mistake about where his own good lies and someone who has thus and to that extent excluded himself from human relationships.[27]

Gustafson, of course, does not define the shared good (the relational good, the good of the whole) as the good of a way of life in a particular community, but broadens it to include the creation. But the notion of a good that is neither yours nor mine in a private sense but is relational underlies Gustafson's as well as MacIntyre's account. At the level of commitment to the whole, my good and yours are not antagonistic, while at the level of a determination of the benefits and burdens of existence within the common whole, your good and mine may pull apart. At this point both MacIntyre and Gustafson recognize that justice and other moral notions are necessary.

The important point to see is that, like MacIntyre, Gustafson appeals to desire and valuation to establish the basic good of community, not to a neo-Kantian theory based on reason or metaphysics. In contrast, Thomas Nagel argued in *The Possibility of Altruism* that unless one gives up a view of oneself as one person among others, one must admit that reasons for acting are "objective"; that is, suffering is a reason for acting whether it occurs in you or me or perhaps in any sentient being. Whether Nagel is correct or not, his is a neo-Kantian attempt to show that, given a type of metaphysical belief that we would be reluctant to abandon, practical reason provides us with a motive for "altruism." If I am prepared to alleviate my own suffering, I should be pre-

---

[27]MacIntyre, *After Virtue*, 229; cf. 158.

pared to alleviate any suffering. What Nagel attempts to provide in neo-Kantian fashion, MacIntyre and Gustafson try to establish as a basic valuation. Nagel's objective reasons tie my good and the good of others together in a way that is functionally similar to the cohesion established by the value of community or creation. On both sorts of theories a moral floor is established—we should be concerned with the good of all who comprise the whole—that is then further specified through distributive justice (what Nagel calls combinatorial principles) and other moral notions.

But of course MacIntyre and Gustafson do not posit the same valuation. MacIntyre seems to see us valuing a common life in particular communities or social groupings based on views about human good. But ways of life may differ, and despite his hopes for a common ethic of the search, in the postscript to the second edition of *After Virtue* MacIntyre clearly says that he cannot guarantee any eventual agreement about human good.[28] The question remains, why should I value someone else's well-being if I do not value the way of life and vision of the good embodied in their community? When Gustafson makes the valued common good broader, he avoids this difficulty. Thus, his stance is like MacIntyre's in that it is a valuation, but it is more like Nagel's in its content and scope. In fact, it is even broader since it includes nonsentient creation. The fact, however, of the disagreement between MacIntyre and Gustafson is what should concern us now. The disagreement signals precisely the difficulty in coming to an agreement about values, a difficulty that liberal theorists try to account for in their own theories of the good. In their moral proposals, moreover, liberal theorists assume only the most minimal of instrumental and moral goods about which agents who have different relational goods or do not acknowledge any such good at all could agree.[29] Even Wong, who wants to include a neo-Aristotelian element in his ethic, does not believe that Aristotelianism provides the basis for claiming that there is one true morality. In the end, there is the problem of the "plasticity of our desires and interests."[30]

Gustafson, in any case, has a place to stand in one dimension of his ethic. Those who share his valuation will stand with him, even if they do not share

---

[28]Ibid. MacIntyre appeals to the virtues of the "search" for the good, but why should we expect that communities will have a common view of the good of the search and, hence, its constitutive virtues?

[29]See Harlan R. Beckley, "A Christian Affirmation of Rawls's Idea of Justice as Fairness: Part I," *The Journal of Religious Ethics* 13:2 (Fall 1985): 210-42.

[30]David Wong, *Moral Relativity* (Berkeley: University of California Press, 1984) 99.

his theism. If we then assume something like Gustafson's commitment to the good of the whole, at the other side of his ethic are the functional requisites. There are important questions here: by functional requisite does one signify only such necessities as a division of labor or some mode of child rearing, or does one want to include more specific institutions, such as family or state, that themselves can take different forms?[31] If functional requisites include some notion of justice, is this purely formal (like cases alike) or does it encompass concepts such as equality?[32] But I think there is more prospect of agreement in this dimension than in the middle, so let us bypass the requisites and discuss how Gustafson fills the middle space.

I interpreted Gustafson as offering an ethic of flourishing, shaped by but by no means determined by what we know of the requisites of individual, social, and cosmic well-being. Gustafson's view is that there are certain functional requisites such as "caring for the very young"; in addition, as "participants in patterns and processes of interdependence" in particular cultural communities we can use our developing knowledge to learn what is good for ourselves and other parts of creation, what makes for well-being or flourishing. Insight into flourishing furnishes a number of duties but no meta-principles. At this level Gustafson would introduce, as MacIntyre does, the value of ways of life in particular communities. But Gustafson would not only disagree with MacIntyre's claim that given the starting point of a good community based on a vision of the human good, one must adopt a reward-according-to-contribution notion of justice. He would also reject the idea that such a starting point itself furnishes any determinate principle of justice. Rawlsian and utilitarian considerations remain in tension within the human realm, and human good may conflict with the good of other sentient beings and nonsentient creation.

Gustafson's operative view here is very much like that of many distinguished philosophers, whether or not they would conceptualize it under the rubric of conflicting goods.[33] The key to this view is an unwillingness to erect a Rawlsian inviolability or to fall into utilitarianism. The moral life (in the middle dimension) is seen as a field of competing forces or considerations—

---

[31]Gustafson, *Ethics,* 2:298.

[32]Ibid., 1:340.

[33]For example, Nagel and Wong. Gustafson, unlike Wong, does not suggest that one hold together Aristotelian and Kantian elements. As I read him, Gustafson interprets neo-Kantian notions such as respect for persons in Aristotelian terms, that is, as one among several basic values, goods, or loves.

for example, increase happiness or respect persons and the relation of these considerations has to be determined without the aid of any overarching principle. Far from regretting the failure to find or develop an ordering principle, philosophers of this conviction view the effort to find such a principle as being similar to the misguided search for an immutable epistemic foundation. These philosophers and Gustafson do not think that any final "combinatorial" principles (which order goods and answer the question whose good) have been established (even as a matter of reflective equilibrium), and some would claim they should not be. I think Gustafson shares the view that it is a mistake to look for such an ordering principle under the conditions of finitude. As far as our experience goes, goods are incommensurate, there is no metavalue for ranking them, and there is no metavalue or principle to relate the goods of the various parties who belong to the whole. We experience genuine moral dilemmas that we must resolve from case to case.[34]

Thus, in some cases we could allow liberty to be overridden for the sake of other goods; in other cases, we might not. Gustafson could admit that if we maintain a value judgment—for example, in a case of experimentation on children—consistency would require that we hold to it in similar cases. But the judgment can change, and in any case, even within specific areas of concern such as experimentation, there is no guarantee that the circumstances in which we made the first decision will recur. What we do not possess and will probably not possess—efforts of those like Rawls notwithstanding—is a persuasive view of how to order the convictions we have about particular cases. I do not intend to suggest that for Gustafson one makes *arbitrary* decisions. Following Putnam, Gustafson could suggest that the various considerations underlying a decision simply fit together in a certain way in one's psychology on a given occasion. Or as Robert Johann suggests in this volume, a decision or judgment for Gustafson is like the work of an artist who molds materials until the final product is satisfactory.

The difficulty with this view of flourishing, however, is that it not only leaves room for disputes about conflicts between the values Gustafson iden-

---

[34]See Edmund Santurri, *Perplexity in the Moral Life: Philosophical and Theological Considerations* (Charlottesville VA: University of Virginia Press, 1987), regarding the distinction between genuine moral dilemmas and those that are "apparent" due to the limitations of our moral knowledge in contrast to God's. See Gustafson, *Ethics,* 1:329-30, 338, on the powers of discernment through which the agent achieves a coherent moral vision: "There is a final moment of perception that sees the parts in relation to the whole, expresses sensibilities as well as reasoning, and is made in conditions of human finitude."

tifies but it anchors values only within particular webs of belief. The difficulty we identified at the level of the rationale reappears in the middle dimension: why choose one set of values rather than another? MacIntyre's notion of valued ways of life, for example, makes justice relative to a prior valuation; thus, there seems to be nothing in MacIntyre's theory that rules out patriarchal relations as a valued way of life. In Gustafson's theory of well-being or flourishing, notions of justice and other moral duties are filled out by insights into what is good for particular beings. But the values of liberty or respect for persons, for example, might not be accepted by others who have different values, different ideals of human excellence.[35] The question is not merely one of instrumental values: is the nuclear family or the kibbutz better for children? The issue is whether or not children or male-female sexual relations or male-female relations of a certain sort (sexually exclusive and lifelong) should be included in our pantheon of intrinsic goods or ends.[36] Granted that biological and social scientific knowledge might help us—for example, when we ask what is best for children—do the "patterns and processes of interdependence" furnish us with any definite guidelines for what we should value as intrinsically good for sentient and nonsentient life? Gustafson is trying to find a middle way between an Augustinian-Thomistic theory of goods or ends grounded in the nature of things and a liberal theory that rests values on preference and denies the notion of essential good. For him work such as Mary Midgley's argues the case for structures of desire and motive that guide our search for the good. Opponents would find the evidence less compelling and, with Wong, would stress the "plasticity of our desires and interests."[37]

Moreover, some would say (Kantians and others) that duties such as respect for persons are not grounded in human good at all but have independent

---

[35]See Gilbert Harman, "Human Flourishing, Ethics, and Liberty," *Philosophy and Public Affairs* 12 (Fall 1983): 312-13, 320.

[36]See Robert Audi, "Axiological Foundationalism," *Canadian Journal of Philosophy* 12 (March 1982): 165-68, regarding the concepts of intrinsic and directly justified value.

[37]See Stephen R. L. Clark, "The Gap Between 'Is' and 'Ought,' " *Aristotelian Society Supplementary Volume* 54 (1980): 207-40, and Farley's query in this volume about "self-evident" value. Gustafson, *Ethics*, 2:292-98, distinguishes between the "patterns and processes of interdependence" that are "functional requisites" or "necessary conditions" and the additional layers of value through which humans shape their existence.

roots.[38] We do not so much identify respect for persons, for example, as one element in a complex of goods that satisfies needs and desires, as we recognize a demand that constrains how we seek the good.

Thus, Gustafson faces in the middle dimension, first, the question of why we choose one vision of good rather than another, and, second, the critic's doubt that certain moral categories should be considered as values or goods at all. He recognizes these issues, of course. Nonetheless, he believes that we communicate with others and share what reasons we can. We are not left with relativism in Bernstein's sense: hermetically sealed systems with no communication and no standards in common. For Gustafson, there is evidence of dialogical convergence as well as divergence. He can criticize others from his perspective, and he can find grounds for toleration in his own view.[39] He can continue the search for common concepts in order to understand and perhaps even mutually to persuade. For example, he could try to persuade or perhaps be persuaded by feminist critics of his view of the goods of marriage.

Therefore, Gustafson would not endorse the radical relativism suggested by George Lindbeck.

> Adherents of different religions do not merely diversely thematize the same experience; rather, they have different experiences. Buddhist compassion, Christian love, and—if I may cite a quasi-religious example—French Revolutionary *fraternité* are not diverse modifications of a single fundamental human awareness, emotion, or sentiment, but are radically (i.e., from the root) distinct ways of experiencing and being oriented toward self, neighbor, and cosmos. The affective features they have in common are part, so to speak, of their raw materials, functions of those feelings of closeness to one's immediate fellows shared by all human beings including Nazis and headhunters.[40]

Lindbeck's error is to think that this statement follows from the general theory that religious and moral traditions are systems of language and culture that shape experience. While it is true that no core is uninterpreted, it may be that there is a case for a thicker core than Lindbeck acknowledges, for example, Peter Singer's argument for the evolution of dispositions to several sorts of be-

---

[38]Harman, "Human Flourishing, Ethics, and Liberty," 320. See Gustafson, *Ethics,* 2:305-306.

[39]Cf. Wong, *Moral Relativity,* ch. 12.

[40]Lindbeck, *The Nature of Doctrine,* 40.

nevolence or Gustafson's sense of elements in human flourishing.[41] Overlaps, in other words, are not necessarily purely contingent, random similarities between radically different cultures.

Conclusion

Gustafson has identified the right foci for ethics: the commitment to the good of all and the requisites. The meaning of both categories, of course, is controversial. But those who do not share his views can still overlap with him considerably; fellow pragmatists at least could see themselves comparing rafts and even sharing parts. As for the middle dimension, he identifies crucial tensions between utilitarian and Rawlsian considerations. I share his view that, at present, we have no convincing way to unite these considerations in a way that resolves or eliminates conflicts between them. Taking either sort as definitive, of course, removes the difficulty, but if neither seems convincing alone, then one is left with a moral inventory that contains elements that are sometimes irreconcilable. Adding the good of other sentient beings and the rest of creation compounds the difficulty of deciding which and whose good to promote. But there might be a way forward. There might be other resources for working out the problems of the middle. Perhaps some view will be forthcoming that combines a richer view of flourishing or well-being than liberals have allowed and distributive considerations based on beliefs about the relation of sentient beings to one another and their common relation to nonsentient creation. This is perhaps a vain hope, and Gustafson may well be right that we must live with possibly conflicting considerations that we have to balance as well as we can from case to case without any metaprinciple. If he is right, then our task is to concentrate on the concrete, to enlarge our sensitivities, and to do what good we can.[42]

REEDER DISCUSSION

Robert Audi: You suggest that for Gustafson there are incommensurable values, and there is no metavalue or metaprinciple by which these goods can be ranked. More-

[41]Peter Singer, *The Expanding Circle: Ethics and Sociobiology* (New York: New American Library, 1981).

[42]I would like to acknowledge discussions about Gustafson and matters treated in this paper with students and faculty during the Luce Seminars in comparative ethics at Amherst College in 1984-1985, in particular Professors Susan Niditch and David Wills of the Department of Religion and David P. Saybolt, 1985.

over, you say there is no in-principled way of adjudicating a conflict, and there is no single metaprinciple we can use. Let's take a scientific analogy. Suppose we have two competing theories. Couldn't we say much the same thing? We will be interested in predictive power for explaining the data in accord with well-established beliefs, and we are going to have to make a weighted comparison. Shall we say there is no in-principled way of adjudicating or just that there is no metaprinciple? Maybe there is a method, and it involves weighing a finite number of factors in historical perspective. On the other hand, there is no simple principle, though we could say there is a principle, if that principle is to take the main criteria (presumably finite) and weigh them in as informed a way as possible in debate with opposing views. Suppose there is no principle even of that sort or that we don't want to call that a principle. Does a rational decision between so-called incommensurable goods presuppose that we have a metaprinciple or would saying that betray a deductivist bias?

To add one datum from your own treatment, you mention that for Gustafson (and I think for just about all of us) it would be in some objective way a mistake to make one decision on experimentation with human subjects and then make an entirely different decision where all the relevant facts are the same. What is the notion of mistake there? It sounds rather objective, though we might not be able to get an overarching principle to justify the decision that we think we should make consistently.

Reeder: Perhaps I confuse saying there is no metaprinciple with saying there is no way. I think Jim means that there is a way without there being a metaprinciple. The way has to be understood by analogy to the artist shaping a number of elements or to Putnam's notion of a number of considerations that one finally puts together on a particular occasion in terms of a psychological criterion of satisfaction.

As for changing one's judgment in a particular situation even if the relevant facts remain the same, I think that Jim will have to allow you to do that. Take a case where you had to decide between respecting the liberty of a patient and respecting the health of a patient. It seems that he says that on some occasions, even when in one sense or another the basic facts are similar, one could come up with different artistic wholes. One time you should shape the elements in one way, and another time you would shape them in another. You would have used the same method in both cases, but the resulting product would be different because of giving weight to one factor as opposed to the other.

Audi: Let me ask about the scientific analogy. The analogy might be two theories being equally well confirmed and equally plausible on all the criteria. But we would probably say that one of them will sooner or later turn out to be wrong. Now in the moral case, would we say that one of these decisions is wrong, although they are equally well confirmed? So we are acting within our rights and making a forgivable mistake, but we are either making a mistake now or we made one before. I am asking two questions. Will he say the same thing as will be said about the scientific case? Will he say something broadly realistic or something that is not so realistic?

Reeder: I think he would say that when using one's method, one has a right to pick the theory one did on a particular occasion. One might realize later that one had weighed the elements in a way that reflected mood or some other extraneous factor, and then one could now look back at the decision and say, "Well, I would weigh those elements now in a way that I would not have before." That is the only sense in the moral realm that one would say, "My decision about what to do with that patient was wrong; today I would relate the elements in a different way."[43]

Paul Ramsey (Princeton University): The issue is not simply finding our way in this middle range and the possibility of agreement among people, but also the possibility of agreement with myself over time, that is, the possibility of a total life plan that has some consistency. It seems that you go so far as to make that impossible. I don't think you could mean that. You speak as if, without there being morally relevant and important differences between my decision at one time and my decision at a later time, I might nevertheless make a different decision in terms of this wholeness. Could you possibly have said such a thing? If that is the case, I pay attention to that book in the Bible that tells me to be faithful to the wife of my youth in one situation, and in another situation I pay attention to leading the more abundant life with another spouse; and I claim that I can do both things and still be a continuous moral agent. You spoke as if the two decisions might be different, and that, I think, you ought to withdraw.

Reeder: No, I cannot withdraw it, at least as an interpretation of Jim, and I am not sure whether there is any other stronger view that can be justified. As I understand Jim, we have needs and desires; on the basis of that we value things as good. We should not confuse the relatively secure kinds of things one can say at the level of the requisites with what one can say in the middle space. In the middle space, I will value liberty and I will value health, but the configurations in which I value those over a lifetime might vary widely.

Ramsey: Morally significant configurations will differ?

Reeder: Yes, and I answered Professor Audi that the sense in which you could say you were wrong was that you would not feel that you had weighed those matters well enough in the past. I am not sure I answered Professor Audi as well as I should have. We have got to be clear about two senses of wrong. I think you could say, even in

---

[43]I modify this judgment in my answer to Paul Ramsey below.

Gustafson's view, that you now see things differently than you did because you have greater insights (for example, about health and liberty) and look back at your previous weighing as wrong. But you don't blame yourself for it, as you might if you looked back at a previous occasion and said, "I made that weighing because I was angry at somebody or there was some nonrelevant reason for having made it."[44]

Midgley: Does it help here to consider that we are commonly in movement, that is, we are beginning to get uneasy and inarticulate about something we used to think was all right? One is inevitably going to misrepresent what is happening if you should not make a change unless you have a clear principle. Consider the increasing uneasiness about punishment in general, particularly punishment of children, in the last couple of hundred years. Some would not have punished their child at many stages of this movement, not being quite sure that the principles they previously had were wrong but increasingly feeling uneasy. They ought, of course, to be trying to move towards a further principle. They ought in the end to be able to articulate what it is they now think. But for a time they have not got there, so the impression of irrationality would be undeserved. One wants both to say that we cannot fully articulate our moral insights all the time and that we ought to try to.

Reeder: I think I follow you, but I am not certain whether Gustafson could say that you are working to a new principle. He can say, "On the basis of my method I am working through to a new configuration that satisfies me in an aesthetic sense or in the psychological sense that Putnam presented." But I am not certain whether he can say, "I am working my way toward a newly articulated principle."

Midgley: If you say there is a principle, it sounds kind of ontological, and, moreover, you might not find one in the end. But it seems right to say, "I am groping towards a new principle," or at least, "I am moving towards a new set of priorities."

Gustafson: May I ask a question? Could you say that I am moving toward a reason and avoid the word *principle?* I think part of the hang-up is on the word *principle.*

Reeder: We must all remember the intentional fallacy; the author never knows what he says, only the literary critic can know! As I read you, nothing prevents you from saying that in a good deal of the moral life one moves to an articulated principle or reason. But I think you do want to say that on certain occasions one has conflicts of goods where all one can do is use the aesthetic or the psychological criterion. In those

---

[44]And even with new insight into liberty or health as goods, one will not necessarily come up with the same ranking or distribution even in similar circumstances; one can find different configurations satisfying.

cases there would not be any articulated principle or reason as to how the case had been resolved.

Gustafson: But you could still give reasons.

Reeder: You could have stated reasons. As with Audi's theories, you would have presented various reasons and compared them.[45]

---

[45]You would present reasons for one or another ranking or distribution; each alternative would have certain advantages and disadvantages. But you would not be able to give a reason for choosing one alternative over the other that will necessarily hold for all similar situations.

BELLAH
Robert N.

Gustafson as Critic
of Culture

O ne finishes a reading of the two volumes of James Gustafson's *Ethics from a Theocentric Perspective* with a sense of awe. So measured a reconnaissance, with careful attention to predecessors and contemporaries, and so leisured a pace, with many pauses, interludes, and transitions, is not what we expect from twentieth-century writers. The display of technical expertise and the effort to be relevant that we so often do see do not seem to be the focus of Gustafson's concern, though the book is expert and relevant. Rather there is a perspective that is broad, not to say cosmic, giving a sense of calm detachment. The detachment is refreshing, but it does raise questions about the kind of critic of culture Gustafson is or wants to be.

At first glance one might expect Gustafson to be a rather sharp critic of contemporary culture. The stance he advocates is radically theocentric, while, as he says in chapter one of volume one, the culture in which we live is determinedly anthropocentric. And indeed there are comments throughout both volumes that indicate the ways in which contemporary culture goes astray, comments that I will discuss further below. But criticism never becomes central to Gustafson's enterprise, nor does he identify with the critics of our culture, religious or otherwise. On the whole, he rather carefully disavows any desire to be "prophetic." We will need to look carefully at the critical implications of Gustafson's argument for contemporary culture and also at how he rather consistently mutes those implications. But before doing that we must consider another respect in which Gustafson is a critic of culture.

For Gustafson it is not only the world, in the sense of contemporary secular culture, that has gone astray, it is also the church. The charge is the same. Religion like the rest of culture has been too anthropocentric. The church has given a centrality to the human project that it cannot have in a genuinely theocentric perspective. Not only have Christians imagined that God has a greater concern for us collectively and individually than is warranted, we also have continued to live in an anthropocentric cosmos long after modern science has deprived us of any warrant for doing so. Thus, in his critique of religious culture Gustafson uses science, an element of secular culture, that, properly interpreted, which is to say interpreted in the light of piety, can help us gain a more properly theocentric perspective. Gustafson is actually more assiduous in carrying out this second kind of culture critique than he is the first one. This is perhaps because, as a Christian theologian, he feels the special responsibility of purging his own house of self-satisfaction and dishonesty.

"A Network of Dependencies"[1]

A central and persistent theme of both volumes is dependence and interdependence. A sense of dependence on God is close to the very heart of what it means to be theocentric, and one of the broader implications of theocentrism is that we recognize the "network of dependencies" that ties us not only to God but to other individuals, to society, and to nature. A profound sense of interdependence, reaching out in time and space, is essential to Gustafson's conception of theocentric ethics.

Modern culture generally and American culture in particular are committed to conceptions of individual autonomy with consequences that are utterly antithetical to the theocentric perspective. Gustafson points this out, as we shall see, but his way of doing so is surprisingly hesitant, gentle, and, in the end, peripheral, or so it seems to me. In the eighty-five pages of the first chapter of volume one, entitled, significantly enough, "An Interpretation of Our Circumstances," the conflict between theocentric ethics and contemporary secular culture is not pointed out. It is only in chapter two that the conflict becomes explicit. The consequences of "an extreme anthropocentrism"

---

[1]James M. Gustafson, *Theology and Ethics,* vol. 1 of *Ethics from a Theocentric Perspective* (Chicago: University of Chicago Press, 1981) 4.

for our treatment of both nature and society are indeed perilous. "The conditions of dependency of man on the rest of nature are such that violation of them leads to a threat to human well-being and, in extreme instances, in threats to human survival." And, a little later, "The high value placed on individual human dignity, if this warrants unlimited individual rights and liberties, is also, in the extreme, self-destructive."[2] Yet almost at once Gustafson cautions against the romanticization of nature or the use of the notion of a "larger good" to oppress individuals.[3] The critique is sharp enough, but it is quite general and quickly qualified.

Perhaps we are wrong to look for an extensive critique of contemporary culture in the sections of the book setting out the general perspective. Perhaps we should turn to the chapters in volume two that illustrate the application of the general approach to specific ethical questions. These four chapters are among the most impressive in the book. They show us the process of ethical discernment in practice, and the treatment is subtle and persuasive. If the proof of the pudding is in the eating these practical chapters augur well for the general approach. Yet if we look to them for a criticism of contemporary culture, we will find a very circumspect criticism indeed. For one thing, a number of areas where our society is especially vulnerable to criticism are not discussed, such as race relations, economic inequality, or the use of our military and economic power with respect to weaker and more vulnerable nations.

Even in the illustrative areas chosen for discussion, the ethically dubious practices of our culture are not highlighted. For example, in the discussion of marriage and the family two ideal types are formulated. The first type involves "an egocentric, hedonistic interpretation of the ends of family life" in which the relatively immediate satisfactions of individuals take precedence over the stability and continuity of relationships.[4] The second type is a patriarchal, hierarchical interpretation of the family in which individuals are subordinated to authority and sacrificed for the common good as interpreted by the dominant member.[5] In an important sense, these two ideal types are used as straw men relative to the much more extensively treated third type where individual and group needs are delicately and complexly balanced.[6] But in America the

---

[2]Ibid., 1:104-105.

[3]Ibid., 1:105-106.

[4]James M. Gustafson, *Ethics and Theology,* vol. 2 of *Ethics from a Theocentric Perspective* (Chicago: University of Chicago Press, 1984) 157.

[5]Ibid., 2:158.

[6]Ibid., 2:158ff.

first two types are extremely common, and the pathologies produced by them are extensive. In *Habits of the Heart,* a book much more explicitly concerned with the criticism of culture, these two types, particularly the first one, are examined at length.[7] Gustafson's very different strategy is to focus largely on the constructive description of the third type as a model of right relationships in marriage and the family, though in so doing he points repeatedly to the ways in which things can go wrong. In substance, Gustafson's position is quite close to that of *Habits of the Heart;* the difference in emphasis may be the sort that occurs between ethically sensitive sociologists who are concerned with understanding the American family as it exists and a socially sensitive ethicist who is concerned with depicting the right relationships appropriate to the contemporary family. Gustafson's strategy means that his criticism of what exists is largely by implication.

Gustafson's treatment of suicide is subtle, comprehensive, and persuasive. He is fully aware that it is often the breakdown in social relationships that contributes to the despair that can lead to suicide, and he is eloquent concerning our responsibilities in that situation: "From my theocentric perspective the first requirement and possibility is to attend to the patterns and processes of interdependence, to attempt to discern from them the conditions that are necessary to mitigate despair, and to govern actions and relationships accordingly."[8] But he does not point out those features of our society that make social relationships fragile and leave so many people isolated. Nor does he hold up for critical examination the widespread belief among educated young people that they have a right to commit suicide because freedom of individual decision takes priority over obligation to others. There can be no doubt that Gustafson disapproves of these features of contemporary culture, but he prefers to leave his disapproval implicit.

The third illustrative example, population and nutrition,[9] is interesting because the element of criticism is more explicit. The norm in this area is clear: "The general obligation based upon our participation in the patterns and processes of interdependence is that the production and distribution of food on the one hand and the size of the human population on the other ought to be correlated so as to avoid malnutrition and famine in any generation and place,

---

[7]Robert N. Bellah, et al., *Habits of the Heart: Individualism and Commitment in American Life* (Berkeley: University of California Press, 1985) ch. 4.

[8]Gustafson, *Ethics,* 2:207.

[9]Ibid., 2:219-50.

but also so as to avoid possible severe outcomes in the future."[10] But in this chapter, more often than usual, Gustafson points to the many factors leading to violations of this norm, such as national or regional selfishness, reliance on the free market without concern for its human consequences, and (here the criticism is primarily of certain religious views) indiscriminate opposition to birth control on the basis of doctrinaire ideas and without regard to the network of dependencies. Yet Gustafson's criticism remains highly general. His call is for general responsibility, not laying particular blame: "It is intellectually naive for moralists not to attend to these complex patterns and processes just as it is naive to isolate within them a single set of institutions as responsible for the famine, malnutrition, and poverty that exist on earth."[11]

Finally, the treatment of biological research funding is balanced and judicious, but it hardly touches on the transformation of American medicine that is being brought about through increasing scientific and technical specialization on the one hand and the growing power of for-profit corporations in medical research and treatment on the other. Thus any criticism of contemporary culture that the chapter contains remains largely implicit.

If one seeks to understand why Gustafson is so muted and indirect a critic of contemporary secular culture there are several places one can look (aside from the fact that in "A Response to Critics"[12] he calls himself an irenicist rather than a controversialist). For one thing, Gustafson seems to be as critical of the critics as of that which the critics criticize. He recognizes, for example, that religion is often used in the service of nationalism or racism, but he believes that absolutizing in the name of religion the interests of the poor or racial minorities or women is equally distorted.[13] Both are forms of utilitarian and, therefore, anthropocentric religion.

Gustafson recognizes the validity of a prophetic approach to Christian ethics, but he is quick to point out the defects of such an approach. He connects a prophetic ethics with an emphasis on "global questions," general questions of ethos, rather than on specific and delimited ethical issues: "Certainly it is a legitimate function of the Christian ethician to engage in a critique of ethos— to make prophetic evaluations of what he or she conceives the current ethos is

---

[10]Ibid., 2:236.

[11]Ibid., 2:240.

[12]James M. Gustafson, "A Response to Critics," *Journal of Religious Ethics* 13:2 (Fall 1985): 185-209.

[13]Ibid., 1:22-23.

in the light of some beliefs garnered from the religious tradition or from contemporary philosophical movements."[14] He even suggests a certain affinity with his own position, since in a world dominated by anthropocentrism, "a theocentric perspective would require a radical shift in thinking and attitude, and consequently in action."[15] Yet he goes on to say that a radical transformation of perspective (conversion) on a large scale is difficult to achieve and that such an approach is not much good in focusing our attention on issues that can be defined precisely enough to facilitate action.

Later in volume one he points out that prophetic moral discourse is better at pointing out "the evil of present social arrangements" than at helping us see precisely what to do about it.[16] In volume two in the treatment of population and nutrition, he points out the tendency of certain "very vocal segments of the Christian churches" to blame poverty, malnutrition, and starvation on certain "patterns of international economic relations." Economic institutions, Gustafson writes, "are highly visible in the world and thus make good targets for moral blame. But the tendency toward simplified causal analysis and therefore toward simplified moral responsibility distorts interpretation in many cases."[17] For Gustafson, then, the "complex patterns and processes" on which theocentric ethics concentrates do not lend themselves to simple causal analysis. The Christian ethicist, aware of the enormous web of interdependence, should be hesitant in assessing general blame, rather he should move toward better balance in specific contexts that can be understood well enough to be amenable to reasonable policy changes. Or at least that is what I understand Gustafson to be saying. It is a position that supports specific policy suggestions more than sweeping cultural criticism. But we must now turn to Gustafson's second form of cultural criticism, the criticism of the religious tradition, which in turn may shed a further ray of light on the peculiarly hesistant form of his criticism of contemporary secular culture.

God, Not Man,
at the Center

Ethics from a Theocentric Perspective, particularly volume one, is not only an essay in constructive theology, it is also a theory of religion. It is certainly not

---

[14]Ibid., 1:71.

[15]Ibid., 1:72.

[16]Ibid., 1:332.

[17]Ibid., 2:222.

possible in this paper to do justice to either of those aspects of the book. But to get at the criticism of religious culture I must at least allude to Gustafson's "religious anthropology," if I may call it that.[18] Gustafson believes that a kind of natural piety is characteristic of human beings generally, however differently it is phrased in different religious traditions. He is quite aware that there is no such thing as pure religious experience, but that all such experience is shaped by cultural traditions and social contexts. Nevertheless, he believes that certain moments of natural piety are generic to the human condition, are part of the very structure of reality for human beings. But if there are aspects of our situation that call out a generic piety that is by definition theocentric, there are also other aspects of the human situation that pull all humans into self-centered distortion, into anthropocentrism.[19] This tendency is what Gustafson calls the "human fault," and the metaphor he likes best for it is, drawing from Jonathan Edwards, the "contraction" of the human spirit.[20] It does not seem to me to push very far beyond what Gustafson actually says to argue that his project with respect to religion is to correct historic Christianity by the standard of a natural piety, a natural piety that is itself based on the best available knowledge of the universe, which means today, among other things, natural science.

In the section of volume one, chapter five, entitled "The Use of Scientific Explanations in the Retrieval and Reconstruction of Theology,"[21] we learn which anthropocentric features of Christianity must be eliminated. Because the place of our planet, not to speak of our species, is so very much more limited in time than once was thought, the doctrine of creation, as well as Christian eschatology, no longer makes sense. There is a problem about attributing agency to God,[22] but even if we can speak of God as Creator, there is no reason to think that His intention in creating the universe is specifically linked to man, as liberal theologians, as well as fundamentalists, have believed. Human beings are simply too miniscule a part of the universe to imagine that they are its purpose. Indeed it is well within possibility that some beings on some other planets are as superior to us as we are to the primates, giving them a better claim than we have to being the objects of God's intention. Similarly, the end

---

[18]Developed most completely in ibid., 1: chs. 3, 5, and 6.

[19]Ibid., 1:293-306.

[20]Ibid., 1:304.

[21]Ibid., 1:251-79.

[22]Ibid., 1:270.

of our species is certain to occur long before the end of the universe, so that our inherited notions of the eschaton are hardly justified.

Even more goes. Jesus, we are told, "incarnates theocentric piety and fidelity."[23] Gustafson is sufficiently careful in his use of words that we can be sure that for him Jesus is not an incarnation of God. Indeed, it would be hard to see what it would mean to say that anything could be an "incarnation" of the God of the vast cosmos of modern science understood in the light of natural piety. It is not surprising, then, that "salvation" goes, though "conversion" remains.[24] Jesus is not the God/man who has come to take upon himself the sins of the world; he is an exemplar of theocentric piety who can call us to conversion, that is, to a "transformation of the perspectives of those who are oriented finally toward God."[25]

What is the purpose of this cleansing of Christian belief in the light of theocentric piety? Honesty and the very deepening of our piety. We are to put away childish things, the illusion that God is more concerned with us than we have any right to believe. We are to turn from ourselves and magnify God. Concretely it means that we cannot use ourselves as individuals or even as a species as the measure of divine ordering. We must sustain a piety toward the whole of being that gives us no special claim. We must not, therefore, violate the natural order for the sake of our own interests. The natural world requires our respect even beyond the long-term interests of the human species.

But I think there is another implication, though Gustafson never says so explicitly. I think it is Gustafson's cosmic piety that makes him somewhat remote from the conflict of human interests and values, that makes him see the complexity of all issues, that mutes his role as a critic of secular culture. Gustafson is a profoundly religious man, and it is his intention to call us away from an exclusive preoccupation with the human species to a life in the presence of the grandeur and majesty of God. That, it seems to me, is the message of both volumes.

Conclusion

As must be evident, I am impressed and instructed by Gustafson's achievement, yet I am dissatisfied with his criticism of both secular and religious culture. Here I can only suggest very briefly what I think is wrong

---

[23]Ibid., 1:276.

[24]Ibid., 1:185, 192.

[25]Ibid., 1:192.

with his critique of religion and what the consequences are for his critique of culture.

George A. Lindbeck, in *The Nature of Doctrine,* a book too recent to have influenced Gustafson, contrasts two approaches to religion, the experiential-expressive and the cultural-linguistic. What Lindbeck calls the experiential-expressive theory of religion would seem to be rather close to what I have called Gustafson's religious anthropology. In both cases there is an attempt to describe features of fundamental human experience that are understood as religious and to which particular religions can be seen as responses. Lindbeck objects to this approach because it imagines a realm of human experience that is precultural and prelinguistic, essentially private. He insists that rather than actual religion being a response to experience, particular religions shape experience and give it form. Lindbeck's argument is polemical, attempting to make a strong case for his cultural-linguistic approach in a situation he believes is dominated by the experiential-expressive model. He tends to argue that the experiential-expressive theory is quite recent, beginning perhaps with Schleiermacher, but he does recognize that it has precursors going back virtually to the beginning of Christianity, as, for example, in Paul's speech on the Areopagus. For Lindbeck the great danger of the experiential-expressive approach is that it will recast the particular religious vision, in this case Christianity, in the alien terms of secular culture (often some form of phenomenological psychology) and thereby vitiate the integrity of the religious message. The cultural-linguistic approach, on the other hand, views the world in terms of the religious tradition and thus maintains its integrity and also its applicability in the contemporary world.

The interesting thing about Gustafson is that, while his religious anthropology is heavily experiential-expressive, it is never exclusively so. At point after point he qualifies experiential-expressivism with a clear sense of the cultural-linguistic aspect of religion. But where Lindbeck wants to make these two approaches antithetical, Gustafson brings them together. For Gustafson it is not a case of either/or but of both/and. He sees that "human experience has a deeply social character,"[26] that we are indelibly affected by the fact that we are members of particular communities with particular traditions.[27] He is especially close to Lindbeck in his frequent reliance on a notion of Julian Hartt that theology is "a way of construing the world."[28]

---

[26]Ibid., 1:120.

[27]Ibid., 1:128.

[28]Ibid., 1:3 and passim.

And yet when it comes to priorities, Gustafson consistently emphasizes experience, even while recognizing that experience is never "pure": "Experience is prior to reflection. This is not to deny that there are reflective elements present in the ordering of even very primary experiences; the human mind or brain is not an unorganized and unorganizing receptor of all the sensations that it can possibly receive. For theology particularly, I believe it is necessary to stress this priority of experience."[29] It is, indeed, the priority of experience that allows Gustafson to assess the religious tradition, what he sometimes calls "first-order religious language," from the point of view of a well-informed contemporary natural piety and thus prune the tradition of what are, from that point of view, its anthropocentric errors.

With Gustafson I believe that, with respect to the experiential-expressive and cultural-linguistic approaches to religion, it is a matter of both/and, but with Lindbeck I would place priority on the latter rather than the former. As a modern intellectual I live in a world in which the experiential-expressive approach makes sense. If I am to deal with my students and my colleagues I must, to some extent, be at home in that approach. I also recognize that this approach has long been valuable in apologetics and is at present essential for interreligious understanding. But as a Christian I think it is my primary responsibility to sustain in thought and practice the vigor of the cultural-linguistic approach. I must try to "construe the world" radically in terms of the religious tradition. As Lindbeck puts it, "For those who are steeped in them [the canonical writings of religious communities], no world is more real than the world they create. A scriptural world is thus able to absorb the universe. . . . It is the text, so to speak, which absorbs the world, rather than the world the text."[30] By text here, Lindbeck means to include the living practice of the religious community as informed by the text, and I would include not only Scripture but also tradition as part of the text.

My reason for making this choice, and I realize that in the world in which we live it is a choice, is that I have more confidence in the validity of the religious tradition, the first-order religious language, than I do in the experience of living in the modern world, which I find in many ways deceptive and illusory (as does, by the way, Gustafson). I recognize that the task of understanding, interpreting, and applying the language of tradition to the modern world is enormous, and one must use all one can from the contemporary sciences to do so. I also recognize that in the very act of continuing the tradition

---

[29]Ibid., 1:116.

[30]George A. Lindbeck, *The Nature of Doctrine: Religion and Theology in a Postliberal Age* (Philadelphia: Westminster Press, 1984) 117-18.

we constantly change, select, and ignore aspects of it, as Gustafson points out.[31] The crux comes, however, where an aspect of the tradition, particularly a central aspect, does not make much sense in terms of a natural piety based on contemporary science. In that case, I would hesitate to jettison the problematic aspect of tradition. The task of interpretation may be very difficult, but we can also remember that contemporary science, however hard, is in constant flux. It is possible that tomorrow's scientific theories may make much more intelligible what today is hard to understand.

In the case of the incarnation, for example, it is not after all modern science that makes it hard to understand. It was quite hard for the pagan Celsus, so Origen tells us, to understand why an obscure Jew in Palestine should be the incarnation of God, already in the second century.[32] On the other hand, neo-Platonism in the hands of Origen, or its modern reworking in the hands of Hegel, seems to make a strong Christology intelligible even in the light of twentieth-century science. My point is not to give priority to neo-Platonism, but rather to argue that we should struggle to understand the first-order religious language, to which I would give priority.

But my problem with Gustafson's theory and criticism of religion may not, after all, have to do with the conflict between modern science and first-order religious language, or at least not exclusively so. Perhaps, in spite of the priority Gustafson gives to experience, the real conflict between us concerns the choice of theological traditions. I would argue that Gustafson's preference for the Reformed tradition is a major source of what I conceive to be his present difficulties. The austerity of the Reformed tradition, the remoteness of its idea of God, even, if you will, its radical monotheism, or theocentrism, lead to the Stoicism toward which Gustafson is tempted ("One moves closer to some aspects of the Stoic tradition than most of Christian theology and ethics has"[33]) or to the "common sense" mentioned in the "A Response to Critics" that has not infrequently followed Calvinism. I would even go so far as to say that the Reformation is one of those happy mistakes that served an important function, but whose usefulness is now at an end. Or almost at an end, since the unlimited monarchical polity of the Roman Church, which justified the Reformation in the first place, has still not been abandoned. But certainly in a post-Vatican II world we can draw on a variety of theological resources, Or-

---

[31]Gustafson, *Ethics,* 2:34 and passim.

[32]Origen, *Contra Celsum,* III, trans. Henry Chadwick (Cambridge: Cambridge University Press, 1965) 22-25.

[33]Gustafson, *Ethics,* 1:190.

thodox and Catholic, Lutheran and Anglican, to mitigate the harshness of the Reformed tradition. A vital incarnational piety, rooted in a living sacramental practice of the church, would seem to me to be a viable starting point for theological reflection and for theological ethics today. (Even in the Reformed tradition the Platonic note in Edwards and Schleiermacher mitigates the harshness and makes them attractive, perhaps even to Gustafson, though he does not dwell on this side of their piety.)

Such a piety and practice would necessitate a rather sharp criticism of contemporary secular culture, which otherwise would invade and destroy the life of the church itself.[34] But out of a vision of a humanity redeemed in Jesus Christ can also come projects for the transformation of secular society itself, even rather modest projects of the middle range, such as Gustafson, I think, would approve.

However differently I would myself approach the constructive task, I would do so now under a great debt to James Gustafson. The Reformed tradition, however it may need supplementing in its rejection of every tendency toward idolatry, is something we forget at our peril. Gustafson has vividly made it live again for us today.

BELLAH DISCUSSION

Questioner: Can you actually fault Gustafson's use of second-order language, or is it just your preference for Platonic language?

Bellah: It's not the use of second-order language that is at stake. We are all involved in interpretation; we obviously don't speak first-century Greek. I would struggle with every resource that I have to continue to try to understand certain whole realms of our first-order language that I think Jim is tempted to pare out. Perhaps it is really a question of feeling an obligation to the text. This is a complex question because Jim is obviously feeling a moral obligation to other things. As I understand his position, I would try to keep more of the primary first-order language than he does, with whatever resources I had to use to do so.

W. D. White (St. Andrews Presbyterian College): I was interested in your reference to the structure of scientific revolutions and the ways that would give you pause in understanding the exact implications of modern scientific findings for Christian the-

---

[34]See Lindbeck, *The Nature of Doctrine,* 24, regarding this problem.

ology. That strikes me as so crucial that I would appreciate it if you would elaborate on it a bit.

Bellah: I think it relates to what John Yoder was saying earlier. We have "facts" and "hard" data from natural science, and we have great interpretive frameworks. If Thomas Kuhn and others are to be believed, those things do not always go hand in hand. You can go on building facts with a conceptual scheme that people have profound doubts about. The whole scientific world view doesn't shift until some radically new reformulation comes along. I am not raising this suggestion because I have some hope that science is going to prove Christianity true in the twenty-first century. That seems absolutely wrong and hopelessly impossible to me. Unfortunately a lot of people now are looking for some soft-headed, aging physicist to come up with a nice comforting scientific vision that allows us to believe that Christianity is really true after all—because this great Nobel prize winner says so. That is the last thing on earth I want to affirm. I am not by any means entirely opposing Jim's strategy here. There are clearly aspects of first-order religious language that we simply can't take literally anymore. We know the world is not built that way. I think the sciences have some things to say about putting restraints on our use of first-order language. What I would try to suggest is that larger scale, cosmological theories are constantly being revised. What was believed to be true twenty years ago is not what is believed to be true today. It is very dubious that theoretical physicists will ever have an absolutely finished theory. We ought to be knowledgeable and responsibly receptive to those things, yet we would be deeply irresponsible if we allowed them to dictate our ability to use our primary language. They are theories that are going to be revised. I would have to go through Gustafson's two volumes very carefully to see at what points I would fault Jim on this, or not. But more than specific statements, I think there is a kind of sense in *Ethics from a Theocentric Perspective* that the imperatives of natural science are perhaps more strongly constraining on our primary religious language than I feel.

Mary Midgley: The ways in which Gustafson uses science are actually very varied. Where the science in question tells us about human evolution, a whole range of things makes it likely that we should conceive our own emotional constitution in one way rather than another. Of course, the whole theory of evolution isn't an infallible and complete whole, but it does happen that most of us in fact accept much of it most of the time. It seems to be bad faith to start saying that this is fallible and uncertain if we in fact accept it. That seems to me to be the area where it is most important for Gustafson, and indeed for me, to say that the facts that I accept as the scientific facts are relevant to my metaphysics and thereby to my ethics.

I don't think what is happening about the cosmological thing is much different. There was an old cosmology that expressed an old ethics and metaphysics. The fact that modern science is contrary to that is adequate to cause us to have to shake up that sort of obvious belief. If anybody finds that they can't keep their religious belief without keeping those factual beliefs, then they have to do what the creationists do and form their science from their religion. Again, it seems to me bad faith for such a person to say, "Oh well, your theory is just your theory and my theory is my theory." That is what creationist-science people say. That seems to be quite disreputable.

There is another and different point, one that I am still slightly puzzled about. Here, it seems to me that Gustafson doesn't finally want to conclude things from science. For example, we are not in the center of the universe. We were thought to be in the center of the universe in the Ptolemaic system, and that was thought to have a special importance. Now if by chance the astronomers actually decide we are in the center of the universe, that wouldn't matter very much. Some of these big cosmological things seem to me simply not to matter, but it is still worthwhile pointing out that the old beliefs were false. That's a way of sort of shaking their symbolic force.

Then there is the other point. Gustafson does want to use a cosmological belief that says that the human race will ultimately die out. According to him, it follows that humans cannot have been a very central part of God's plan. Here I have difficulty being sure that does follow. For one thing, this ties up with the trouble about immortality. Doesn't the other alternative not exist, that the souls are immortal, so it was always known that the heavens would be rolled up as a garment? If we are now told that by the scientists too, it makes no difference. Or one might have some sort of panpsychist view in which, you know, life is all one thing, and it all goes back, and if there is some life in Alpha Centauri, then good luck to it; there it still is. So I am a little worried at this point; I am not clear about which use Jim Gustafson wants to make of this. But for both the other things, for quite opposite reasons, it does not seem to me that he is doing anything illicit with the sciences.

Bellah: Well, that may well be. It is just my anxiety about using science to limit first-order religious language in what that . . . Well, the incarnation . . .

Midgley: Could you explain this term? I don't know what first-order religious language is.

Bellah: It is the language of the biblical text as opposed to the language of sophisticated theology. Of course, incarnation is not, I think, in the Bible either. It's first and sort of first-order language.

Midgley: What is Plato's, what is anybody else's language?

Bellah: I think Plato is the first-order language of another religio-philosophical tradition. I think you are quite right that evolution is generally more central than cosmology to Jim. On the issue of how important humans are in the cosmic spectrum as revealed by evolution and the knowledge of the history of the solar system, one move that Jim doesn't make is in line with Platonic-Hegelian tradition. This tradition appeals to me. It does not matter how much one sees the emergence of human existence as in one sense a natural evolutionary development—as conscious, self-conscious, and objectifiable through language and discourse. Nonetheless, that tells us something terribly important about the nature of reality. To me it is unthinkable that it doesn't tell us something about God in some way. Now, if there are some creatures somewhere else in the cosmos who have levels of complexity beyond ours, that also would tell me something about God. I am not arguing anthropocentrically. I am not saying we are the crown of all the beings. Nonetheless, in terms of the species we know, it would be foolish not to see that humans have certain potentialities for conscious relationship to an enormously dependent and interdependent universe, precisely along the lines that Gustafson is most interested in. I am profoundly instructed by your book never to make any simple distinctions between us and the animals because they have the beginnings of everything we have. Nonetheless, in certain things we do have more, and that more is to me instructive about ultimate reality. I would even think in terms of first-order religious language about the meaning of the Logos and things like that. That is the point I would make. I would not adopt creation-science.

<u>Ian McPherson</u> (Covenant Presbyterian Church, Phoenix): Would you reflect on the fact that not only has science gone through great revision, but what's behind first-order language in the Christian faith has also gone through fantastic revision, through historical research and reflection?

<u>Bellah</u>: I think that's very much the case. I think that part of the problem is the invasion of a central strand of American Protestantism by secular orientations that have left the primary language pretty gutted. Part of the problem is to retrieve a living sense of the tradition. My present inclination is to move toward a more active liturgical kind of piety than the almost exclusively word-oriented verbalism of the tradition out of which I come. On the other hand, one of the most stunning things in our recent history is what you might even call a revolution in biblical studies. Out of the very heart of higher criticism—which carried a kind of positivistic scientism almost to the point of destroying the Scriptures by reducing them to the bits and pieces of the archaeology out of which they came—came a series of movements in the last thirty years to recover the religious meaning of those texts. The one that has impressed me most recently, because it is so sociologically sensitive, is the new emphasis on canon and the appreciation of the fact that the text is the text of the living community. The community lives in the light of the text, and the text is carried only by a living community. That is one enormous resource for revivifying a very deep capacity to live in that primary language without sacrificing the intellect and without renouncing the

achievements of higher criticism. It is informed very richly by this powerful language in ways more effective—and less intellectual or purely ethical—than much of the liberal Protestant tradition.

Tod Swanson (graduate student, University of Chicago): Augustine, Origen, or Thomas Aquinas might well want to mitigate the austerity of Gustafson's version of the Reformed tradition. Although they were speaking out of tradition, they argued in terms that could be shared with the scientists and the philosophers of their times. They could enter into argument with others about whether austerity should be mitigated, but on other than cultural-linguistic or confessional grounds. It seems that you can't be very prophetic from a Lindbeck-type position because there aren't transtribal truth claims. Why could you not make your argument on grounds similar to Augustine and Aquinas, and not try to make them from a purely canonical or cultural-linguistic perspective?

Bellah: First, I think Lindbeck is deeply influenced by certain developments in the social sciences. He draws heavily on Clifford Geertz, for example. So I think the cultural-linguistic theory of religion is not necessarily a completely parochial one. I think Lindbeck feels the pressure of universalization. He is prepared to deal with the relationship among Christianity and Judaism and even Islam, because all of them share certain fundamental terms. I am in no sense committed down the line to be a follower of Lindbeck. It's precisely at that point that I have problems with Lindbeck. I think each of the great religious traditions necessarily has a horizon of universality, that we are speaking to all human beings. In that sense, I would affirm John Yoder's missionary or evangelical mode. We are not speaking just to our own community. We are speaking because we bear something that we feel is true for all human beings. The last thing I want to be is simply a pietistic confessionalist. I am certainly prepared to argue in the public forum with theologians and with social scientists about these matters. What has struck me is the extent to which one will be heard if one makes a strong case, even in the heavily secularized and really quite hostile world of social science.

AUDI
Robert

Theology, Science, and Ethics in Gustafson's Theocentric Vision

T aken in the widest sense, a theology is an attempt to provide a holistic account of our experience and our world; it seeks to develop a comprehensive vision that includes not only our religious practices, but also the other major aspects of our culture, including science and art and the social forms of civilized life. James Gustafson has constructed a theology in this broad sense. He pursues questions of great religious significance, for instance, questions about the proper objects of confidence and trust, of loyalty, of hope, and of our loves and desires.[1] He treats these questions in the widest context, connecting them to developments in science, in philosophy, in the history of religion, and in other fields. He also refines and extends a religious outlook—the Reformed tradition—but he is openly willing to give up parts of his religious tradition, to combine it with new elements, and to develop it in re-

---

[1] For Gustafson's setting out of these questions see James M. Gustafson, *Theology and Ethics*, vol. 1 of *Ethics from a Theocentric Perspective* (Chicago: University of Chicago Press, 1981) 224-25.

lation to "other ways of explaining and construing the significance of 'the world.' "[2]

Gustafson's theology is many faceted, and in *Ethics from a Theocentric Perspective* it is set out in the context of his philosophical, historical, and scientific views. I cannot summarize even the theology of volume one, but by exploring a major aspect of that theology I hope to clarify its structure and content. My focus will be Gustafson's view of the connections between theology and the sciences, and of both to ethics. I shall first briefly explicate his view of the relation between theology, as he practices it, and science. The next section will explore how he takes the resulting theocentric view of the world to bear on ethics. And the final section will critically assess some major points that have emerged and will pose a number of problems that I believe should be pursued in further developing Gustafson's overall theoretical perspective.

Gustafson on Science and Theology

Gustafson's views on science and theology are developed above all in his section entitled "The Use of Scientific Explanations in the Retrieval and Reconstruction of Theology." It is no accident that he opens the section with Calvin's striking assertion that "it can be said reverently, provided that it proceeds from a reverent mind, that nature is God."[3] Even with Calvin's qualification, duly noted by Gustafson, that this statement might lead to "confusion between God and 'the inferior course of his works,' "[4] the statement is still important in understanding Gustafson's view of the relation between science and theology. Before articulating that view, I should note Gustafson's typology for classifying the uses of science that a theology may make. There are five categories.

First, a theology may, so to speak, absorb science and take theological propositions to *be* scientific, as in the case of creationist cosmology.[5] Second, theology may give a certain primacy to science and draw "theological deductions from scientific explanations of the world";[6] the Stoics and Deists represent this strategy. A third, intermediate position is based on a realistic epistemology and metaphysics and sees scientific explanations as ultimately

---

[2]Ibid., 1:154.

[3]Ibid., 1:251.

[4]Ibid.

[5]Ibid., 1:252.

[6]Ibid., 1:253.

leading to a limitless ground on which those explanations are based.[7] In the fourth view, theology and science are sources of independent truths; indeed, the truths may, as for Paul Holmer, be incommensurable.[8] The fifth view is Gustafson's own:

> Relative to the first type . . . one cannot draw scientific conclusions or hypotheses from theological statements. Theology cannot explain the world scientifically. Relative to the second type . . . one cannot draw theological conclusions deductively from scientific data and theories; there is a measure of autonomy in religion; it makes sense only with the acknowledgement of piety. . . . Yet theology cannot make claims about God's relations with the world that are incongruous with well-established scientific data and theories.[9]

This last point is so important that it is worth citing in another formulation, in which Gustafson uses terms from Troeltsch: "the 'substantial content' of ideas of God cannot be incongruous (rather than [as for Troeltsch] must be 'in harmony') with well-established data and explanatory principles established by relevant sciences, and must 'be in some way indicated by these.' "[10]

Keeping in mind Gustafson's view of the relation between science and theology, let us ask what he takes theology to have learned from science. One important point is simply that "the religious sense of dependence upon powers beyond ourselves is supported by many of the data and theories of many sciences. In nonreligious terms, this simply indicates that human life is a part of nature."[11] A second major point is, "A rudimentary understanding of the natural sciences is sufficient to indicate that ordering exists in nature."[12] To be sure, this ordering does not "warrant belief in a Designer. At most one might say that a 'governance' is occurring. Its presence, however, evokes awe and respect, natural piety, toward nature. And it warrants the affirmation *within piety* that the powers and the ultimate power are ordering; they are not

---

[7]Ibid., 1:254. Gustafson does not precisely characterize the view. I infer what I say here from both what he says himself and what he quotes from Jaki.

[8]Ibid., 1:255-56.

[9]Ibid., 1:257-58.

[10]Ibid., 1:257.

[11]Ibid., 1:260.

[12]Ibid., 1:262.

purely contingent or chaotic."[13] This ultimate power, of course, Gustafson takes to be God. Not surprisingly, then, after discussing in more detail how various sciences "contribute to the substance of theology,"[14] he asserts that

> enough has been said about what can be said about God from the various sciences to sustain the general point: "God" refers to the power that bears down upon us, sustains us, sets an ordering of relationships, provides conditions of possibilities for human activity and even a sense of direction. The evidences from the various sciences suggest ["within piety?"] the plausibility of viewing God in these terms.[15]

So far, we have considered what theology might gain from a proper interpretation of the sciences. There is also much that it must give up in the light of such an interpretation if it pursues a hard question Gustafson believes many theologians have avoided, namely, "What if a rational assessment of the structure of the world requires that we consider the form of life that is appropriate to *it?* What if there is a deep incongruity between what we know about nature and the continuities of man with nature on the one hand, and on the other hand a life-policy of humanizing and personalizing the world?"[16] Gustafson is intent on pursuing this question in relation to the sciences, and he concludes that there is much that theology must give up as a result. Let us consider some major changes that he takes to be in order.

First, theology has traditionally been too anthropocentric: "a number of things attributed to God in the Christian tradition that sustain this anthropocentric view and the morality that is derived from it must be called into question in the light of some of what we learn from the various sciences."[17] Most important is "the anthropocentric centering of value, reinforced by the view that the divine intention is finally focused on our species. . . . Do the [scientific] accounts of billions of years of development of the universe . . . alter in any way the claims that have traditionally been made for the place of the human species in the intention of God?"[18] Gustafson grants that there is

---

[13]Ibid. My emphasis.

[14]Ibid., 1:263.

[15]Ibid., 1:264-65.

[16]Ibid., 1:266.

[17]Ibid., 1:267.

[18]Ibid.

room for disagreement here, but the point is that theology cannot ignore the question. His own conclusion is that "if there was divine 'foreknowledge' of human life, there was no particular merit in bringing it into being through such an inefficient and lengthy process."[19]

There are other theological revisions Gustafson takes to be indicated by evidences from the sciences. Consider Christian eschatology. Clearly, scientific evidence about the demise of the earth is relevant; and "since the forecasted demise is so long in the future that it has no significant bearing on present conduct, some wonder whether the human values and aspirations that traditional eschatologies sustain need be questioned at this time and in the light of current scientific speculations."[20] Gustafson also cites "counterevidences from biology, for example, that with the demise of the brain the center of personal identity is gone."[21] The suggestion here is apparently that resurrection is not a rational hope.

Scientific developments also bear on human freedom. He asks, "Are individual actions to be interpreted more as the directing of natural impulses, desires, and capacities or as the fruits of 'free' acts? . . . some of the traditional and contemporary claims for radical freedom, such as those espoused in theologies influenced by existentialism, cannot be sustained in the light of what we are learning not only about the biological nature of human life but about other aspects of life as well."[22] The evidence from the sciences shows that we are shaped by biological and social factors that affect our capacities and aspirations in ways that theology must take into account if it is to understand our freedom.[23] While "human accountability is not abolished from this point of view . . . persons have been held accountable in the past for more than they actually should have been . . . for events and effects for which they were only partially causally accountable."[24]

Even a theologian's conception of God should be responsive to evidences from the sciences. Take the model of personal agency. This is central in Christian theological conceptions of God, and it implies "that the ultimate power has intelligence similar to our own and can exert its will in ways comparable

---

[19]Ibid.

[20]Ibid., 1:268.

[21]Ibid., 1:252.

[22]Ibid., 1:268-69.

[23]Ibid., 1:269.

[24]Ibid., 1:290-91.

to ours."[25] If scientific findings about our species are taken to heart and "man is conceived more in terms of the continuities of action and agency with 'nature' . . . both the scope of human agency and, by analogy, of divine agency are more limited. Since, as I have previously argued, all of our construals of the deity emerge out of our interpretations of human experiences of the world it is not possible to think about God as God might be in his aseity."[26] One major conclusion Gustafson draws here is that while "we can discern through experience . . . and through our knowledge of life in the world what some of the divine purposes are for creation,"[27] we do not have sufficient reason to posit an intelligence similar to ours or a capacity for radical agency similar to that sometimes claimed for us.[28] By undermining our anthropocentrism, then, taking scientific results seriously also undermines our anthropomorphic conception of God.

In the realm of value, too, if theology takes science seriously enough, it must again relinquish its traditional anthropocentrism. Given a clear realization of our place in the empirical universe, we should not view our own good as God's central purpose: "My argument radically qualifies the traditional Christian claim that the ultimate power seeks the human good as its central focus of activity."[29] This does not lead to utter relativism; for instance, "Murder is always wrong."[30] Nor does it require doubting that God's purposes are good. But as the Genesis account itself suggests in its reference to God's viewing the whole creation as good, we must not suppose that our own good is the sole or central focus of divine concern.

So far, my exposition of Gustafson's use of scientific evidence in developing theology has been closely tied to the text. I now want to be more speculative in suggesting how he takes science to bear on theology. In some cases, I can cite passages to support my interpretations; in others, I count on the reader to discern the view in implications of what Gustafson says. There are at least five major ways in which, for Gustafson, science bears on theology: it is an antidote to anthropocentrism; it qualifies—or thoroughly undermines—absolutes; it contributes to a more nearly adequate conception of God; it con-

----

[25]Ibid., 1:269.

[26]Ibid., 1:269-70.

[27]Ibid., 1:271.

[28]Ibid.

[29]Ibid.

[30]Ibid.

stitutes a model for theology; and it serves, in a complicated way, as a guide in ethics.

Science against Anthropocentrism. We have seen some of the ways in which scientific evidence undermines anthropocentrism, but the point deserves elaboration. Let us assume the conception of God as the ultimate power, with dominion over nature as well as humanity; this minimal characterization of God is generally not controversial among most theologians in the West, or at least is common ground between Gustafson and most of his theological colleagues. In the light of this conception, scientific developments suggest profound continuities between ourselves and lower animals. They also indicate a degree of order even in inanimate processes. Together, this continuity and order make the natural world an appropriate object of divine concern and a possible locus of divine activity. If one also construes our makeup as essentially biological and therefore physical, one finds it still more plausible to regard us as part of nature and, hence, even if we are one focus of divine concern, integrally bound up with the external world—a world Christians have often regarded as a domain created for our welfare. Here, then, science is a *leveler;* it undermines the hierarchical notions that are easily sustained by those who see us as radically discontinuous with the rest of the world.[31]

Science versus Absolutism. Once a theology takes responsibility for giving due weight to scientific evidence, the absolutism characteristic of some religious thinkers tends to be undermined. If, for instance, scientific evidence weighs strongly against statements based on literalistic readings of the Bible, or against deductions about the divine will from observations that seem scientifically explainable, then one is far more likely to be cautious in drawing theological conclusions. This applies both to religiously based assertions about the natural world and to moral matters. Indeed, scientific sophistication is likely to

---

[31]Gustafson says, for example, that "the dignity of the species is protected by those precepts which require that we favor man over animals in all instances where human life is threatened" (ibid., 1:100), whereas "any interpretation of life which excessively accents the similarities rather than the distinctive differences between man and the rest of creation is likely to find reasons in certain circumstances to curb human activities that enhance human dignity" (ibid.). Science supports such an interpretation: for example, "A religious interpretation of special providence was undercut by the development of science in the seventeenth century; it was replaced by a religious interpretation of the Deity as the clockmaker. The Deity as the clockmaker had an agonizing death during the nineteenth century when evidence from geology, biology, and other sciences pointed toward the importance of processes of development in nature" (ibid., 1:122).

incline one to regard "moral rules and principles" as "general rules whose application must be addressed to changing historical conditions. This is the case for two principal reasons. One is that it is not given to people to know inerrantly what the divine governance requires under some special circumstances. . . . The other is that the divine governance is an ordering and not an immutable eternal order; rules and principles have to be open to revision and extension."[32]

Scientific Progress and the Conception of God. The point that scientific understanding can help us toward a more nearly adequate conception of God can be developed in a number of directions. For one thing, if there is any sense in which nature *is* God, then in helping us understand nature, science can help us understand God. I am reluctant to take this identification as more than a powerful metaphor, though Gustafson cites it more than once here and also cites it in his other writings.[33] But even if nature is only ordered by God, our understanding of it can aid us in understanding God: if it does not by itself warrant inferences about God, it at least helps us avoid unjustified conclusions based on scientifically falsifiable views of the world or unjustified postulations of supernatural agency where scientific explanation is available. Moreover, if God is somehow manifest in nature, then there may be a sense in which he is perceivable, or at least discernible, therein: to grasp the order in nature, perhaps, is to come as close as one can to grasping the divine ordering, or that aspect of it embodied in the parts of the universe that are accessible to us. Science, then, might lead to one kind of understanding of God. Note, too, that as Gustafson often stresses, the scientific understanding of nature tends to evoke natural piety,[34] perhaps partly because such understanding is so easily felt to reveal the ordering of the ultimate power in virtue of which scientific laws have their universality. Natural piety, in turn, helps us understand God. It does this, in part, by opening us to seeing and accepting "the powers that bear down upon us and sustain us." We approach neither nature nor the concept of the divine with rigid preconceived ideas. Liberated from the need to confirm a fixed outlook, we are better able to learn. As Schleiermacher put the point, in part, "It can never be necessary in the interests of religion so to in-

---

[32]Ibid., 1:316.

[33]For instance, in "Nature: Its Status in Theological Ethics," *Logos* 3 (1982), Gustafson says that "if . . . as Calvin averred, 'nature is God,' and ethics is to be theological, then there is no way of avoiding the difficult task of finding out what clues, or indications of the divine governance are present in nature" (22).

[34]Gustafson, *Ethics,* 1:262.

terpret a fact that its dependence on God absolutely excludes its being conditioned by the system of Nature."[35]

Science as a Model for Theology. Surely science can also inform theology by serving as a model for it. If Gustafson does not explicitly say this, he implies it. It is noteworthy, for instance, that he conceives theology and science as both involving "activity of the practical reason."[36] He also suggests that "theology *has* developed in ways that have some similarity to the processes by which scientific thought develops."[37] Part of the point here may be this: just as scientific theories develop only when *imagination* is brought to bear on the data—to which the application of logic alone would not yield explanatory hypotheses—so theology develops when, within piety, nature is taken not as a fixed domain of objects put there for our exploitation, but as a sphere of divine ordering in which, to some degree at least, what God is enabling and requiring us to do may be discerned. Consider also the need for retrieval and recombination in theology. "Selection of what is to be retrieved or sustained is relative to knowledge and understanding present in the culture that pertains to matters of concern to theology. . . . Selection is made in the light of other areas of knowledge. So also, then, the processes of recombination, reinterpretation, and innovation take these into account."[38] Much the same could be said, of course, of science—as the history of science, for example of astronomy, amply shows. Science is also *fallibilistic,* in the sense that even well-confirmed theories are regarded as open to revision and, in principle, falsifiable. Indeed, it is arguable that, whatever a scientist's private convictions, scientists qua scientists do not believe hypotheses but simply note their degrees of confirmation, rank them, and act on them accordingly: testing them further if they merit it, preferring better-confirmed hypotheses if the tests so indicate, and so forth. This doxastic restraint is reminiscent of Gustafson's substitution of piety, as an attitude, for belief, as a cognitive commitment, in his development of Troeltsch's ideas. Lastly, note that science is impersonal; even when it deals with individual phenomena, it construes them as instances of kinds of

---

[35]The quotation is given by Gustafson (ibid., 1:177). I assume that he quotes assentingly. I might add that the possibility of overdetermination supports Schleiermacher: an event can have two simultaneous, independent, sufficient conditions and can be adequately explainable by appeal to either. Presumably, one could be supernatural, one natural.

[36]Ibid., 1:158.

[37]Ibid., 1:139.

[38]Ibid., 1:142-43.

phenomena. The individuality of a thing can be scientifically captured, but only by attributing to it a unique combination of general properties. Similarly, theology, at least as Gustafson and many others practice it, is unlike faith in speaking of God impersonally, sometimes even in a technical way; and if, in the end, "there is no escaping the 'subjectivist trap,' "[39] science at least provides a model for the study of complex individual phenomena in terms that are both intersubjective and anchored in a framework of objective procedures for confirmation and explanation.

The Ethical Bearing of Science

We come now to the assessment, from a theocentric perspective, of the significance of science for ethics. This significance may or may not be mediated by theological reflections, and Gustafson sometimes discusses it in the light of such reflections, sometimes not. One might think that what really determines the connection between science and ethics for Gustafson is his commitment to a modern version of natural law theory in ethics: rightness supervenes on certain natural adjustments, such as the affectional structure of normal families, and science enables us to discern these basic patterns. But Gustafson is not a natural law theorist in this sense. He takes a proper conception of nature to be highly relevant to ethics, but he does not think that moral principles can be read off natural patterns.

Perhaps the first point to be made here is that if science tends to evoke and develop natural piety, then it supports what we might regard as the natural counterpart of *respect for persons,* an attitude that some moral theorists have taken to be fundamental in ethics, and to which virtually all of them have accorded a significant place. Indeed, if persons are continuous with nature, then piety toward nature should be expected to extend toward them. Moreover, if we have a sense of dependence on nature and a related sense of gratitude,[40] we are much less likely to consider nature merely a means to our own ends. The resulting attitude of respect and dependence can readily extend to persons. A third important point is that if *ought* implies *can,* then in helping us see what is possible for us science helps us circumscribe the domain in which attributions of moral obligation are applicable. If we are as limited in what we can do as some behavioral scientists seem to think, then many theological accounts of human obligation are too strong. Thus, a theocentric view informed by contemporary science tends to negate "the aspiration for the perfectibility of man, if only

---

[39]Ibid., 1:264.

[40]Ibid., 1;130.

because man in nature, culture, history, and society is in a process of change."[41] On the other hand, if we have undiscovered potential, then what we should do may go beyond what anyone now proposes. In this regard, the example of Christ is relevant: "His teaching, ministry, and life are a historical embodiment of what we are to be and to do—indeed, of what God is enabling and requiring us to be and do."[42]

A fourth, related point is that scientific understanding can help us oppose what is bad as well as discern what is good, in us and in nature. Scientific inquiry can help us root out human faults. Consider the four faults Gustafson mentions as failings that the Christian tradition has treated with insight: misplaced trust; misplaced valuations of the objects of desire; erroneous perceptions of the interrelations of things; and unfulfilled obligations. Misplaced trust is obviously less likely if one is scientifically well informed, for one is more likely to know what one can and cannot count on. Misplaced valuations, while apparently possible given any degree of purely cognitive sophistication, are far less likely if one does not have mistaken beliefs about the properties of things— for example, about what benefits they will bring. Erroneous perceptions are largely correctable by scientific inquiry. And unfulfilled obligations are in general more likely to be fulfilled in proportion to the extent of one's relevant knowledge: knowledge of one's own capacities, of what options to pursue for a given end, of how to remove obstacles to one's actions, and so on. Such knowledge is of course much the sort of thing Gustafson speaks of in relation to discerning the divine governance (discussed in detail in volume two). "What can be discerned, to put the matter abstractly, are the necessary conditions for life to be sustained and developed . . . not only for individual and interpersonal life but also for social institutional life and the life of the species."[43]

It should not escape our attention as we discuss the bearing of science on theology that, in Gustafson's scheme, theology also bears on science. If we take a theocentric view of the world, not only are we more inclined to develop natural piety than in an anthropocentric view that puts nature at our disposal, we are also more inclined to view science itself theocentrically: as an exploration of the divine order, capable, at times, of revealing aspects of the divine ordering conceived dynamically and diachronically. Indeed, if our theology is theocentric, the ways of nature may be in some respects a better indication of the divine order than the ways of humanity: they are universal, or more nearly

---

[41]Ibid., 1:310.

[42]Ibid., 1:276.

[43]Ibid., 1:339.

so, and they are unaffected by the intervention of our own free and sometimes misguided agency. It is a little as if one were to compare reading a writer's text directly with reading it through interpreters who express their own personalities in framing their interpretations. On the other hand, the conception of nature as divinely ordered may be scientifically useful. It may be heuristically valuable in that it suggests explanatory hypotheses that might not otherwise be conceived. It may inspire a search for connections among apparently disparate phenomena whose similarity might otherwise be overlooked. And it may help motivate a search for progressively deeper and better explanations; for a theocentrically oriented scientist, there is no limit to the order to be discovered in nature. If there is at some point an inclination to regard Gustafson as having scientized theology and perhaps even God, it must be remembered that he has gone at least as far toward divinizing science.

It will not be possible to pursue in detail any of Gustafson's ethical discussion in volume two, but there are a few general points that are in order here and are essential for understanding his conception of the relation between science and theology. Above all, a major element in Gustafson's theology is his view that, from his theocentric perspective it follows that we are to relate all things in a way appropriate to their relations to God, though there are no divinely revealed prescriptions of conduct.[44] Nature does not provide a blueprint to which we must conform our actions. What it does provide is much less determinate. As Gustafson says in chapter nine, for example, God orders life through patterns and processes of interdependence in which individuals, institutions, and communities participate; and these patterns and processes, whether in the individual or the family or society, are, though not a sufficient basis of ethics, necessary conditions for the fulfillment of other values and ends. They are, then, an essential part of the basis of ethics. They form part of the factual superstructure within which a sound ethics must guide us, and we must therefore conceptualize them as accurately as possible. Science is indispensable in this task, whether the subject is obligations among mutually dependent family members or priorities in biomedical research or, even more globally, patterns of world population. But indispensable though it is, it does not by itself provide moral principles.[45] Both in developing and in applying such

---

[44]This point is expressed in ch. 8 of James M. Gustafson, *Ethics and Theology*, vol. 2 of *Ethics from a Theocentric Perspective* (Chicago: University of Chicago Press, 1984) 253-77.

[45]Gustafson points out, in *Can Ethics Be Christian?* (Chicago: University of Chicago Press, 1975) that "the *dependence* of the finite-created life on the superior power

principles, theological reflection may influence our use of scientific findings. This is another respect in which theology, though it should take careful account of scientific results, may help to take us beyond them.

Some Problems in the Interpretation and Assessment of Gustafson's View

Far more could be said to indicate the subtlety and power of Gustafson's theocentric position, but we already have before us more than can be assessed in a short space. My procedure will be simply to recall some central points, discuss them critically, and summarize some issues that deserve further study.

Let us begin with a puzzle. On the one hand, Gustafson revises Troeltsch's view that the content of ideas about God must be "in harmony" with well-established scientific results; yet he agrees with Troeltsch that they must be in some way indicated by these scientific results. One would think that such an indication would entail some degree of harmony. I imagine that what Gustafson is rejecting here is (among other things) a demand that scientific data either be accounted for theologically or, on the other hand, be the major basis on which people come to believe in God, or the major source of attributions of divine properties—as if those properties were posited simply to explain natural phenomena. What, then, is the relevant kind of indication? Is it something like an evidential relation between nature and its Orderer? Let us explore this.

The closest Gustafson seems to come to endorsing a version of the Design Argument is in the context of rejecting that argument as fully cogent. Not even the remarkable ordering of nature nor "the even more remarkable capacity of the human mind to understand it in greater and greater detail and accuracy, is sufficient *in itself* to warrant belief in a Designer. At most one might say that a 'governance' is occurring. Its presence, however, evokes . . . natural piety. . . . And it warrants the affirmation *within piety* that the powers and the ultimate power are ordering."[46] On the face of it, this suggests that while the order of nature does not by itself warrant belief in a Designer, it evokes, in those with a deep understanding, a natural piety in a context of which one *may* justifiably believe in an ultimate ordering power. If I understand Gustafson, however, he is rightly not taking this justification to be a

---

of the Creator is a condition that requires the ordering of the created forms of life in correspondence with their Creator's will" (87) and that "certain action-guiding values and principles can be inferred from religious beliefs as normative for those who share some common Christian experience of the reality of God" (173).

[46]Gustafson, *Ethics,* 1:262. Emphasis mine.

matter of objective probability, and he is certainly not conceiving it as entailment; it is more like the sort of justification William James had in mind in "The Will to Believe." One is not intellectually compelled to believe in an ultimate power, but one may; and, *given* sufficient natural piety and deep enough scientific understanding, one tends to. If we add that in this context one's belief in an ultimate power need have no direct implications concerning the moral properties associated with God, we may conclude that Gustafson is not offering a disguised Design Argument. But he *is*, in a Jamesian spirit, taking seriously the underlying inspiration of that argument.

Having noted these points, we are in a good position to pursue Gustafson's views about the bearing of science on our conception of God. I have already suggested that if we regard the natural world as even manifesting the divine nature, then scientific understanding of the former can contribute to our conception of the latter. But nature surely cannot be plausibly thought to exhaust God, at least if, like Gustafson, one wants to preserve a moderately strong connection with the Hebraic-Christian tradition. How, then, might we salvage, within the theocentric framework, any notion of a personal God? One might think that because Gustafson rejects an anthropomorphic conception as part of an untenable anthropocentrism, he leaves us with no basis for attributing personal characteristics to God. This impression is reinforced by his remark that "since . . . all our construals of the Deity emerge out of our interpretations of human experience of the world, it is not possible to think about God as God might be in his aseity. . . . The question is the choice of analogies, metaphors, or symbols."[47] On the other hand, Gustafson repeatedly speaks of what God is enabling and requiring us to do, and he uses other terms expressing agency, for example, "ordering," "creating conditions for possibilities," and so forth.[48]

Gustafson's considered view, I think, is not that we cannot speak of God as an agent, but that "if we choose to use the analogy of agency for construing the Deity, it must be developed with great circumspection. Insofar as the analogy leads us to assert that God has intelligence, like but superior to our own, and that God has a will, a capacity to control events comparable to [that asserted in?] the more radical claims made for human beings, the claims are excessive."[49] But if this is so, how can we speak of what God is enabling and requiring us to do, or of God's purposes—for even if we distinguish purposes

---

[47]Ibid., 1:270.

[48]Ibid., 1:271.

[49]Ibid., 1:270.

from intentions,[50] do not purposes imply something at least similar to a will, particularly if we are referring to God rather than lower animals? (One might also question whether, even if having a given purpose, say, to A, does not imply the corresponding intention, namely, to A, a being can have purposes without having *some* intentions.) Gustafson seems to face a serious dilemma here: if he adheres to his strong rejection of anthropomorphism in the conception of God, he is hard pressed to make the connection between science and ethics required by this theocentric view; if he allows the apparently necessary anthropomorphism, he is hard pressed to sustain his view about the ultimate power.

I believe, however, that a careful reading may yield a way out. Note that he prescribes our attributing to God an intelligence *like* our own and a controlling capacity *comparable to* our capacity to control events. These terms are vague; but I think he is above all rejecting a kind of *assimilationism:* a tendency to regard God as essentially like us, only infinitely greater in the degree of his possession of the same virtues. Now one can reject assimilationism and the associated anthropomorphism in conceiving God without denying that there are *any* substantive similarities between us and God. For example, whereas we know the world through perception, God perhaps knows it in some direct way; and whereas we control events through the instrumentality of our bodily movement, God's actions are perhaps all basic: he never has to do anything *by* doing anything else, such as using an instrument, but the disposition of his will does produce change. Would God then have intelligence and agency *like* ours or not? In some ways, yes, in others, no. But we do not know the ways precisely, and it is better to resort to metaphor and to suspend judgment on certain specific descriptions of God than to risk assimilating the divine to the human. It may be a mistake to say that "it is not possible to think about God as God might be in his aseity," but Gustafson's more guarded statement on this matter is surely plausible: there are not "sufficient reasons to move from our perceptions of the purposes of the divine governance to the assertion that these imply an intelligence similar to our own."[51] I agree that the evidence does not justify such inferences. But that their conclusions attributing limited similarities between the human and the divine are utterly unintelligible without unwarranted anthropomorphism is not established—and perhaps not meant to be established—by Gustafson's arguments.

If these considerations about the divine nature are correct, then neither Gustafson's rejection of anthropocentrism nor his rejection of assimilation of

---

[50]Ibid.

[51]Ibid., 1:270.

God's nature to ours requires wholly giving up the conception of God as a personal being. Indeed, if what God enables and requires us to do is to be sufficiently intelligible to us to help us in making moral decisions, it looks as if we must posit *some* broadly personal divine characteristics, perhaps most notably a kind of agency. Perhaps Gustafson could accept this last point; I certainly do not see it as inconsistent with his central views. But the impression created by some of what he says is that he cannot countenance a personal God, and that is why I am at pains to suggest that his central views do not entail that God be identified with nature or otherwise conceived as lacking intelligence or agency. There may, however, be other major theological views that must be rejected given his central points. Let us explore three cases: eschatology, freedom, and the place of humanity in nature.

In interpreting what Gustafson says about the eschatological bearing of scientific evidence, it is well to remember that his position does not require rejecting a theological view simply because it is not confirmed by scientific evidence; rather, incongruity with that evidence is the scientific basis he countenances as demanding theological retraction or revision. In this light, his statement that "we may not be able to say what the end will be, but, as Troeltsch stated, it will not be the Apocalypse of traditional Christian thought"[52] may presumably be seen as a denial that the relevant events, conceived literally, will occur. Is he, however, committed to denying that *anything* "apocalyptic" will occur, perhaps something marked by extraordinary events, though without suspension of natural law? Or would his view be that there is no reason to affirm that such events will take place and that, even apart from the absence of scientific indications, the inclination to believe it stems from anthropocentrism? I suspect this would be his view.

A crucial consideration here is the status of personal identity, for if our nature does not preclude resurrection, then what seems the most important strand in traditional eschatology perhaps need not be severed. Gustafson's own view of the human person is physicalistic: we are biological creatures. I have already quoted him as saying that "with the demise of the brain the center of personal identity is gone,"[53] and in chapter two of volume two he goes so far as to speak of the "nature of the person" as " 'physicalist' or 'biologistic' in character." Two points should be made here. First, what the biological evidence strictly confirms is the limited conclusion that certain brain functions are *closely correlated* with certain mental functions. Second, it is only through the use of Occam's razor that one can rule out a parallelist account of the cor-

---

[52]Ibid., 1:268.

[53]Ibid., 1:252.

relations: there is no purely scientific, as opposed to metaphysical, sufficient reason to *identify* mental properties with physical ones.

Gustafson might object here that Occam's razor is surely common to science and metaphysics. I would agree, and in any case I believe that for him a theological view that goes against a theory established by ordinary scientific evidence *combined with* Occam's razor is to be rejected or revised. It should not be assumed, however, that resurrection preserves personal identity conceived as rooted in bodily substance. John Hick, for example, argues that at the very time of bodily death one might receive a resurrection body; and while he does not describe the relevant "material" in detail, one might suppose that it shares with biological matter whatever it is that serves as a basis of mental life. [54] This is highly speculative, however; and it must be admitted that if one accepts a biological conception of the person—which many scientists and scientifically informed philosophers do not—then, while resurrection can still be consistently held to be possible, the prospects for a plausible account of it are dim. It is important to see, however, that it is one thing to reject disembodied personhood; it is another to conceive personhood as entailing *biological* embodiment. Neither of these views is confirmed by scientific considerations alone, and one could accept biological embodiment as a necessary condition for human personhood and reject it as a condition for divine personhood. God is not a biological entity.

There is also room for dispute regarding how much of a blow Gustafson's theocentrism deals to the traditional view that we are (normally) free agents. It should certainly be granted that scientific advances have shown us limitations on what we can do and have helped us see that agents may be compelled to do certain things by factors of which they are unaware. But is there any reason to conclude that we are not normally free when we reflectively suppose we are? If freedom is inconsistent with determinism, that is, with every event's being produced by an antecedent or simultaneous event in accordance with a universal law of nature, then *if* science is confirming determinism, it is thereby undermining our traditional conception of our own freedom. Now there are times when Gustafson speaks as if he did think freedom and determinism incompatible. At one point, for example, he says that "if the determinism is not absolute, if the systems [of religious views] leave some small places and times for human accountability for actions (as all the major ones do), they also

---

[54] See John Hick's "Theology and Falsification," *Theology Today* 17 (1960). I have critically assessed Hick's views in this article in "Eschatological Verification and Personal Identity," *International Journal for the Philosophy of Religion* 7 (1976).

acknowledge a sense of possibility."[55] On the other hand, he does not seem to think that determinism *is* true, nor is there general agreement among scientists regarding the extent to which scientific developments even confirm determinism: indeed, many think that at least some of the basic laws of nature are statistical rather than deterministic.

What Gustafson does say about the bearing of scientific progress on freedom is limited and probably open to more than one interpretation. One main point is to the effect that there is a tension between, on the one hand, the scientific conception of our actions as the directing of natural impulses and responses to social and cultural "conditioning," and, on the other hand, the traditional view according to which our conduct exhibits the "fruits of 'free' acts." I believe that this tension is easily exaggerated: scientific progress may be confirming that our actions tend to be predictable from a detailed knowledge of our biological and sociopsychological makeup, but to infer that such progress should undermine our sense of freedom is unwarranted. Indeed, in my judgment, as in the view of many philosophers, particularly since Hume, freedom and determinism are compatible, and whether an action is free is a matter of the kind of thing that produces it and does not depend on whether it is generated by antecedent variables in a way that renders it subsumable under universal laws.[56] Moreover, I would argue that although there are certainly pressures that limit the scope of our freedom, and while we are sometimes unknowingly compelled, it is easy to exaggerate the extent to which psychological, social, and cultural factors diminish the freedom of our actions.[57] On the question of freedom, then, I conclude that Gustafson simply shows the relevance of scientific developments to our assessment of the extent of our freedom; he does not show, and is probably not trying to show, that every plausible conception of the extent of our freedom, whether theologically based or not, is undermined by scientific findings.

If the many philosophers who hold compatibilism (the view that freedom and determinism are compatible) are right in doing so, then even if deter-

---

[55]Gustafson, *Ethics,* 1:133.

[56]For an account of freedom and moral responsibility in which they are compatible with determinism, see my "Moral Responsibility, Freedom, and Compulsion," *American Philosophical Quarterly* 11 (1974). I have critically assessed some plausible arguments for incompatibilism in a study, forthcoming in *Faith and Philosophy,* of Peter van Inwagen's *An Essay on Free Will.*

[57]For discussion of the scope of moral responsibility and some defense of the view that it is often unduly narrowed, see my "Self-Deception, Action, and Will," *Erkenntnis* 18 (1982).

minism should be true and even if we are simply biological creatures, it would not follow that we are not free or not morally responsible for our conduct. I would argue, then, that even a thoroughgoing deterministic naturalism need not undermine human dignity. Perhaps Gustafson could agree in this. If so, then even though his rejection of anthropomorphism undermines the idea that we are created in God's image, a notion that "has protected the dignity of the human species and the dignity of the individual,"[58] one important pillar of human dignity—our freedom—is perfectly consistent with his theology.

Whatever we conclude about how much room Gustafson's theocentrism leaves for human freedom, there remains a question about the extent to which theocentric perspective can take humanity as a focus of divine concern. It might seem that even if it is not committed to a biological conception of the human person, it "radically qualifies the traditional Christian claims that the ultimate power seeks the human good as the central focus of its activity."[59] The word *central* is crucial here. To see how, suppose that God is infinite, at least in thought, knowledge, and potential activity. Just what is the center of an infinite "field "of concern or potential activity? And what is it for something to be central in the attention and concern of an infinite being? Centrality is merely metaphorical in such a context: God can hold every detail of our existence vividly before his mind at once, while attending to infinitely many other things at the same time. Gustafson need not deny this; for, if I am not mistaken, his main point is that in a theocentric view we are not God's *exclusive* concern, or his dominant concern in the way children may be the dominant concern of their parents. Gustafson is not committed, I think, to construing theocentrism as forcing us to reduce, in absolute terms, our sense of God's concern for us. We can be of infinite concern to him, even if nature is also.

I am of course presupposing what some might call a philosopher's conception of God; but if it is a philosopher's conception, it certainly has appeared in the thinking of many theistic nonphilosophers. In any event, even if we do not take God to be infinite in the suggested ways, any plausible conception of Him as ultimate power leaves room for humanity to be a very significant focus of divine concern, whatever other concerns He may have. I agree with Gustafson, then, in rejecting the parent-child model if it is to be more than a suggestive metaphor. But I cannot see that scientific evidence, or even a naturalistic construal of the human person, must place us too low among God's concerns to sustain a sense of His love for us, a sense strong enough to

---

[58]Gustafson, *Ethics,* 1:100.

[59]Ibid., 1:271.

cohere with a proper reading of the New Testament. The exclusivity of anthropocentricism must go; the sense that we stand in a unique relation to God, one pervaded by his inexhaustible love, can be sustained.

The last general problem I want to explore is the connection between Gustafson's theocentric perspective and his ethics. I shall be brief. The problem that concerns me—which I believe should be addressed in more detail by Gustafson himself—is how the theocentric perspective helps us derive ethical guidance from scientific findings. I have already cited his point that we cannot read moral principles off from any scientific description of natural phenomena. How does theocentrism do any more than exhort us to treat our environment with respect—which seems prudent in any case—and remind us that scientific knowledge is indispensable in adapting means to ends? What ends, for instance, are supported by a theocentric perspective? Precisely what would it have us ultimately seek?

There is much to say in dealing with these problems. My first point is simply that if the theocentric perspective leads us to respect our environment more, and to adopt better means to our (legitimate) ends, that is a significant accomplishment. But we may go further, to the question of ultimate ends. The theocentric perspective nurtures respect for persons. As I have stressed, it does this in part because it helps generate and sustain natural piety, which, in a biological conception of persons as continuous with the lower animals and as part of nature, itself tends to generate and sustain respect for persons. That respect, in turn, tends to support the Kantian idea, which many moral theorists endorse in some form, that we are not to treat persons merely as means to an end. But there is perhaps a more direct way that the theocentric perspective supports respect for persons. By overcoming our anthropocentric notion that we are God's chief concern—and the often resulting sense that we *as* Christians or Jews or Moslems or whatever are theologically or otherwise privileged—it reduces bigotry and enhances our sense of our connectedness with persons of other creeds and other nations.

This is not to affirm any particular moral principle. What the theocentric perspective leads us to is more a framework for formulating and refining moral principles than specific moral principles themselves, if indeed it leads us to any specific principles. But that is no mean accomplishment. The view may not decide between, say, utilitarianism and Kantianism; indeed, as far as I can see, it is in the spirit of the view to select elements from each in an effort to accord maximal respect for persons. But it may enable us to reject seductive but false principles, for example those that treat people in radically unequal ways: for this is, among other things, a counterpart of one kind of bad science—making unreasonable distinctions between objects of the same natural kind. A kind of *universalizability,* then, should be a criterion for sound ethical principles insofar as scientific theorizing is taken as a model for ethics. The sort of unequal treatment of persons that fails to pass the test of ethical universalizability can perhaps also be regarded as exhibiting a kind of disorder; if so, then insofar as a scientifically informed theocentrism leads one to seek to formulate principles of conduct that like scientific laws, exhibit *order,* one will also tend to reject principles that distinguish among persons on the basis of the culturally and biologically variable properties so often underlying discriminatory conduct: creed, color, nationality, social class, and the like.

If we add to this the fact that a theocentric perspective will share with science a fallibilistic outlook, then that perspective may be expected to adopt tolerance as a goal in a mutually supporting relation to the end of respect for persons. This, too, is an important implication. But in one case I am not sure Gustafson draws the right inference from his reflections on science. Pointing out that he "does not share the confidence in realistic epistemology and metaphysics that are essential to Jaki and others,"[60] he says, "That confidence is cast into doubt by the evidence for social and cultural relativism in perceptions of the nature of ultimate reality."[61] The supposed basis of doubt is not specified, but I see no reason to give up realism as an *ontological* view if it is conjoined with an *epistemological* fallibilism: there is a reality, and there are objective truths about it, but we, and our methods of inquiry, are limited and fallible.

It is true that one can view the history of science as suggesting that there is no objective truth to be found. But surely it is at least equally plausible to take seriously how much has been preserved in the way of *approximate* formulations of laws of nature, to note the degree to which there seems to be convergence in at least physical science, and to conclude that we may be approaching a progressively more adequate view of the natural world. Quite apart from this, however, even if science does not give us final precise formulations, it does give us formulations that hold approximately throughout the world and, so far as we know, the universe. The counterpart of this is a universalistic, though fallibilistic, ethics, with approximate rather than unqualified formulations. From this perspective, we can also plausibly resist the inference from the constancy of change in human history and culture to the rejection of "the aspiration for the perfectibility of man."[62] We may be unable to achieve absolute clarity or justified certainty regarding criteria of human excellence,

---

[60]Ibid., 1:258.

[61]Ibid.

[62]Ibid., 1:310.

but we may still be warranted in framing, in broad terms, a substantial number of lasting ideals.

This is not to deny Gustafson's weaker suggestion, which does not license the inference just rejected, that *"eternal* criteria of human perfection are impossible to *establish."*[63] That is an epistemological point, and its scientific counterpart *is* true. My point is ontological: just as there may be universal scientific truths that we progressively approach, so there are apparently universal human ideals and cross-culturally valid moral truths that may be progressively clarified and, in principle, more and more nearly realized. Our conduct, of course, may not keep pace with our ideals, and in some instances it will not be clear just what resolution of a conceptual problem our principles imply. But our engineering may not keep pace with our physics; and it is by no means always clear how to apply our physics to solving a practical problem.

I believe, then, that the reflection on the nature of science does not suggest, nor does any enduring feature of scientific method suggest, that the moral counterpart of science is a relativistic ethics in which the *warrant* for moral principles has no cross-cultural validity. Note that Gustafson himself says of murder, for example, that it is always wrong; and I do not think that his considered view is relativistic in the sense just specified. But I would like to see a stronger dissociation between that kind of relativism and theocentric ethics, and a related emphasis on the point that neither fallibilism nor the constancy of social change entails relativism, any more than its scientific counterpart is entailed by fallibilism in science or the natural and social evolution. I am not speaking of *relativity of content*—the view that *what* one ought to do depends on circumstances, for example on one's having made promises or accepted culturally defined duties as, say, parent. Some version of content relativism is surely true. But it does not imply *relativity of status*—the view that (roughly speaking) the *basis* of moral obligation depends on, and is no deeper than, variable features of culture, such as customs, folkways, and prevailing attitudes. I do not see that Gustafson's apparent affirmation of relativity of status runs deep in his position, and I doubt that the view is sound.

One might think that fallibilism and tolerance do not go well with the sort of moral realism I have suggested is appropriate in the ethical counterpart of science, realistically conceived. But that is simply not so: indeed, the sense that one might be wrong because the world, or the truth, really is otherwise than one thinks is likely to be more humbling than the instrumentalist view that all we can hope for is progressively more adequate principles for organizing experience. Risking error would better support tolerance and caution than

---

[63]Ibid. Emphasis mine.

risking superannuation. Moreover, if one has a truly theocentric vision, presumably one would expect the ultimate power to create or sustain a structure of some determinate, even if in principle alterable, kind. And is not natural piety greater when its presumed object is such a reality? My suggestion is that Gustafson should perhaps think of realism less monolithically. Rather than link epistemological and metaphysical realism in the way he apparently does, he might accept a sophisticated metaphysical and scientific realism and endorse a fallibilistic epistemology that eschews the naive epistemological realism according to which things are uncritically taken to be generally as we perceive them to be and certainty is often obtainable even on complicated matters. The moral counterpart of such a view would seem to correspond to what he appears to hold in ethics: a fallibilistic, approximative, but cross-culturally valid—and in that sense "realistic"—moral theory.

Conclusion

The theocentric perspective that Gustafson has given us provides a plausible framework for theological reflection, for ethical inquiry, and for constructing a coherent theistic world view. More than any other major theological framework I know, it takes science seriously. It is indeed quite suited to offering us a possible way to retain both a scientific habit of mind and a theistic outlook. It should, in addition, interest nontheists. For even if one does not believe in any ultimate power in the universe, one may want to know how a world view that does can illuminate ethical and other concerns. The analogy Gustafson suggests between ethics and science—for instance, between scientific discernment of a structure underlying disparate data and ethical discernment of moral principles implicit in patterns of natural and social dependence—also has independent interest. One can also agree with a number of Gustafson's conclusions even if one does not arrive at them in the same way; if one does arrive at them differently, much may be learned by tracing them to different starting points. One's view may emerge better justified, more readily communicable, and more easily connected with other positions.

As I have interpreted Gustafson, he is a kind of theological naturalist. There are at least three reasons for interpreting him in this manner. First, his strongest (or at least basic) commitment is apparently to reason, in a very broad sense of the term, with science representing its highest form of application to the natural world. He says, for example, that "the only good reason for claiming to be Christian is that we continue to be empowered, sustained, renewed, informed, and judged by Jesus' incarnation of theocentric piety and fidelity."[64]

---

[64]Ibid., 1:277.

Second, he conceives virtually everything, including persons and probably God as well, as continuous with nature. Third, while he conceives God as in some way transcending the physical world, he apparently also takes God to be an ultimate *natural* power.

It may be that Gustafson should also be considered a *metatheologian*. For in much of what he does he is providing a structure for theology, not producing a specific theology from a particular religious point of view, and in providing this structure he freely uses techniques and results drawn from philosophy, science, and other sources. As this might suggest, his preference for the Reformed tradition emerges from, as much as it inspires, his metatheology.

These points concern Gustafson the theologian, not Gustafson the man. As an individual he counts himself a Christian. Does his theological framework really allow for a Christian theology, or is Christian theology by its nature too anthropocentric? Or is he at most *religious,* as opposed to having a particular (theistic) *religion*? These questions will be controversial, since there are many conceptions of religions and many plausible versions of Christian theology, including a number that are too literalistic or too dogmatic to be theocentric in Gustafson's sense. But if I have been right in suggesting that what is in some sense a personal God can be conceived in Gustafson's theocentric framework, then the largest obstacle to a Christian theology's being worked out theocentrically is eliminated.[65] The status of eschatology remains a problem. A traditional Christian theology (like a number of others) must presumably provide for some kind of possible endurance of persons beyond bodily death. But I fail to see why a theocentric perspective cannot meet the minimal eschatological requirements, for it surely *can* account for the centrality of the great commandments to love God with all one's heart and to love one's neighbor as oneself. These and other problems—particularly the specific connections between ethics and science in a theocentric perspective—surely

---

[65]In "Remarks on a Theological Program Instructed by Science," *The Thomist* 47 (1983), Gene Outka says of Gustafson's volume one that "at times the book renders a theistic doctrine of God otiose" (591) and that in Gustafson's "attack on religion as the gospel of egocentric human fulfillment . . . divine agency is jeopardized" (591). Some of the problems I have raised regarding Gustafson's theology are very similar to some raised by Outka, but I differ from Outka in my assessment of Gustafson's resources for dealing with them. For instance, although Gustafson does not give an account of divine agency, nothing to which he is deeply committed seems to me to preclude it; and while his naturalism may sometimes appear to provide only a heuristic role for a theistic doctrine of God, its overall thrust seems to require the notion of a personal—though not anthropomorphic—deity.

deserve more study. One purpose of this paper is to generate, and perhaps in some way direct, that study. But I have also sought to show that contrary to what one might think on the basis of some of Gustafson's major points, certain strands in traditional theism may be both more resilient and more easily reconciled with a scientific outlook on the world than many naturalistic thinkers believe.[66]

AUDI DISCUSSION

Frederick Ferré (University of Georgia): I want to make what I hope is just a clarifying remark. Regarding your speculation about what Jim might have thought about science, I think I want to defend him against speculations that I think show a naive attitude toward science. For example, is science a help in countering anthropocentrism? It is true that science looks at mankind through the wrong end of the telescope, and we turn out to be rather small in terms of the content of science. On the other hand, the methodology and the epistemology of science is deeply anthropocentric. The knowing "I" is sharply distinct from that which is known. The I/it relationship of the scientific explorer to the object of his or her knowledge, and so the potential for a radical anthropocentrism, is perhaps exaggerated by Theodore Roszak and others of the last decade. But I think we should remember that there has been within the Cartesian framework, in Galileo, and all the rest, a great deal of anthropocentrism that is right at the very heart of modern science.

In addition, I think we may well be reminded that real live scientists are seldom those who simply withhold belief or disbelief from their favorite hypotheses. They are full of commitments and excitement and enthusiasms and beliefs, just like any other human beings. I think we ought not idealize science in the way that Jacob Bronowski and others have by supposing that all is sweetness, tolerance, and light. I do not think Jim holds that view either. He is more tentative and more genuinely open to many possibilities than most of the scientists that I know.

Let me make one last point regarding the way in which science is alleged to bring about a natural piety towards nature. That is true for some geniuses like Spinoza and Einstein, but let's not forget that science tends to designate that which is explored. As a rule, science looks at its objects of experimentation quite unfeelingly. The sci-

---

[66]For helpful comments on this paper I want to thank Robert McKim and William Lad Sessions. My thinking on the overall topic has also benefited from discussion with James Gustafson and with many of the symposium participants.

entific exploiter of knowledge can be compared to the conquistador during the time in which the Western world was out to ravage the New World. Science can, in fact, be morally related to what Bacon was urging in the early days of science, that is, a way of getting knowledge and power. For almost all of the points that could be made in support of Gustafson's having a benign view of science, I would argue that there are other things that can be derived from science. We must not, therefore, take a naive attitude toward science. I am glad to speak on Jim's behalf so that perhaps he can be distinct from those speculations.

Audi: You have made valuable points. Let me respond to them, starting with the second with which I wholeheartedly agree. Live scientists are full of commitments. So far as the thesis I expressed is plausible, it is a thesis about the scientist qua scientist. You always have a person doing science, but we can talk about the scientist qua scientist when we talk about the scientific agent acting properly within the methodological principles of the discipline. So we don't disagree substantively, and I don't really assert the thesis that I suggested in the paper. However, it is a plausible one, and I think Gustafson could hold it; but he certainly has not affirmed it.

Your third point was that science does not automatically evoke natural piety; science can look at nature unfeelingly. That is most certainly true. My suggestion, and perhaps Gustafson's, was that doing science in a systematic and thorough way *tends* to evoke natural piety. It would be an empirical question whether it does and under what conditions the tendency is inhibited. I would be prepared to defend the view that doing science systematically at a high level tends to evoke natural piety.

On your first point concerning the anthropocentrism of scientific method, I believe we need a distinction. I have been thinking of anthropocentrism as a matter of content, though a method can also be anthropocentric. For instance, the view that we are central in God's concern is anthropocentric by virtue of its content. What is it for a view to be methodologically anthropocentric, such that it must make us central? I don't think science is like that. It is true that we have to use the telescope, but we don't want to take the fact that *we* are using the method as a sufficient condition for the method's being anthropocentric. You have to be on the using end of the telescope, the microscope, or whatever in any method. Whether being on the using end makes us central is a controversial question; I think it does not.

R. Neville Richardson (University of Natal, South Africa): My question is about the sources of natural piety. Professor Ferré mentioned that not all scientists would share a naturally pious view of the world. You seem to suggest that there is a normative science that, if only seen by those engaged with scientific method, would naturally lead to natural piety. I see scientific method as a natural thing that does not carry values with it, and so I go along with Professor Ferré. Even in terms of the illustration he used, Einstein and Spinoza would probably draw their values from Judaism, but even that would have a pole of domination over the other pole of stewardship. So there are many possible sources from outside and within their religions that could rise to natural piety within the sciences. I am interested in your idea of high-level science that seems to lead to natural piety.

<u>Audi:</u> I resisted a temptation to construct an a priori account of what it is to use a scientific method properly and then get a deductive result that entails natural piety (except where there are specifiable interferences). I really meant it when I said the question is empirical whether the systematic use of scientific method and the sophisticated pursuit of science tends to evoke natural piety. I think Jim has also resisted the tendency to make the connection a priori. One interesting empirical question here is whether the tendency in question would exist, if it were not for our religious history. If it would not, we cannot conclude that the tendency is somehow illegitimate. Nevertheless, that is an interesting question.

To speak directly to your question about a scientific method being neutral, how about this instrumental context? If you use tools day in and day out as means to an end, we need not suppose you enjoy your work and love the shiny surfaces of the tools to suppose that you acquire a kind of respect for them. Respect for the material with which you work daily is a natural attitude. When we consider the whole of nature, which we instrumentally manipulate but relate to aesthetically in our use of leisure time, it does appear that natural piety is natural to us insofar as we are rational creatures trying fully to realize our capacities. It looks as though natural piety *is* natural and not merely grounded in our religious traditions.

<u>James Day</u> (Allegheny College): With the respect to the use that Jim may be making of a Design Argument, does he reject every form of an ontological argument in favor of a cosmological argument? I think this depends upon whether we read Jim's work as primarily apologetic or as explicative for those who share some form of natural piety.

<u>Audi:</u> As I read Jim, he is not at all attracted to the idea that there is a deductive path from nature to God. The argument from design has traditionally been read as an inductive argument: the premises yield a conclusion with a degree of probability appropriate to warrant believing the conclusion. I don't see him as offering the argument from design. My suggestion is that he is sympathetic with the spirit of that argument. In his own complicated way, he supposes that the things that would be taken into account by someone constructing a good argument from design may warrant theistic belief within piety. But "within piety" is a crucial qualification. It doesn't seem that he is endorsing a version of the argument from design if we are thinking of the ordinary starting point of the nonskeptical philosopher against the skeptic, with no religious tradition in the background and no piety presupposed.

The Paradox of Humanism

What Is Anthropocentrism?

I s man, strictly speaking, the only thing that has value or importance in this world or out of it? Does man contain the whole value of the universe? This is the question that first brought me into print, and it is one with which I am still deeply engaged. My answer to it has always been no. So has James Gustafson's. But we have come to this answer from very different angles, as it were from different countries.

He has pointed out that besides man there is also God. He probably speaks in the first place to people who are already convinced that indeed God is there, and he points out how strange it is, if so, not to treat God as central. What I have been saying, meanwhile, is that the natural world is also there, with its great wealth of living things and its contribution to our own nature. I have suggested that it is somewhat odd to regard this whole physical universe either as valueless or as having value only as a plaything for the human will. This argument of mine speaks, in principle, to the godless as much as the God-fearing, and I am myself greatly puzzled about religion, though by no means indifferent to it. But I have been interested to find that a number of other religious thinkers, besides Gustafson, have responded to my suggestions. I am sure that anyone who follows up the ways of thinking about value that my arguments suggest is likely to reach territory that borders on land occupied by the religions. This territory is very difficult and badly needs mapping. But, since I did not start out convinced that all religion is a creation of the devil, I would like to join Gustafson in making some effort to explore it.

Since each of us probably represents the position of a fair number of other concerned people, it seems worthwhile to examine some of the points on which our paths have converged. And it is probably best, as usual, to start from the negative angle because that is likely to be the clearest. What, then, essentially, is the thing that we are both *against?*

The simplest name for it, and the one Gustafson commonly uses, is *anthropocentrism*—the notion that everything centers on man. What does this involve? We must pause first for a small, tiresome, semantic point. I say man and not humanity deliberately. The way in which this doctrine has been developed has always involved a notion of the human race that did not include women. The special virtues and capacities that were cited as justifying humanity's supreme status were those seen as peculiarly male. This assumption flows partly from patriarchal Judaism, partly from the special notion of democracy that the Greeks bequeathed to the Enlightenment—a notion expressed in phrases like "the rights of man," "one man, one vote," "a man's a man for all that." Male intellect and will provided the passport that took "man" to his special place in the universe and that caused some influential sages (such as Comte and Nietzsche) actually to promote him to the seat of God. In spite of occasional official concessions, he never really took woman there with him.

This is by no means just a matter affecting the position of actual women. It is a special propagandist ideal proposed for human life generally. It involves the dominance of one set of human qualities over another—a dominance so complete that I do not think the idea of *centrality* does it justice. This objectionable, hypertrophied current variety of humanism does not just paint the universe as centering on the human will and intellect, but exalts them to the point of apotheosis. It reduces all values other than those it favors—both inside and outside human life—to instrumental status. This impoverished way of thought seems to me to be better described as reductive or exclusive humanism than merely as anthropocentrism.

The notion of centrality is perhaps not strong enough to convey the charge that needs to be made here because it is too flexible and open to compromise. In any system, different elements can be viewed as central according to the angle from which we consider it at a given time. Indeed, it seems possible that part of the controversy about Gustafson's ethical views may flow from a false antithesis. Ought there really to be a competition between God and man for a single central position in ethics? Is there perhaps a sense in which each is central, in which due attention to each complements, and does not detract from, attention to the other?

Humanism—Reductive and Otherwise

However this may be, no such compromise is possible for a doctrine that declares a priori that nothing can possibly have value except members of our own group. This is essentially a competitive position. Of course, humanism as such does not have to take this pugnacious stance. Humanism can be a thoroughly positive attitude, calling simply for the due celebration of human life and the avoidance of misanthropy. With Aristotle, and again with the early Renaissance humanists, this call was found to be compatible with theism. Very strong forces, however, always tended to drive it into more polemical and competive forms. Enlightenment thinkers, becoming increasingly critical of the church and increasingly drawn to pagan Greece and Rome, came to see the celebration of man more and more as an attack on the Christian God. Their aim, therefore, was not just to celebrate humanity, but to avoid celebrating anything else. It became exclusive and reductive.

At first, man's main competitor was God. At that time, nonhuman nature appeared largely as an ally of mankind and received a certain amount of celebration as an aspect of the present world (Rousseau). During the Romantic Revival, however, this celebration threatened to make nature a rival, not only to God, but to man himself. So nature, too, became suspect to humanists, as it had long been to monotheists. Man imitated God's famous jealousy. The modern exaltation of the supreme and solitary human will, stemming from Kant and flowing through Nietzsche to Sartre and Jacques Monod, is as much directed against rivalry from nature as it is against that from God. Humanism has reached this extreme competitive stage just at the point where it becomes really disastrous for it to do so—the point, namely, where our species has begun genuinely to threaten its environment, and accordingly to need restraints on its confident expansion as it never did before.

This is the emergency that Gustafson sees, and it is one that calls for changes in nearly every aspect of our practical thinking, not just in theology. It cuts right across the boundaries that normally separate different disciplines and also across those between religious and secular thinking. Exclusive humanism has been nourished in both camps equally. How has that come about? Very often, I think, this mean view makes its mark mainly by a certain stern and ascetic tone, an assumption that what it asks us to give up is a mere weakness, an indulgence, flowing from sentimentality and superstition. When we hear this kind of voice telling us, in the name of the law of parsimony, to economize by giving up some way of thinking as a luxury, we should always be suspicious. We should ask not just whether it actually is a luxury, but also what other expenditure these savings will be used to fund. (Economy, after all, is not an end in itself except for full-time misers.) In thought as in politics, brutal reduction in one place is often a cover for illicit expansion in another.

In the case before us, it seems clear that rank superstition about human destiny is replacing that respect for the biosphere that we have been told to dismiss as mere sentimentality and "nature mysticism." Groundless fantasies about a dazzling human future, both on this planet and off it, are developed to justify our chronic abuse of nature. Most of them rest on extrapolating graphs of human development that contain nothing to justify any such extension. Evolution itself is imagined, quite contrary to Darwin, as following such a graph. It is viewed mythically, in Lamarckian style, as an endless escalator bearing our species infallibly on to supernatural levels of intelligence. Omega Man, once the despised property of Teilhard de Chardin, is back in business, invoked now by certified scientists as our destined evolutionary goal. This future superperson will, they tell us, "transcend to new dimensions of time and space . . . as much beyond our imagination as our world was to the emerging eucaryotes." (This prediction comes from a recent handbook by a molecular biologist about primal soup.[1] Obviously, all this Lamarckian melodrama is as contrary to official Darwinian scientific theory as it is to traditional religion. One reason it is indeed necessary to attend to physical science is to explode the distortions of it that often power ideas that we need to resist. Bad metaphysics often uses bad science. Obviously, again, these distortions are not an integral part of modern scientific humanism. But superstitious fantasies of this kind are now quite common in writings produced by people who see themselves as expounding that humanism. The worship of man is at present taking some very extravagant forms.

The Quest for Maturity

These forms are worth noting, especially for people who are inclined to welcome reductive humanism as an infallible cure for superstition. The surgical procedures of cutting out God and outlawing reverence for nature do not, unfortunately, remove the habit of forming wild cosmic fantasies. These clinging weeds will still grow around, and distort, whatever is left as the center of value in our thought system. If nothing is left but man, then he will be their focus. The reason the cults of God and of nature have in their time ac-

---

[1] William Day, *Genesis on Planet Earth: The Search for Life's Beginning* (East Lansing MI: House of Talos, 1979) 390-92.

quired similar outgrowths is not that either God or nature is an unsuitable object for reverence, but that reverence itself is a complex attitude that, unless carefully watched, tends to nourish these weeds. Whatever objects we revere—even machines—we are liable to build myths around them that are both pernicious and surprisingly silly.

In its sterner, morning-after mood, reductive humanism gives this problem a simple, surgical answer. We ought, it says, to give up reverence altogether. Like the Stoics, we should admire nothing, should acknowledge nothing as greater than ourselves. In order to convince us of this, humanism has itself generated a very powerful myth based on the human life cycle. It portrays reverence itself as childish, as part of an infantile weakness that we must outgrow and transcend. Auguste Comte presented this story in a peculiarly flattering form, by linking it to the relationship between European culture and that of less-favored races. The rest of the world, he said, is inhabited by primitives, who are children in the grip of religion and magic. Europeans alone have reached adolescence and are working their way through the slightly more respectable paths of metaphysics. But they must next move on to become real adults strong enough to use only science, no longer venerating either God or Nature. This story contains endless interesting confusions, but I want to concentrate here on just two points—first, the shallowness of its psychology, and second, the political overtones that have made it, both in its own time and still today, so influential.

That the psychology is shallow can be most simply seen by noting how regularly its proponents fail to take their own medicine. Comte himself notoriously founded a Religion of Humanity, with temples, saints, rituals, and all the rest of the childish paraphernalia. Freud, who developed Comte's reductive view with peculiar sternness and fervor in *The Future of an Illusion,* expounded in his later metapsychology a vast drama of cosmic war between Love and Death that puts Greek religious mythology entirely in the shade. Marxism is no less mythogenic. Sartre bows down before the supernatural human will. Jacques Monod, with exceptional nerve, celebrates the death of animism and the utter meaninglessness of all values by telling us to devote ourselves unquestioningly and completely to the service of something called Science. Doctrines like these are myths. They are not just convenient ways of summarizing groups of ordinary social interactions among human beings, logical constructions out of humdrum empirical elements. They deal with large aspects of life in a way that simply cannot be understood if we outlaw, or neglect, our natural tendency to see human life as only part of a much larger pattern, and to bow down in reverence before certain aspects of that pattern.

This tendency is certainly not just childish. It may well have its roots in childhood, drawing strength from the wonder with which we first encountered the world—from our uncorrupted response to things we had not then begun to pretend that we understood or knew how to master. But in that sense, the childish vision is part of all that we most value in life. It powers the imaginative activity out of which arises not only art, but also science. In that sense, we cannot take St. Paul's line and say, "when I became a man I put off childish things "(1 Cor. 13:11). That simple idea of a complete and final switch of interests upon reaching maturity is false to our experience. The arrogance that goes with it constantly misleads us—most obviously in our personal lives, but also, just as badly, in the kind of large questions we are now considering. People whose idea of maturity is to lose that childish vision, to stop looking for any wider pattern, and to limit their attention to things that directly affect them, do not become very fully developed human beings.

The Political Slant

This blinkered existence is not, of course, exactly what people who want to abolish reverence normally have in mind. Their central interest is usually political. Here we turn from the shallow psychology to the wider social model that tends to cover up for it. Reducers want to get rid of all social relations other than those between freely contracting equals—"fraternity." Everything parental and hierarchical ought, they feel, to go. Independent adults are then seen as detached entities, always liable to take off at any moment, fearing nothing and needing nobody. In political life, where release from illicit authority is an important aim, this ideal has good roots. But transferred to private life, where intricate networks of mutual dependence are normal and salutary, and to the inner life of the spirit, it works very oddly. Not only are children now effectively outlawed, but parents and faithful friends are in trouble too, not to speak of marriage, which was an obvious target from the first. Some of those who preach the solitary ideal, such as Nietzsche, are themselves real hermits, renouncing the world. Others, like Sartre, live in the world but want to avoid any deep commitment to it, such as marriage or children. Both parties tend to use the same sternly reductive tone I spoke of earlier. They imply that ordinary, sociable people are self-indulgent infants, lacking what it takes to became properly adult.

We do not have to be impressed by this. The solitary ideal is only one among many possible ones, and these people's personal choice of it evidently flows very much from their own taste. They have not been brought to it by an objective consideration of what human maturity demands. In fact, if one tried to consider objectively what maturity does demand, one would most likely give more weight to the idea that a mature person is one on whom others can rely, one who plays a positive part in creating and sustaining the necessary social networks, than to the negative idea of standing outside those networks.

Biologists may be a bit simple-minded in treating the power to rear offspring as a central mark of maturity. But it seems quite as simple-minded to suppose that refusing to rear them is the mark of maturity.

At this point we notice an alarming development. Reductive humanism, steadily narrowing the field of our concern, has cut short our natural human interests in three stages. It first attacked the heavens, cutting out our idea of God and of nonhuman spirits. Next it amputated the earth, ruling that non-human nature was alien and did not concern us. But now third, and most alarming, it attacks the structure of human life itself, isolating each individual in the supposedly impregnable fortress of his own autonomous will. The world appears, finally, as a jumble of disconnected social atoms. This strange existentialist picture does not seem to be either a true description of the world we actually live in or a plausible ideal for something that we might want to turn it into. How did we come to be landed with so bizarre an ideal?

The Chimera
of Human Self-Sufficiency

We reach here the paradox I have noted in my title. Humanism exists to celebrate and increase the glory of human life, undistracted by reverence for any entities outside it. But as soon as we begin to cut away those entities, valuable elements in human life itself start to go, too. The center begins to bleed. The patterns essential to human life turn out to be ones that cannot be altogether contained within it. They must, if given their full scope, lead out far beyond it. To be fully human seems to involve being interested in other things as well as human ones, and sometimes more than human ones.

The first hints of this difficulty appear in what may be called the paradox of individualism just noted—the awkward fact that an individual who isolates himself from the world to concentrate on his own development and happiness may be prevented by that very isolation from being developed or happy at all. "Happiness," as Butler pointed out sadly, "does not consist in self-love. People may love themselves with the most entire and unbounded affection, and yet be extremely miserable."[2] Individualism, therefore, cannot stand alone; it has to be only a balancing element in people's attitudes, setting proper attention to self against the claims of others, but not trying to deny these altogether. Reductive individualism, as preached at times by both libertarians such as Nietzsche and by social-contract theorists such as Hobbes, is a mean and claustrophobic view. It narrows and darkens human life instead of enriching it. In fact, in spite of its great political uses, both past and present,

---

[2]Bishop Joseph Butler, Sermon 11, *Upon the Love of Our Neighbor,* sec. 9.

the social atomism that underlies it is no sort of an adequate model of human life, even for political purposes. And for many essential purposes that are not political, it is a disaster. There is, I suggest, an exactly parallel difficulty about the current attempt to respect man while altogether despising the natural world to which he belongs. If that is so, however, what do we now need to do about changing it? What must we now see and acknowledge that we have been neglecting?

Many suggestions are needed before new models can be evolved. One such suggestion, brought forward at present by many people, including Gustafson and myself, stresses our need to recognize our kinship and continuity with other animals and the rest of the natural world, and the respect due them. This must involve not only that we act differently towards them, but also that we take a different view of ourselves. We need to concentrate rather less on our own achievements and rather more on the vastness and splendor of what we have been given. This involves admitting that our will is not the only valuable thing in the world, nor the creator of everything that is valuable. We did not, for example, even create our own talents or our own intellect. Kant has certainly had an unlucky effect here by overstating the value of will. Indeed, he gave an impossible account of will (practical reason) when he represented it as something quite separate from and opposed to all feeling, even to the desire for ends. Like all great moral philosophers, Kant emphasized one side—the one that was needed in his day—and neglected others that did not at that time call for so much attention. There is not much sense in continually battering him for this today—a pastime that is now rather a favorite one among moral philosophers. What is needed is to be clear about the general faults of the model of human maturity that he proposed, and still more clear about those added by his successors, and to move on towards a better one.

The faulty model, which is still very influential, is that in which the relations of reason or the will to feeling is that of master to slave or ringmaster to circus animal, rather than that of conceptually linked aspects of a single whole. Our freedom to choose needs to be seen not as the ringmaster's freedom to subdue the animal, but as the freedom of the whole person to understand and control what he or she is doing. Our natural feelings are an essential aspect of our freedom. Without them we could not begin to be free, because we would want nothing and have no alternatives to choose between. And we did not create those desires. We owe our basic motives, as well as the objects in the world by which we are moved, to powers that are not our own at all. Failure to recognize this is radical blindness and dishonesty. The spiritual pride that denies it is, therefore, still a vice even without God, and gratitude and humility before the natural world are still virtues. We live in a world that we did not make, a world that, though we vary it by culture, is still given.

Who Gave the Given?

In this way, I and many others have been emphasizing the given element in life. Gustafson has emphasized the giver and makes him central. Can these two things be separated? Could there be a given world without a personal giver? I do not know. This is a vast question about the personhood of God. There are plenty of very serious world views where the giver is seen as so impersonal that the word *god* may be out of place, and there is real doubt about whether or not to use it. Aristotle and the Stoics did not usually use that word. Spinoza did and was attacked as an atheist and blasphemer for doing so. Such views can be called "pantheist." As such, they tend today to get rather a bad press, as do also views called "deist."

Critics are inclined to dismiss impersonal views of this kind as in some way watered down and intellectualized, as mere evasive substitutes for religion, attempts to palter with Occam's razor, to eat the religious cake while still keeping the credit for intellectual self-denial. From the religious side in particular, these critics tend to say, "Come, come, you must get off the fence; are you a Christian or not?" People who have found a belief system that satisfies them as a whole very naturally tend to take this kind of line with those outside it, but this brisk approach can hardly settle the matter. Religious experience does, as William James pointed out, differ amazingly from person to person as well as from culture to culture. And response to the intensely personal element in traditional Christianity and Judaism seems to be one of the points on which temperamental variation is especially wide. Pantheistic views may be somewhat mysterious, indeed obscure, but for all that they can certainly be real faiths by which people live. The cases of Aristotle and Spinoza ought, I think, to settle that point. The word *god* is not simply being hijacked and misused here; it is invoked with good reason to indicate a deeply religious awe and wonder. I think I live somewhere out here myself, and I can only testify that I find the atmosphere in those regions easier to breathe than the more personalized aspects of my native Anglicanism.

Scientists and the Ultimate Mystery

Besides pantheism, Western thought contains at present an interesting range of positions that lie slightly further out from religion as we know it, but unmistakably still keep some religious elements. These are the attitudes of good and serious scientists to nature. Awe, veneration, and wonder, rising from a deep sense that (as Aristotle put it) man is certainly not the greatest thing in the cosmos, were very powerful in Darwin even when his conventional religious faith had weakened, and are still so in many scientists today. Some, ranging from Julian Huxley and Theodosius Dobzhansky to Edward

O. Wilson, have seen this veneration as a proper foundation for religion or for mythology, explicitly so-called. Many more, who might recoil from that suggestion, fall back on something like it when the question is raised asking just why science is so valuable—what makes it so important an activity? Reductive humanists have a real difficulty in answering this question because for them the world that physical science studies is in itself completely without value. If all value really lies in man, the proper study of mankind can only be man. The social sciences and even the humanities would be superior. One could then only defend the superiority of physical science by maintaining that the actual intellectual contortions that it requires are a superior human performance, so that the physical world is needed only in order to provoke these activities. The stars and the seas, in fact, exist and matter solely as an elaborate piece of apparatus in the human intellectual gymnasium. This is not the spirit in which physical scientists in general actually approach their work, and they tend to find the claustrophobic, short-sighted human conceit that it expresses to be somewhat repulsive.

There is, therefore, a real difficulty about endowing reductive humanism with the flattering title, which is often given it, of "scientific." It is not scientific, but it has been developed to fit a certain current image of science as the path to the apotheosis of man. The way in which this has happened is quite complicated and would repay investigation. It probably starts from the oddity of Auguste Comte's initial move. When Comte nominated science as the successor to both religion and metaphysics, he in effect gave it some extremely ambitious functions in the formation of the belief systems by which people live. In theory, the idea was that no such general belief system would any longer be needed, that only particular facts would be used. But that idea is deeply confused. Facts always have to be assembled and selected, and general ideas play a crucial part in this process. However, the physical sciences are, strictly speaking, not capable of dealing in any such general ideas. They owe their strength to confining themselves firmly, from their textbooks on, to certain limited sets of questions about the physical world. They disown all wider inquiries.

If, then, there is to be such a thing as the scientific world view, its shaping is always a metaphysical matter. But Comte had represented metaphysics as merely a kind of methadone for weaning people gradually from the heroin of religion. And the followers of Karl Popper rejected it still more flatly as entirely alien to science. Since, in fact, metaphysics is the branch of thought by which the relation of science to life and to the rest of the world has to be understood, this was unfortunate. People have not stopped needing general ideas or the world pictures and belief systems that grow out of them. And the obvious importance of physical science in the modern world means that it must now play a prominent part in any such world picture. But the nature of that part is at present determined much more by our undisciplined imagination than by critical thinking. A welter of technological fantasies about what is called "the future" get believed simply because they look "scientific" in the sense of using the apparatus of science. On the important questions of human nature and destiny, these fantasies cluster around extraordinary Lamarckian visions like the future evolution of Omega Man. When we ask what this paragon will be like, it turns out, by a remarkable coincidence, that he will simply be a super-scientist. Heaven on earth, as scientifically predicted, will be an enormous and indefinitely expanding laboratory. When we ask why any such progressive development at all should be expected, science proper rejects the question as extraneous. Darwinian theory gives no sort of ground for such predictions. What produces them is unbridled, uncriticized, superstitious humanism, using imagery drawn partly from superficial aspects of science, but partly also, as it seems, from religious ideas of heaven and salvation. Anyone who expected ascetic economy of the imagination from the isolation of man is due to be disappointed.

Briefly and crudely, then, this is how the objectionable attitude that Gustafson usually calls anthropocentrism, and that I have been calling reductive humanism, seems to me to work and to be so powerful today. I am interested to learn from him—what was news to me—how far it has infiltrated theology. I agree with Gustafson that this attitude combines the worst of both of the main ways open to us in which vast cosmic questions can be approached—the scientific way and the religious one. It has neither the realism, parsimony, modesty, and pragmatism of true science nor the profundity of serious religion. It is, as he says, cheap faith. It owes a great deal of its strength to its flattering optimism, resting on empirical predictions with no visible basis. In an expansive age, when both our own culture and to some extent human life generally have seemed to be constantly growing and prospering, this current form of humanism has treated that growth as the norm and has promised that it will continue forever. When the growth flags, as it is already doing, unnecessary distress and confusion ensue. If the growth is reversed, which seems almost equally inevitable, for many people the spiritual floor will fall through altogether. They have not been trained, as people in less hopeful cultures are, to look for the meaning of life anywhere else than in continually increasing prosperity. Moreover, the physical world picture currently accepted leaves no doubt that in the end the human race is bound to become extinct anyway. "Scientific humanists" who notice this obvious fact tend to collapse in helpless horror. Thus both Jacques Monod and Steven Weinberg tell us that this fact alone is enough to make life meaningless. What it actually involves is that we need to stop locating the meaning of life always on the jam-tomorrow pattern, somewhere in the distant future, and to look for it, as other cultures have had to, also in the whole pattern of past and present and in eternity.

But how, you may ask, is all this absurd exaltation of mankind relevant to Gustafson? The crudities I have been exhibiting all belong, do they not, to secular scientific humanism? They are surely a disease from which Christianity, with its temperate habits and well-regulated life, is entirely immune. I only wish that this were so. But it seems clear that, on the contrary, this very powerful strand in modern thought has, ever since the Enlightenment, deeply infiltrated Christian thinking. In the first place, Kant's influence here has plainly been enormous. His technical, but never fully explained, use of the word *person* to convey an obscure but somehow supreme kind of value crops up continually in religious controversial contentions today and is evidently widely seen as an unanswerable argument. It is, in fact, often almost impossible now to get religious disputants to stop talking about *persons* for a moment and consider *souls*. This linguistic fact puzzled me until I saw the explicit arguments for cosmic human supremacy that Gustafson and his critics quote from theologians. For instance, Karl Barth (according to Father McCormick) calmly observes that all creation is just a "theater of the covenant" between God and man, that this same creation is "radically incapable of serving any other purpose," and he finally writes as follows: "It is the divine will and accomplishment in relation to man—and nothing else—which really stands at the beginning of all things. It was in this way—and no other—that heaven and earth originated."[3] This sounds to me quite simply mad, and mad for entirely traditional reasons. Where, after all, was Karl Barth when the Lord laid the foundations of the earth? How could any creature stand in such a relation to its creator as to be sure that it knows the entire range of his interests and purposes? How can any thoughtful person not suspect that it is our own natural self-love and conceit that give us the impression of ourselves as central and tempt us to harden that impression into the claim that we have actually no competitors?

I must conclude. It will perhaps do Gustafson little good with some of his colleagues to have outsiders like me applauding his central move and saying that it is a necessary one. All the same, I would like, if possible, to bypass these tribal considerations and suggest that it is both necessary and a move that many of us, in our day-to-day thinking, have already made, though we still officially possess moral principles that clash with it. (Hence, perhaps, the reason for some of the applause for Gustafson's honesty, which he understand-

---

[3]Richard A. McCormick, "Gustafson's God: Who? What? Where? (Etc.)," *Journal of Religious Ethics* 13:1 (Spring 1985): 57.

ably finds a little alarming; has lying become the norm?) Many of us already do—or do we not?—think it monstrously wrong for our species to wreck and destroy the earth without scruple. And we think—or do we not?—that it would still be wrong to do so even if we stood some sort of chance of getting away with it. As we probably do not stand that chance, the point *can* be conveyed indirectly, as merely a matter of human prudence. But this kind of vast, indirect, long-term prudence is just as foreign to our normal thinking as the more direct scruples are, and without them, it is inclined to sound forced and unrealistic. It seems urgent for all of us, both inside and outside the religious denominations, to reshape those parts of our conceptual schemes that, though they may have been innocent in past ages, now block our response to the supreme and central trial of our age.

MIDGLEY DISCUSSION

Douglas F. Ottati (Union Theological Seminary, Virginia): Reductive humanism certainly gets up a big head of steam in the modern period. If that roughly corresponds with what Gustafson means by anthropocentrism, and if there are connections between theology and wider patterns of thought in culture, might it not be the case that theology could make common cause with the more classical traditions in criticizing anthropocentrism? It may be that theology doesn't start with a highly anthropocentric base, but that the anthropocentrism of some Christian traditions has been intensified more recently and badly needs criticism now in a way it may not have needed at an earlier time.

Midgley: Yes, indeed. I am suggesting that the really disastrous things come from outside the Christian tradition, though they have found ground to grow there too. I do not suppose that any other culture has felt as confident as we have since the Renaissance in the way we treat the physical nature around us. Of course, we have become more powerful technologically. Descartes is a watershed, though he did not stand alone in dividing off objectified physical matter from ourselves as selves. He licensed a way of regarding a physical world that has made modern science possible. One must give him that tribute. No other culture has produced any such science. Whatever its faults, it is an amazing achievement. This is why I want to say that I think there are two strands in science or in the idea of science. One aspect is awe-struck wonder. There is also the reductive and rather contemptuous aspect by which people refuse to be impressed. The latter has gotten out of hand. Christianity would not have gone so far without that aspect, though certainly it is very strongly biased in favor of man.

Keith Keeling (Rockford College): You did a marvelous job of showing us how reductive humanism has risen historically, and its absurdity. But that seems to be the only reason you gave for giving intrinic value to the nonhuman world. That is, the reason we should see the value of trees, animals, rivers, and so forth, is the absurdity of reductive humanism. It seems that the characteristics of reductive humanism are so deeply entrenched that we are going to have to have some very powerful and direct reason for valuing the nonhuman other than the absurdity of anthropocentrism. John Passmore and others have provided one avenue for doing that—in the long run we as humans will suffer if we damage and destroy our environment. Some forms of classical Christianity, and James Gustafson in a somewhat different mode, have provided yet another way of getting at that, in terms of God's valuing of the entire creation. Though you have no objection, you did not really accept that way of coming at the intrinsic value of the nonhuman either. I wonder if you have some other good in mind to get at intrinsic value?

Midgley: I didn't, of course, discuss this. When one asks for an argument to prove that something is valuable without explaining from what position one starts, it tends to be a bit unrealistic. We are not in this situation about the nonhuman world. In the context of attitudes we already have, indirect explanations of why we value the nonhuman world look artifical and unconvincing. Take someone who loves horses. If it is put to them that they can't really love horses, but rather the horse is serviceable and brings out splendid frames of mind, they will not be impressed. Similarly, it is not now the first time that we got out of our buildings and met the nonhuman world. People have always been deeply entangled with it. They are naturally adapted to react to it in certain ways, to love some things and to hate others. These are not just matters of use. They are direct affections. The model that has often been accepted—the model of what benefits you are going to get from this—is too simple. To give that kind of indirect explanation of already existing and varied phenomena and interactions is unconvincing. Take Kant's example about cruelty to animals. Kant was obviously sensitive to the ill-treatment of animals. Yet he says, "It can't be because the animal has rights. The animal isn't an end in itself. It must be because it would be bad for me if I were cruel to the animal." But it might not be, who knows? That's an empirical question. This simply is not the path that our thinking takes. To introduce this bent artificially merely to preserve one's theory is not reputable.

John P. Reeder, Jr.: Could you say something more about natural feelings, desires, and basic motives? Exactly how do those sorts of desires or motives contribute to our choice of ends and to our sense of moral principles? How does one identify what desires and feelings are natural, and how do they figure in deciding what we want?

Midgley: Perhaps it is best to start from issues that actually make a difference to people. The notion of absolute human freedom—of an infinite range of choices before us, which has been put before us by existentialists and similar people—is held to show that we are not by nature endowed with feelings that could limit either what we can choose or what we ought to choose. Perhaps a fair example is the matter of parenthood and family. Plato thought it would be a pretty good idea to bring up babies without their parents; this link should not be allowed to develop. He is echoed by some modern feminists such as Shulamith Firestone. To say that you have to have a factual belief that people could be brought up in this way (that this would not prevent them from becoming satisfactory people) and also a value judgment that this would be a good thing (that either nothing is lost or that which is lost is less important than what is gained) seems to be a fair case where the facts can be relevant to the values.

In fact, when one tries to understand it, one will not find that one is using factual judgments written down in blue and value judgments written down in red. One is constantly using terms that have both sorts of connotations, and this is not because one is being obscure and confused, but because these are the proper ways to discuss such a matter. It is striking, I think, that these recommendations are made without anybody having tried them. Of course, you are not allowed to experiment on human beings. However, there is still a great range of evidence available from what you might call natural cases—people who have had various kinds of parenting, and the like. I think most of us would think those facts were relevant. I suppose even Plato, if it had been put to him that it is not likely to work well, would have said something like, "Oh well, then we will have to leave it as it is. What a pity." I am sure that Shulamith Firestone would be interested in experiments. People argue from the kibbutz and things of that sort. Then there are these cases where people have had more or less natural parenting in various ways, and it becomes necessary to study those—not just as one might study pebbles, but with sympathy and insight, as if one might be finding oneself in these situations and sort out what is going on.

It is my contention that if one does that in such a case, after a time one will have in one sense descriptions of facts, but facts that commit one to one value judgment or the other. We do not start this without any systems of value. We start it with a priority system, an idea about what matters and what doesn't, partly formed by our society, partly by our nature, and partly by our wills. This is public in the sense that we share it with those around us to some extent. We can communicate with them and ask them what they think. In that way, it seems to me that one would find oneself with good grounds at each stage for moving over toward the value judgments. Now I do not think I can be bothered to do the science fiction bit and say what would cause us to say, "Hooray, this is the right way." I think it is probably more realistic to think what one would probably do, and that would be to say, "Well, in spite of Plato and Shulamith Firestone, actually the parental bond is valuable and necessary." For one thing, the babies like it, and crude facts like that.

Reeder: Perhaps the disagreement between yourself and others, then, might be in the degree of confidence one has about what one discovers in these empirical investigations. There are plenty of people who would argue that though certain forms of bonding and affection are necessary, why should they take place in the nuclear family? Why should one sort of individual rather than another play those sorts of psychological roles? In other words, we would be involved in very complicated disputes about what is necessary or advisable for raising infants.

Midgley: It is complicated all right, but so is the program to be gone through if we say a priori that this is wrong. The burden of proof is not necessarily always on someone who produces some facts, as against someone who has a bloody great theory. The burden of proof can lie either way, and it seems to me that in view of what the facts clearly are in all sorts of different cases, one should send Plato and Shulamith Firestone back to do their homework.

Stewart W. Herman (graduate student, University of Chicago): You stated that we live in a world that we did not make. I take it that this is an expression of piety as well as a description. It illustrated for me your general theme that humans need a faith, a relatedness to something not themselves, in order to be human. My question is where you draw the line between the human and the nonhuman. Gustafson, in his account of the world, will say that human interventions have altered the world; the otherness we encounter in the world is, in part, the unintended consequences of our own actions. We conceive divine ordering in the playing out of human actions in ways we did not intend. I saw what I thought was a difference in your viewpoint. I had the sense that you discerned this otherness operating chiefly in a realm of nature that is not affected by human interventions. Perhaps Gustafson fuzzes the line between nature and the realm of the human in a way you would like to keep more clear.

Midgley: It was certainly not my intention to sound as though I was interested in nature only insofar as it has not been affected by people. Though we know perfectly well that people had a great deal to do with making a garden, we know also that people could not create a bush. There is a great deal that comes from outside. About human nature, I am concerned to say that we didn't produce our talents. We didn't produce our bodies or indeed our wills. We have all these things as a result of natural processes that we don't know very much about. I think we do not understand ourselves at all well. So there is an enormous amount of what is given in human life too. This strikes me particularly about talents because the importance of talents is prominent in present-day thinking. We venerate artists. We do not really think that a great painter or pianist is produced by somebody going out to condition and create them. They just happen; that is given. It appears to be a matter of heredity. Some can become great pianists, some can't. I do not even wish to think there is a line here, even a fuzzy one.

GUSTAFSON
James M.

Response

I t is commonplace, but nonetheless true, to say that the greatest satisfaction that can come from one's publications is to have them taken seriously. Even when, as Farley aptly says, they have been praised with shouted damns one knows that issues have been raised that cannot be totally ignored. I feel deeply honored by this event and grateful to Washington and Lee University, and especially to Harlan Beckley, and to the Institute for the Advanced Study of Religion of the University of Chicago for sponsoring it. I am grateful to the planning committee for its work. For one thing, I doubt if any of the contributors would have written such careful pieces in response to my work if they had not been invited to participate in this symposium. Second, Harlan Beckley's conception of the symposium, from the first I knew about it, directed its intention not only to assessments of my work but also to how issues raised by it can be dealt with or built upon by my fellow scholars. The symposium is to look forward and not only backward. Thus I am deeply grateful to all of the participants for the care they took in reading those six hundred pages and in engaging in detailed and careful analysis of them and their implications. I never anticipated that a symposium such as this would take place, and my own aspiration for it is that it will make some difference in subsequent deliberations about various issues in the ongoing work of theology and ethics, including my own.

My purpose in writing the book was to address more than fellow scholars; as I indicated in the Preface, I aspired to speak to clergy and to laypersons who thoughtfully ponder religious and ethical matters. I get much satisfaction from evidences that at least a few such persons have been led to reflect in different ways after studying my work. There is no evidence that those who might worry about possible deleterious consequences of my book on readers or the church have anything to be alarmed about. To the best of my knowledge, only one person agrees with the work as a whole without a significant exception.

The contributors to this symposium, save Yoder (whose presence here is especially important for this reason), are fundamentally empathic with what I have written. This makes the internal criticisms of my work very cogent and not easy to respond to adequately in the time of this lecture. I am instructed by these papers in important ways, and while I have, thus far, not been persuaded to alter what I have written in a fundamental way, I am sure that I would have written parts of both volumes differently in order to resolve better than I have some ambiguities, to meet head-on some of the arguments of these contributors and to develop implications these papers have helped me see.

Reeder's characterization of my work as having a "composite rationale" very aptly characterizes in language other than my own the fundamental process and pattern of the book. I think his characterization also fits the ways in which especially Audi, Farley, Johann, and Kaufman have analyzed and reconstructed what I have done. Yoder does not deny that a composite rationale is appropriate, but he claims that for a Christian theologian (and I anticipated what has been charged to me by other critics, namely that I am no longer a Christian) I begin the composite in the wrong place, and even as I pursue it I have not adequately taken into account what ought to be there for a Christian theologian nor argued sufficiently for rejecting what I reject and including what I include.

I chose to write a book of theological ethics, and not one about how theological ethics ought to be written; and its strengths and weaknesses depend not only on how it meets certain formal criteria but also on the decisions I made about the substance or subject matter of theology and ethics. My own assessment of the serious critical reviews, including the papers presented here, is that although there are well-developed critiques of ambiguities in the argument and fundamental rejections of it, the coherence of the work as a whole has not been seriously challenged. I attempted to be forthright in writing about implications of my position and assumptions I made, though I did not argue fully for many of them; in this respect I have the audacity to claim that I have been more straightforward than many of my colleagues writing in theology and ethics. I attempted to be clear about my selection of criteria by showing how they are related to the theocentric perspective as I develop it, and to state their implications.

In this written Response to the papers, I have chosen to treat them as a kind of composite as well. This has the disadvantage of not addressing each paper individually, but it might better contribute to the forward-looking intention of the planners of this symposium. If, by responding in this way, I seem to skirt some of the problems raised by the papers, I hope that will not be understood as a sign of intellectual cowardice; indeed, I shall attempt to bring in as many critical and detailed points as possible.

The critical issues in a work such as mine are several, and they form the outline of my Response.

(1) What sources are used, selected from, and why?

(2) What weight is given to aspects of the composition, and what is determinative?

(3) Around what does the position cohere, and what are the strains to coherence?

(4) What are its implications for traditional or standard criteria for judging theological ethics?

(5) Are its practical implications desirable or undesirable and why?

I hope, in following this order, to avoid simply restating my position as articulated in the book.

Sources

Comments have been made about all of the four sources I had stated as important for theological ethics in chapter five of *Protestant and Roman Catholic Ethics,* and recapitulated in *Ethics from a Theocentric Perspective.*

Bible and Tradition. Many of the shouted damnations of my book are in focus against my rejection of much that is biblical and is part of the tradition theologically and religiously. I think Yoder's most substantive criticism addresses them. Farley gets at it more obliquely when he argues that the tradition is only a matrix for my work and that I deal with it as a social scientist, whereas I deal with sciences as a theologian. (His is a provocative insight for me, and while I might qualify its force to some extent, I feel it.)

I wish briefly to state why I treat the Bible and tradition in the way I do. First, I wanted to avoid claiming that what I wrote is what the Bible and tradition *really* mean. In my case the claim would be patently false to readers, but I have long been skeptical about implicit and explicit claims of some others to this effect. Second, as a number of persons pointed out while I was writing, and subsequently, I could show more clearly and expansively how more of what I have said is at least compatible with aspects of the biblical material and the tradition and could thus have warded off some of the criticisms to which I have been subjected. There are allusions to this in the book, and Kaufman's and Audi's papers particularly suggest ways in which that could be done. I knew, however, from the beginning that what I was writing did not rely on the Bible and tradition for fundamental authorization; I did not intend to claim that what I wrote had to be taken seriously because Bible and tradition backed it. I did say that the Bible and tradition were expressions of persons' and communities' relations to God through human experience, and I take both more seriously than is probably apparent to my readers and critics. But, with Kaufman (especially in his *Theology for a Nuclear Age*) I claim that in the light of modern events, knowledge, and so forth, there are grounds for a radical evaluation of many traditional Christian beliefs. Indeed, I find Kaufman to be an ally in this important respect.

It may be frustrating to have me respond to my colleagues on this matter by setting alternative ways in which the Bible and tradition are used, but that is all I have time to do. Counting my own I can distinguish six positions from the papers.

(1) Determine key symbols from Bible and tradition and interpret them in a way that corrects their usage in light of modern knowledge, fits current concerns, and continues to give direction to religion and morality. I think this is Kaufman's position, elaborated more in *Theology for a Nuclear Age*, where he takes God and Christ to be principal symbols. His interpretation of Christ, incidentally, is quite similiar to mine in *Ethics from a Theocentric Perspective*, of God semicompatible with mine.

(2) Hold to Bible and tradition for the sake of providing Christian identity and a distinctive basis for cultural criticism. I think this is Bellah's position with Lindbeck's backing. To borrow from Farley, I read this as being a social scientific use of tradition and not a theological one. Even Lindbeck does not argue that God has revealed himself in a way that gives this cultural linguistic system unique authority. (My critique of Lindbeck and others is forthcoming in an article entitled "The Sectarian Temptation: Reflections on Theology, the Church and the University."[1])

(3) See the Bible and tradition as revelatory of God and isolate its distinctive element that becomes part of a theology also developed on other grounds. I think this is Farley's position with reference to redemption. If I were to take this position, I would include more than redemption—for example, the wrath of God.

---

[1] James M. Gustafson, "The Sectarian Temptation: Reflections on Theology, the Church and the University," *Proceedings of the Catholic Theological Society* 40 (1985): 83-94.

(4) Take the Bible and tradition as revelatory of God's self-disclosure and thus the starting point and principal context for theological ethics. I think this is Yoder's position; he has identified himself with "biblical realism" and impressively grounds social ethics in biblical materials that are exegeted and interpreted. This position is distinguished from Bellah's and Lindbeck's by the theological claims that back it; I think Yoder would not be satisfied simply with a historical social claim that tradition preserves identity and, therefore, is to be valued. This position is not fundamentalism and not orthodoxy. If I may invoke the name of one of Yoder's mentors, Barth represents this position most fulsomely; it is cogent, comprehensive (one can have a composite rationale from its center), and coherent. I am not susceptible to conversions, but if I were, the lure of Barth could effect one more readily than any other author.

(5) Make theological arguments on philosophical grounds and show how they are compatible with the Bible. I think Audi does this in his brief discussion of God's love. No claims for biblical revelation are *necessary*, but they are possible.

(6) I would describe the position I have taken in the following way: various sources, including the Bible and tradition, are drawn upon to form a composite account that leads to certain general conclusions. These, in turn, ground the inclusion-exclusion criteria for use of the Bible and traditions as they do for other sources as well.

I do not have time to develop a response to each of these positions in this paper, but the agenda is set somewhat by my outline here both for me and for others.

The Sciences. A good deal of the critical discussion of my book has been addressed to the ways in which I use materials from the sciences. In addition to the discussion in the papers for this symposium, this matter has been addressed somewhat extensively by Gene Outka, Stephen Toulmin, Richard A. McCormick, Lisa Sowle Cahill, and others. I have no doubt that the attention given to my use of scientific materials is justified by the role they play in my book. This is the focus of Audi's patient and fair-minded analysis and critique of my book; it is at least touched upon (and mostly more than that) by all the contributors. That scientific materials are used in both aspects of my work, theology and ethics, has not gone unnoticed. I will not summarize, even briefly, my self-understanding on this matter; Audi's descriptive analysis of it is accurate, and since it is present in this volume I trust it can be recalled. I will, however, state tersely why materials from the sciences are so important to me: if God is the ultimate orderer of life in the world, and if this ordering is through the patterns and processes of interdependence of life in the world, then knowledge of those patterns and processes is important for what they indicate about God. If the moral question is "What is God enabling and requiring us to be and to do through these patterns and processes?" then knowledge of them is important for ethics. Our best sources for knowledge of these patterns and processes are the sciences. Farley's account of my "commonsense ontology" and Reeder's description of the middle level of my work especially acknowledge this.

I will defer further discussion of the sciences until I come to the next two major headings of this paper ("Weight Given to Aspects of the Composition and What is Determinative" and "Coherence and Stresses in the Position"—the first major heading being "Sources") because my colleagues have addressed my *usage* of them in those terms.

Philosophical Methods, Insights, and Principles. I have always known that I would have written a better book if I were a better philosopher. I have also always been uncomfortable with theological ethics or moral theology that can be interpreted as having first determined what is the correct or best philosophical position (presumably on philosophical grounds) and then built theology and ethics on the basis of that judgment, or on the presumption of its privileged compatibility with Christianity. I alluded to some historic examples of this in the Christian tradition. Recently I think we have seen Christian ethics shaped by existentialism, for example, Bultmann; by analytical moral philosophy; by phenomology, for example, Howard Harrod; by hermeneutical theory, for example, Gibson Winter's most recent work; by Marxism, and so forth. I am uncomfortable with flat-footed uses of typologies of ethics to create little boxes into which positions can be put, and still more when it seems to be suggested that a theological ethical position has to fit into one of those boxes to be coherent or respectable. Audi, Reeder, and others here have been aware of the "mixed" character of my work with reference to some of these boxes, for example, Kant—the deontological box and utilitarianism—the consequentialist box. The theologian has to be his or her own philosopher in the area of ethics as elsewhere, and, granted my inadequacies, I have tried to be philosophically responsible in developing a theological and ethical position. A question is raised for me by the papers, that is, if the position can be properly described as "pragmatism" (Reeder), is it *necessary* to the theology, or could other types of philosophic work be used and perhaps be even more compatible?

I am not offended by Reeder's characterization of pragmatism; I think Johann's extraordinary praise of aspects of my work is based in part on his sharing a family resemblance to me in this respect. Reeder's use of Richard Bernstein to locate me on one map (it is not the only map he uses) is accurate; Johann's location of my work between the extremes of Nietzsche and Aristotle is correct, and between Aristotle and MacIntyre is more refined and is plausible. I am a bit surprised that none of my colleagues has suggested shades of Spinoza, present but not identified. Only Midgley mentions his name. An important moral philosopher and an intellectual historian who have looked at (I am not sure really read) my work mentioned the affinities they perceived with Spinoza. I read a lot of Spinoza and some secondary literature on him between the times I wrote the volumes and deliberated about using him as a benchmark. I wonder if I would be interpreted differently if I had done that.

Since my colleagues have properly been more concerned with the philosophical aspect of *my own* position than with *the sources* from which I have drawn, no more needs to be said concerning this issue.

Experience. The importance of experience as a source of reflection and as a mediation of what is objective to self and community is clear enough from my work. Johann, among those who have commented on this aspect, is most sympathetic with its use. His redescription of its role is, I think, accurate. Briefly, he has made the following points: rational inquiry is a matter of organizing experience; experience cannot be reduced to something purely cognitive nor something purely affective; it is social in character; reflection on experience can issue in knowledge that can be "in some way" validated in turn by experience. His way of developing further the uses of rationality in relation to experience is agreeable to me. All this suggests in another way the aptness of Reeder's classification of my work as pragmatic. Farley, in his careful reconstruction of what he calls my genetics of piety, also treats experience as a source for my work with fairness and sensitivity.

My delineation of piety, the religious dimension of experience, is, I think, problematic for some of my commentators. One question is whether natural piety needs God or whether it is simply a general human experience. It will not satisfy the critics to explain that this is a point at which the biblical monotheistic tradition becomes an important part of the composite account, a way of organizing the experience of piety. The explanation would not be sufficient *justification* for invoking the monotheistic tradition (Farley). They will still question, I think, whether piety linguistically construed in a tradition is a sufficient warrant for both in our being (our religious affectivity) and our thinking (our articulation of theology) to make a One beyond the many rationally necessary. Bellah, incidentally, is correct in indicating that I do not fit either of the types on which Lindbeck has constructed his argument about the nature of doctrine. (I have a personal letter from Kaufman in response to an earlier book of mine in which he finds my recourse to experience to be "spooky.") One aspect of further self-examination on my part would be to explore whether I am worse off in using piety in my thinking than important theologians such as Calvin, Edwards, Schleiermacher, and, I might add, Bushnell. It is noted that I chose the term *piety* rather than *faith;* I think for a large segment of my critics much of what I have said would pass muster if I had used the term *faith* and left it as ambiguous as it often is in usage.

Weight Given to Aspects of the Composition and What Is Determinative,
and Coherence and Stresses in the Position

For the sake of brevity, and with awareness of the costs involved in making a choice under the conditions of finitude (in this case space limits), I shall collapse two headings that in a more expansive version can be profitably distinguished.

These two headings cover matters that evoke sustained critical analysis from several of the papers and from other critics as well. While different papers approach the question of weighting in different ways, they make it clear that their authors have read my book closely and intensively. Reeder, Audi, and Farley are most comprehensive because they have chosen to get at the issues raised by these headings in the most complex way. Other authors—for example, Kaufman and Johann—chose to focus on more limited matters, each of which opens to these issues. I will not do justice to either the comprehensiveness or the precision of analysis and criticism on this occasion.

Reeder has me trying to keep a raft afloat. I wish he had chosen another image! Maybe a space exploration vessel that would go out of our solar system to the source and center of all that is. (I have thought of various titles for this written Response: "Gustafson's Raft: Can It Still Float?" "Gustafson's Trail: Does It Get You from Here to There? Or to Anywhere?" "Gustafson's Spaceship: Can It Even Get Off the Ground?")

I suppose I could have jazzed up my book if I had made a claim to novelty of sorts by saying I was taking a systems theory approach to theology and ethics and had expounded the commonsense ontology of systems theories, but I have not claimed to be that novel or that au courant. I think one way to get at an answer to the question of whether one element of the composition is finally decisive is to ask: On my barely floating raft, the elimination of which board would make it finally sink? (I do not need to name the boards: Audi, Reeder, Farley, Johann, Kaufman, and I among us have them all named.) There is another implied question about my barely floating raft: Because of how I designed and constructed it, is it tilting dangerously (or perhaps fatally) and why? Here the question is not just the boards but how I have put them together and with what, whether I have used bolts and nuts or baling wire. (As everyone who has lived in rural America knows, baling wire is not to be demeaned.)

Kaufman brings his paper to one of its climaxes by wondering whether I am essentially confessionalistic after all. If I take the *essentially* in one way, I admit that a kind of confessionalism (piety construed from a monotheistic tradition) is a board that is needed to keep the raft steady. I can take *essentially* another way and ask, if the "confessional" board is removed will the raft sink? I think it will not sink, but it will cause a tilt. Farley uses the trail image and carefully points out "breaks" in the trail; one of them he sees as a fideistic appeal in invoking the tradition's formed conviction about God. I think it is a break if I have not adequately justified my use of that conviction and brought it to bear at an earlier point on the trail. (See how I differentiate myself from Jaki.) And whether it is fideism, or something more complex than how I normally use that term, is arguable. I think, obviously, that it does not fit the normal usage of fideism. I think it is more like John Henry Newman's "assent," or what H. Richard Niebuhr called "beliefal realism."

It is possible to construct a theology that avoids that break, if it is one, in the trail. Kaufman has provided an example in his work. For him theology is an activity of the human imagination that analyzes, criticizes, and reconstructs the concept of God in order to develop a framework of interpretation that provides an overall orientation for human life. The symbol "God" performs two indispensable functions: it relativizes and humanizes. (There are passages in his *Theology for a Nuclear Age* that I, at least, can read as aimed at my first volume.) I continue to think that Kaufman's theological method is basically Kantian. Theology is an enterprise of pure practical reason; on the basis of imaginative constructions, transcendental deductions, we provide symbols that perhaps do not refer to any reality but are necessary to support a humane and proper way of life. Kaufman may be correct that I have not been sufficiently self-critical about method, but his, like that of others, has not yet won the day. I think any position between the extremes of theological rationalism and sheer fideism will have a similiar break in the trail. (In a reader's report to the University of Chicago Press on the first volume, the writer—it was, I know, Julian Hartt—pointed out that people were not going to roll over and concede to my arguments, but he kindly added that that has always been true in theology.)

Under the heading for this section of my Response it seems to me that the most persistent question is the relation of God and nature. The questions of my critics are sharp and direct. Farley asks, why affirm God at all? What do I mean by God, especially as a power at work in the processes of life? Reeder asks questions of similiar content and import. Kaufman asks, is this a theological position at all? Is God as important as I claim? Why Other and not nature? I think Kaufman is incorrect in suggesting that the historical source of my error is a radical dualism in the Reformed tradition. Nor do I recognize the grounds for his charge that I have "zeal for God's utter independence from everything human."[2] One ought not read Barth's early work back into his antecedents in that tradition. I still think Calvin always had to be on guard against Stoic metaphysical tendencies in his theology, and Edwards and Schleiermacher have been interpreted as having pantheistic tendencies, if not as pantheists. I also think that Kaufman's and my common mentor, H. Richard Niebuhr, never quite got his relativizing One beyond the many together with his God acting in all actions upon us. (For interpreters of H. Richard Niebuhr I want to note that the proofs for *Radical Monotheism* were delivered to our home in Lund for him to work on when he arrived to visit us after delivering the Robertson Lectures in Glasgow, from which *The Responsible Self* is derived.) Audi does not raise these questions quite as straightforwardly but builds an interpretation that concludes that I am a theological naturalist. He manages with little cuts from as sharp a knife as other critics use to draw the same blood.

The three persons with whom I conversed most regularly and who read rough drafts of volume one virtually day by day (all of whom are here) can testify to the fact that the cluster of questions around the relation of God and nature gave me more intellectual agony than any other part of the work. I think my critics understand how I attempted to resolve the issues: within the context of piety and construed from the monotheistic tradition I moved from the powers, patterns, and processes to the Other, the Ultimate Power. It is in this move that, as I have noted, Farley finds fideism and Kaufman finds confessionalism. Johann rightly points out that in theology as well as ethics I insist on holding the affective and cognitive together. The issues were raised by Cahill and McCormick, especially, in the essays in the *Journal of Religious Ethics*. (I have a letter from one of the editors of that volume that had the title of McCormick's essay as "Gustafson's God*s*"; whether that was a typing error or McCormick's originally submitted title I do not know.) Among the alternatives to what is in print that I rejected were several possibilities. One was an even more confessionalist position than I took: on the basis of God's revelation through the events recorded in the Bible one can incorporate, what I will call here for shorthand purposes, Nature as ways in which the gracious revealed God orders the world. In some ways this is Barth's move; once he has taken away the use of nature to come to knowledge of God and one has confronted the gracious God of revelation, one can engage in a composite rationale using many sources to provide indications of God's ordering power. A second: I could make a move similiar to one Kaufman makes, that is, one needs a final relativizer to make the construction work intellectually, religiously, and morally. If I did that I would have violated a tenet I had established, namely

---

[2]Above, 26.

that one ought to attempt to avoid justifying one's view of God on instrumental grounds. I also rejected the announcement of *sheer* transcendence, though mystery is acknowledged. Other alternatives I rejected are summarized accurately by Audi, and he has included the most pertinent quotations that describe the position I took. Perhaps if I had undertaken to use Spinoza as a benchmark I could have refined my position; I am not sure. I am, candidly, not prepared now to make a better argument for the position I have taken, nor have I quite gotten the help I can use from the papers to develop a different position that coheres with elements I find no reason to give up. But then, my critics were not asked to improve the design of my barely floating raft!

Part of the larger issue of God and nature is the impersonality of the Deity in my work and my invocation of some traditional symbols of a somewhat more personal sort as having (candidly admitted) expressive and utilitarian value in practical religious life. Audi attempts to help me at this point, as he does at many points along the way. (I am grateful to Audi for his interpreting my work, using its ambiguities and possible implications of it, in such a way that I am not quite as heterodox ethically and theologically as I appear. Detailed response to all his work in that regard, I fear, is not possible in this presentation.) At one point Audi seeks to help by pointing out that my use of the verbs *enabling* and *requiring* with reference to God are anthropomorphic, and I need not be too ashamed of that. (See also Farley on *enabling* and *requiring*.) But the country boy left in me came up with the following thought, worthy or unworthy as it may be, that the rich black loam on my wife's family farm in Iowa enables some fine corn and soybean crops to grow, but rain and other things are required to bring that to fruition. Which use of those terms is metaphorical?

Audi has cited the crucial quotations in my work and subjected them to critical analysis and possible reinterpretation. He properly locates my dilemma. "If he adheres to his strong rejection of anthropomorphism in the conception of God, he is hard pressed to make the connection between science and ethics required by his theocentric view; if he allows the apparently necessary anthropomorphism, he is hard pressed to sustain his view about the ultimate power."[3] One resolution of the dilemma that I reject is a right- and left-handed God, working impersonally through the law (Nature) with his left hand, and personally through the gospel of redeeming love with his right. Audi quotes the most crucial material from volume one;[4] those sentences are the

---

[3]Above, 173.

[4]James M. Gustafson, *Theology and Ethics,* vol. 1 of *Ethics from a Theocentric Perspective* (Chicago: University of Chicago Press, 1981) 271.

ones that I have, for some time, judged to be in need of more extensive elaboration, more careful refinement, and perhaps significant rewriting. I have given more traditional anthropomorphic language a high value in that practical order, for the sake of piety and morality, but that has not resolved the issue satisfactorily in the order of theological articulation. In addition to how those matters pertain to thinking about God, Audi raises them with reference to personal identity and immortality and to human agency.

Audi is correct to say that it is one thing to reject disembodied personhood and another to conceive of personhood as entailing biological embodiment. I have for many years read literature on mind/brain, soul/body, and so forth, and no one will dispute that it is not possible to disprove the existence of personal identity persisting objectively after death. I comment on 1 Corinthians 15 in the book, a text I have never used in funeral meditations. I have a strong preference for another Pauline text on these occasions (no doubt wrenched from its broader theological context), namely Romans 14:8: "If we live, we live unto the Lord, and if we die, we die unto the Lord; so then, whether we live or whether we die, we are the Lord's." It may be deficiency in imagination that leaves me so agnostic (to say the least) on this matter: the logical possibility of an alternative is overweighed by my naturalism.

On the matter of personal agency I am not sure how much Audi and I disagree in the end. He appeals to our "sense of freedom," which I would state as our capacities for self-determination. Again that is a literature that has occupied me for years, and I have tried to avoid some traps we get into when we use the radical polarity of determinism and freedom by talking about conditions and conditioning and about capacities for self-determination. Kaufman, in a vigorous discussion in his living room several years ago, argued that I was overreacting to existentialist-like claims. Perhaps I was. But I am also interested in thinking out the consequences for moral accountability of various positions on a continuum. Johann has me quite correct in his reconstruction of the role of ends and desires, and I am no doubt much closer to Edwards than I am to radical libertarians. My observation is that in theological ethics this whole issue is generally left imprecise by most writers; for example, what position is implied about this matter by those who argue that narratives shape character through community? Among some colleagues in theology it has not even been considered. Some Swedish theological students who participated in a seminar I conducted three years ago were excited when I observed that I had never met a Calvinist theologian in Sweden or a Lutheran theologian from the Republic of Ireland. (In Sweden at one point in the seventeenth century Calvinists were judged to be subversive and as dangerous as the Jesuits; the Dutch diplomatic staff was not even permitted to have its own clergy.) Perhaps the deemed radicality of my own writing is evidence for my conviction that capacities for self-determination are real, though the "sense of constraint" from many sources taken into account in my exercise of them shaped what I wrote.

Johann writes that "*God* is the name for the ultimate source of the possibilities for being in experience."[5] I do not disagree with that, but I find it to be more partial than my own view. He does not refer to God as the Ultimate Orderer. I cannot here develop a detailed response to him on this point, but my impression is that he finds less basis for ethics, less guidance for conduct and ordering of life in the world from the natural ordering than I do. The emerging moral order, if my impression is correct, is more a construction out of agents' subjectivity than it is a construction out of *human experience of the patterns and processes* of interdependence. If I am correct, then the theological naturalism that is attributed to me quite properly by several commentators affects not only what I say about God but also what I say about morality more than Johann's position makes possible.

Farley as I noted, like Audi, sees signs of anthropomorphism in the language of God's enabling and requiring, but Farley makes more of the language of purposes, a teleological element in what I say about God. I made a distinction between intentions and purposes, reserving the language of intention for the fruits of our rational activity relative to ends. I speak of God's purposes without claiming that God has intentions like we have—this issue has been only alluded to in my Response but is taken up by Audi and others. By using the term *purpose* I pointed (somewhere) to the functional interdependence of things and attempted to be agnostic about one big telos. My temptation toward a big telos comes from both Thomas Aquinas and Jonathan Edwards; perhaps God's purpose in creation is ultimately to glorify Himself (or the Godself, to avoid another needle from Kaufman), but about that I surely cannot be certain.

Kaufman wants to retain theocentrism and avoid gross anthropomorphism, and I am happy for all the company I can find. His proposal is to use metaphors drawn from history and culture and personal existence in speaking about God. I think this is easier for Kaufman to do than it is for me because one criterion he has for theology is that the symbols ought to enhance humanization. Kaufman is not one of those physico-theologians that Kant wrote about; I am, and thus certain criteria for the adequacy of theology are more important for me. I do not think I neglect human creativity as much as Kaufman seems to think I do; other commentators see more recognition of that in my notion of participation than he does. If I were to write an essay on *Theology for a Nuclear Age,* I would take account of his central observations of our cir-

---

[5]Above, 114.

cumstances, namely the capacity we have to destroy, but I would put it in a texture of interrelationships that is denser than his. (Regarding that book, I think Kaufman's question is not with the sovereignty of God, but with the providence of God.)

I noted at the beginning of these remarks about God and nature, the impersonality of my view of God, and so forth, that these matters gave me agony when I wrote volume one. I think my critics are saying to go home and agonize some more. Whether I can do better while retaining other aspects of the composition that I have not found reasons to jettison remains to be seen. Certainly I need to expand more on the pertinent sections and to make some sharper distinctions to take account of their blows. I think my raft floats, but some changes in construction will make it steadier.

I must hasten to make some comments about the discussion of my ethics under headings two and three. Reeder, Audi, and Johann have developed very empathic reconstructions of this part of my work; I am very grateful to all three for the ways in which I can still see myself, but somewhat differently, in their mirrors.

The relation between my interpretation of God and the ethics is a matter attended to not only by them but also by other writers. It is clear to everyone that one can have a moral outlook, develop moral guidelines, and so forth, similar to mine without invoking the name of God. Midgley's work, among others I have read through the years, is evidence of this. Whether she walks up to some religious vision, or at least a quasi-religious vision of a whole, but does not cross over has interested me ever since I read an interesting footnote at the end of *Beast and Man*. I am not interested in forcing her or anyone else to make a move of pure practical reason, that is, to insist that God is an essential postulate of practical reason to sustain her moral vision; indeed, I would violate my reasons for interest in theology if I did. Reeder is correct to indicate that the "middle" portion of my work as a basis for ethics can stand independently of the theocentricity; Farley's construction of my commonsense ontology makes the same point. Farley, however, comes to a thesis that "if divine activity is simply identical to perceived world processes, with whatever happens, it cannot provide a basis for *moral* content."[6] Johann does not read me as having claimed identity, and I think he is correct. I think that Farley and I are using *basis* in different senses; I attempted to make clear the limits of a *basis* for morality by arguing for its necessity but not sufficiency.

Reeder correctly points out that the ethics I develop is not an ethics of divine command (on which he wrote an important dissertation). A divine

---

[6]Above, 54.

command theory of ethics would not cohere with the theology I have attempted to develop. I have lined out a theology and an ethics on, at least, some of the same ground. That is the import of Farley's development of my commonsense ontology: it relates to and coheres with both the ethical and the theological. If that board is taken from the raft, it will surely sink. Put in terms of classifications, I have a naturalistic basis for theology and a naturalistic basis for ethics—though a box called naturalism is not quite right. But Midgley asks, does the ordering need an Orderer? Is God identified with the patterns and processes of interdependence or is there more to God? This turns the discussion back to that touched on previously in this Response. I do not argue that the ordering logically necessitates an Orderer, but that given a set of observations about life in the world and given piety, the outcome, both affectively and reflectively, is construed from the tradition in a way that I, at least, can affirm an Orderer. Does the piety need a Deity? Not necessarily, but again construing things out of my Reformed theological and religious roots, I assent to saying there is one. Does the Deity act as the ultimate relativizer? Yes, in the sense that all that is is related to God. So what else does God mean for moral life?

If God is the Ultimate Orderer and Power, the determiner of the ultimate destiny of all things, natural piety is both focused and intensified. *If* God, then the language of stewardship and service appropriately point to the awesomeness of human responsibility. I wrote a book not only about theology and ethics, but also about religion and morality. To use metaphors used in Edwards and Puritanism, and in Calvin and others, there is a difference in taste and sight, a difference (to use less "spooky" terms) in perception and valuation, because it is finally God with (if I may resort to a personal term) whom human beings and the world have to deal. There is a difference in human disposition and affectivity. In these respects, at least, I perceive myself to be very much in a biblical tradition.

I have already alluded to what I perceive to be a difference between Johann and me. First, I appreciate his reconstruction of my view of human agency, and I find no difficulty in his using the terms *conscience* and *conscientiousness*, though I do not. My point of difference can be elaborated a bit by observing that his ethics is probably more inventive and creative than mine. I agree that to speak of God is to speak of a reality concerned with the whole, but if God is the Orderer and not merely the condition of possibility, then ethics has to be developed more on the basis of the perceptions of ordering relationships than I detect in his paper. I have no quarrel with "ethics of emergent order" as a general description, but I think I would stress the boundedness of the ordering more than he does.

Audi and Reeder both indicate that my ethics makes possible communication across cultures (including cultures that coexist in our own society). Audi wants to press me toward a statement of stronger ontological realism than I am prepared to make, arguing that one can have epistemological fallibilism with such realism. I have fudged on that question; perhaps more than fudged— I have not been persuaded on philosophic grounds of that possibility (but I acknowledged my limits as a philosopher). Reeder picks up my use of "functional prerequisites," a term I have used throughout my career and drawn from sociological theorists such as Talcott Parsons and Marion Levy. Whether Audi and Reeder are more hopeful about finding a universal basis for morality than I, I am not sure; many have already claimed to have found it. Particularities of cultures as well as the human fault qualify my expectations of the practical effectiveness of such a position. I have read too many books and articles and heard too many lectures that in effect make a strong claim only to find that other rational persons do not agree with the moral theory presented. But it is the case that my work provides at least *a* basis for extending the communication and overcoming some disagreements between *at least some* morally interested groups. Since my own work as a practical moralist has for many years been not with ecclesiastical groups but with others, I have personal evidence to support their observations. (I might add that my nonparticipation in responsible ecclesiastical groups was not of my choosing; what I was writing and still write has tended to be "out of sync" with the contemporary interests of church moralists and thus I, like Ramsey, have seldom, if ever, been invited to participate.)

I shall take time to make a few random comments about Reeder's paper. First, given Geertz's theory of religion, he is correct: I have a general argument going about the webs of belief that ground all ethics. My problem is, still, that on that basis all ethical views are religious, and I do not see what differentiates a religious ethicist from a probing moral philosopher. But this is a side issue on which we understand each other and have gone our own ways. Second, what I call intuition in the discernment process is not quite as cognitive as Reeder suggests; it has some aesthetic-like features, or perhaps one could better appeal to the perception of a gestalt. Third, I do not mind what I have written being called an ethics of human flourishing since it at least poses the possibility of an interpretation that counters the perception that it leads to an inhumane world. Last year I was invited to read a paper at the conference of the British Society for the Study of Christian Ethics; their topic was "human flourishing." I responded that I would prepare a paper if I was permitted to address "The Limits of Human Flourishing," which I was. Reeder's paper does not (and cannot in limited space) fill out what he means by the term; I am wary of it because of the inherent temptation to turn it into a virulent anthropocentrism.

Again, I acknowledge the insufficiency of this Response to the presentations made at this symposium. I summarized my own view of how I manage headings two and three: weight given to aspects of the composition and co-herence issues. Farley, I think, is right on target when he sees the "common-sense ontology" as the center of coherence; the weights given to what is drawn to develop it indicate crucial judgments on my part. This assertion is not meant to resolve the question raised, for example, have I overweighted certain things relative to various criteria that critics bring to bear? Have I succeeded in mak-ing some things, particularly my view of the Deity, coherent with the com-monsense ontology? These papers, on the whole, do not distance themselves as radically from my work as do the published papers by Hauerwas, Mc-Cormick, Cahill, and Ramsey in the *Journal of Religious Ethics.* If that is a mea-sure of some agreement with my enterprise, I am most pleased. I sometimes have been made to feel a bit lonely, theologically, during the past four years.

Implications for Traditional Criteria
for Judging Theological Ethics

This heading is not intended to convey the notion that there is one cri-terion in the tradition, nor to convey a trivialized sense of some standard of orthodoxy. It is simply a shorthand way to comment on the perspectives of critics of my work. Four of the essays in the *Journal of Religious Ethics* address my work from perspectives that use more traditional criteria.

I certainly cannot be accused of hiding what Jarl Hemberg calls an "ex-tremely radical approach" to traditional criteria under systematically ambig-uous usage of traditional biblical and theological language. For example, I used "Nature" in a chapter where most theologians would have used "Creation" and "The Human Fault" where they would have used "Sin." Nor did I ever proclaim that I was taking a radical approach for the sake of novelty. Two tra-ditional criteria are clearly rejected: (1) theological ethics begins with the ex-egesis of Scripture, and (2) theological ethics must be Christocentric. I carefully never used the adjective *Christian* for what I wrote knowing that I would have to stretch the normal usage of the term to make it fit. I have not been sur-prised by the grounds of criticism from more traditional ways of writing theo-logical ethics, nor by the vehemence of some of them. The question this leaves with me is this: have I done something so radically different that there is no common ground on which to converse with my more explicitly traditional (from various traditions) colleagues? Yoder's paper indicates that, at least for some persons, further conversation will be difficult, if not impossible.

Yoder charges that my "own synthesis is so modern and individual that the lived experience of centuries of missionary faith does not register as an al-ternative model. To be 'missionary' . . . or 'evangelical,' as I prefer to say, is not to claim universality as achieved either on the grounds of a revelatory priv-ilege [perhaps contra Barth at this point?] or because one can apologetically subject it to everyone else's concepts of natural reason. It is to discover approximations to universality in the lived experience of transtribal communication and reconciliation."[7] Rightly or wrongly, I take that to be his fundamental substantive charge against me and his most concise statement of an alternative procedure. He speaks not just for himself but seeks to represent a classic Reformed tradition to supplement the imbalance of this symposium. The theological and ethical enterprise proper to the church has a distinctive center of gravity, a clear delineation of what is central and what is peripheral, and possibilities for coherence and inclusiveness around that center. I attempted to indicate not only that I am aware of such an alternative but that it is one of the bases for my compositive enterprise, and clearly biographically the place from whence I come. I suspect both from his critical comments on the inadequacies of my work and from the statement I have quoted that our differences are on the criteria of what one will give up "to discover approximations to universality" and why these are important, and on how the discourse with other "tribes" ought to be conducted for the sake of communication and such reconciliation as is possible.

"What say ye about Christ?" is clearly a critical question. I am sure that Yoder and Kaufman would agree on one point, namely that Christian theology is marked in some way by the significance of Christ. I do not develop Christ as prophet, priest, and king, nor does Christ function as a symbol in the way he does for Kaufman. My position in this regard has evoked many shouted damns; they were not unanticipated by me. A crucial sentence in volume one is more often partially quoted or misquoted than it is correctly quoted. "Jesus incarnates theocentric piety and fidelity." This sentence was chewed over for a long time; one correspondent who was reading the manuscript as I wrote it suggested "Jesus is *the* incarnation of theocentric piety and fidelity." The absence of the article *an* in the sentence is intentionally and systematically ambiguous. I have pointed out in my response to the *Journal of Religious Ethics* papers that people who cite that sentence never seem to take into account the rest of the paragraph. If I had written something that I cannot write, namely that Christ is the revelation of true humanity, I could have passed muster with many more persons.

I indicated earlier in this Response that Kaufman is an ally in the stance of critical evaluation of aspects of the tradition—here the traditional criteria for judging theological ethics. I cannot follow Yoder's proposal to find "approximations to universality in the lived experience of transtribal communication" without being radically open to revisions that might be required in

---

[7] Above, 76-77.

the perspective and the language of my tribe. For example, orally and in writing, several persons have said that one can, on Christological grounds, be theocentric and anthropocentric at the same time; for some this means that grounds for compatibility between evidences from contemporary sciences and traditional theology can be found, in my judgment probably by selection from each source. (There is also a simple linguistic problem: there cannot be two centers to any figure, to the best of my knowledge, unless they are two names for the same point.) Other theologians assimilate views from the other tribe and reinterpret them in traditional theological language, thus providing them with a religious and theological meaning.

If the gulf has become so broad and so deep between my "modern and individualistic synthesis" and Yoder's brief delineation of the classic Reformed tradition, I must wait to see how other persons from that tradition take account of what I have attempted to account for. I have read some efforts to do that, though they are not discussed in the book, for example, by Karl Heim, T. F. Torrance, Wolfhart Pannenberg, papers by Philip Hefner, and others. Perhaps, as some friends have suggested, this is a margin of my work I ought to pursue in more detail. Whether my proposal is as individualistic as it appears to be (that it is my effort and not that of a group is clear) remains to be seen. I do not think it is esoteric; a sociologist of knowledge would probably trace it to the social location of my professional life, a secular university, but that location is an important one in our culture and formative for many who pass through it.

Practical Implications:
Their Desirability or Undesirability

Under this heading I wish to comment on papers by Midgley, Yoder, and Bellah. Midgley's trenchant analysis of the paradox of humanism, with its historical, philosophical, and ethical dimensions, comes from a perspective I share with her; my readers know how much I used her work in volume one, and thus how much she has both informed my work and, with her marvelous turns of phrases, enabled me to highlight features of my own. Perhaps her paper shows Bellah that one can write more radical cultural criticism, be more prophetic, from the perspective of my middle ground (Reeder) than I have been. From a different perspective and using different sources and methods, Gibson Winter, in his *Liberation of Creation,* evokes some of the same judgments; Hans Jonas, in a somewhat apocalyptic vein, in his recent book on responsibility, adds to the literature. Frederick Ferré, Ian Barbour, Stephen Toulmin, and others have also been part of my nourishment on these matters. The force of the analysis of the paradox of humanism is to me not only in the realm of ideas and beliefs but also affective as well. Apart from some evocation and direction of the passion, analyses like that have little social and historical effect. Kaufman's book *Theology for a Nuclear Age* is impregnated with similar passion. Responses to these sorts of analyses are inadequate apart from some sense of remorse and need for repentance, without a crying out in the words of the Psalmist, "Create in me a clean heart, O God, and renew a right spirit within me."

My understanding of the practical implications of my work includes a call for a radical conversion, a deep reorientation of values, attitudes, outlooks, affections, and so forth. Here I think I am much in accord with biblical and traditional Christian and Jewish ways of thinking about our human situation. If I have not gotten the relations of my theological construction to the piety worked out to satisfy my critics, I have at least made a case for the "senses" of dependence, and so forth, that Reeder recalls to our attention, for piety and for the practical significance of traditional monotheistic primary religious language. My theology and ethics can be the basis for some heavy preaching about the wrath of God, and the need for individual and cultural repentance. (Maybe those who faithfully come to hear me preach at Rockefeller Chapel think that is all my theology permits.) My point with reference to Midgley is that it is not only our conceptual schemes that need revision (as she concludes in the last sentence of her paper), but also what loyalties ground our loves. The theocentricity and piety that I have lined out, I think, calls for radical *metanoia*. Midgley's paper is good preaching, as well as trenchant intellectual and historical criticism.

I suppose Bellah is asking, if this is the case why does that note get qualified, tempered, and die a death of untold complexity in my book? I can respond to his query on that point by turning to some things I have written, but not published, since the book was completed. That is: one can distinguish within moral discourse between prophetic discourse, ethical discourse, and policy discourse. (At my place of work these would be called three "moments," but I try to avoid local jargon as much as possible, inflicting only my own!) Prophetic discourse is basically indictment; it describes the evils of the world and points to the factors that cause them, particularly the blameworthiness of responsible human beings. In its sermonic form and in other writings, for example, Schell's book that so impressed Kaufman, evocative symbols and narratives and description are warranted. It is to evoke passion.

Prophetic discourse is not ethical discourse, if ethical discourse means (as I think in normal usage it does) making an argument on the grounds of some human values or moral principles for the rightness or wrongness of a course of action, prospectively or retrospectively. On at least some occasions, responsible individuals or institutions find they cannot determine the course of action simply by the conclusion of an ethical argument. Ethical discourse is not policy discourse, or at least often it is not. Policy discourse has to take into account the position and capacities of agents to effect outcomes, the accumulation of resources to do so, the questions of likely success or failure, and the like.

Now, to return to Bellah's critique of my work, the theology I have developed requires that one move from the prophetic to the ethical to policy discourse. For example, in my chapter on distribution of research funding for biomedical research I do raise a more prophetic question—does our preoccupation with health indicate disorientation of a deep sort? Or, as I sometimes put it, has health replaced salvation and the glorification of God as the chief end of human beings? In the same chapter I do show how ethical arguments work in assessing courses of action. But if my practical ethical question is asked—"What is God enabling and requiring us to be and to do in a particular set of patterns and processes of interdependence of life?"—I have to get involved in what I, above, have called policy discourse. Thus, considerations other than the prophetic and the ethical are important.

The issue raised by Bellah, and perhaps implied by Yoder, is whether this capitulates too much to the modern world with its complexities, and to how things *actually* are, in order to get from point A to point B. I do not rule out more prophetic stances, and I include the ethical, but I believe I and my colleagues have obligations to contribute to the discussion of policy with those who are in positions of specific responsibilities for the outcomes of particular choices. (The few who remember Kenneth Underwood might recognize, if not his influence on me in this regard, at least a reinforcement of an early concern of mine.) My delineation of what I call discernment, as well as the four exemplary chapters, is an effort to show how this can be done. The strange ending to MacIntyre's *After Virtue,* appealing almost romantically to a kind of monasticism, is not coherent with my theological ethics.

Yoder poses some questions about the particular topics I chose as examples. The choices, as I indicated, reflect a number of things: topics I had attended to partly as a matter of choice and partly of circumstances, topics that would require me to take different factors into account and address different kinds of human complexity, and so forth. I did not claim that suicide was more important than war, and while no one of the topics focuses primarily on the political and economic factors, as Yoder recognizes, I do not leave them out of the book, and I bring them into the discussion of medical research and population and nutrition. There may be a kind of natural affinity between the topics I chose and the position I have developed, but I firmly believe that on the basis of it I can deal with revolution and violence, poverty and oppression, and other topics seen more frequently on the current agendas of my colleagues. As a published dialogue with Elmer Johnson shows, I would not be satisfied to pronounce the evil of radical discrepancy between incomes. I would, if not by disposition, by virtue of the sorts of things I read and persons with whom I talk about such matters, be concerned with the requirements for a healthy economy as well as what constitutes fairer distribution of income; on the latter I would be concerned with taxation policies, welfare policies, and other elements that have to be considered to achieve fairer distribution. All of this does not deny the importance of the prophetic indictment or the ethical argument. I think they are deficient but necessary conditions for ethics from a theocentric perspective. I also think that given research time, I could address many more social and moral issues than I have.

It would only take time to speak my thanks again for the papers by my colleagues and again acknowledge the inadequacies of my Response. So, I will just pole my raft to the shore and step off. It might float better without me on it.

Panel Discussion

Farley: I want to press Jim on his language about "discerning what God is doing." The phrase suggests a morally pertinent discernment, and I wonder how specific he is able to be about this. According to Jim, ordering in the world is something human beings can directly perceive. We do not even need the sciences to perceive all sorts of orderings, though the sciences refine this perception enormously. I think that what Jim means by this ordering is some kind of integrating. Ordering is moral process as it obtains integrations of various sorts. If I pressed that, I would want to argue that those integrations themselves contain disorderings. The disorderings are conditions of those integrations, and as soon as an integration is formed, there are forces working toward disintegration. World process is comprised of that.

Now, what is divine ordering? The divine is defined as the source or condition of ordering, perhaps the condition for obtaining these integrations. According to Jim, there is something purposive about this. I also think something about it relates to the good. The question is, what is it that is good in the divine ordering or in obtaining integrations? Is integrating itself good and identified with good? It would seem to me that it is not. We can think of all sorts of phenomena or world processes that require integrating forces. The Third Reich, for instance, is a kind of integration. Just integration, the fact that you had a concatenation of forces and powers so that the Reich arrived, does not itself make that good. Is one better than another simply because of the factor of integration?

If not, are some integrations preferable to others? One might propose that some integrations are better than others if within them one has the least disorder. Or, one of the ways of assessing integrations in relation to each other is that some of them move toward a complexity that produces what might be called a "higher order" of being or existence. But God is then the orderer not just of the condition of world process, but of a certain direction toward complexity of a higher order. The direction of this analysis is that there are at least some criteria, some ways of filling out the meaning of good, that are not simply carried in the language of ordering or integrating. In other words, when we look at the phrase "discerning what God is doing," we are not simply discerning all processes or integrations. We are discerning integrations of a certain sort, or that are going in a certain direction, or that are good in a certain preferable way. If Jim cannot consider these suggested options, I am back to the question I raised in my paper: What is the moral pertinence of discerning what God is doing?

Gustafson: First, I think I nowhere say that we discern what God is doing. That is what my mentor, H. Richard Niebuhr, said, that he could discern what God is doing. I think I have always been very careful to say that we do not discern what God is doing. What I said is that we seek to discern what God is enabling and requiring us to be and to do.

Farley: OK, let's go with that.

Gustafson: It is important to go with that. Now we have a human response, and a community and a subject trying to discern what is being required. One thing you might say is being required is some sense of an ordering that is objective, but that is not the only criterion. What we are enabled and required to do has to be discerned with reference to the historical actualities in which we are a part. That is an important correction; I never say we discern what God is doing.

Secondly, I think my use of the word *ordering* rather than *order* was an effort to include processes in which there are forms of distintegration as well as forms of integration. My intention is to avoid the more static conceptions.

My third comment is that I never talk about the good; I talk about good*s*, ends. I would say, integration is an element of what is involved in what we are required to do; integration itself could obviously lead to repression, as you illustrate. So integration never stands alone. There are pluralities of ends that can be morally backed and supported that do not fall into a kind of natural harmony. So I deal with the plurality of values. Yes, integration is a functional requisite for a community, but that is not the only functional requisite. Other things are needed. So I don't talk about the good; I talk about good*s*.

To get to the theological issue, the reason I can't say that we discern what God is doing is that human agency is there. I don't read off what we ought to do in terms of what I might dimly say is the divine ordering because, as human agents with responsibilities and capacities to order life in a particular way, we are not determined. The divine ordering is not so simple. So far as I can speak about it, it does not have a single end such as integration. It provides conditions of possibilities of flourishing, as Jock Reeder says, and not only of human life but of human life in relation to other areas of life. So I have to draw inferences about the appropriate values that we ought to seek to actualize within the context of our particular situation. I probably am not reading as much into the divine ordering as you see me reading into the divine ordering. An assertion of the divine is not an assertion of a metaphysical order so much as it is an assertion of an empowering and reality that I am not quite willing to define and spell out precisely.

Farley: The same question would still apply, I think, to the language of flourishing. All kinds of things emerge.

Gustafson: Sure, but flourishing isn't one thing. I worry about the term *flourishing*. Jock Reeder amended the first draft of his paper that said that I had an ethic of human flourishing. I was going to take off on that because I don't think I have an ethic of human flourishing in the narrow sense. Flourishing, again, is the flourishing of a lot of things.

Kaufman: Everything?

Gustafson: Well, are we speaking descriptively or normatively?

Kaufman: Normatively.

Gustafson: No, I don't think it is everything, because I don't want evil to flourish.

Kaufman: But all the beings in the world?

Gustafson: No, they can't all flourish because life is such in the world that some things have to be destroyed for the sake of other beings.

Kaufman: So flourishing does not give us a criterion?

Gustafson: In and of itself, it does not give us a criterion. One of the things I learned from our mentor, H. Richard Niebuhr, is that when we say good I have always asked, good for whom? Good for what? Flourishing for whom? Flourishing for what? Those terms always have to be used in relations.

Kaufman: Flourishing is a reference to the being itself, is it not?

Gustafson: I never used it; Jock Reeder used it.

Kaufman: But you accepted it. If we talk about your or my flourishing, or the Third Reich's flourishing, we are talking about its flourishing for itself. To the extent we use the term *flourishing,* the "for whom" doesn't arise. It is already implicit that it is the being itself that is coming to some kind of fulfillment or realization.

Gustafson: I don't use the language of flourishing. I am not prepared at this point to say how I would adapt what I am saying to that vocabulary.

Audi: I appreciate how much you have left open in the course of making a number of commitments. Let me ask two questions that bear on what seems to be open. First, I referred to you as a naturalistic theologian, not a theological naturalist. We both distinguish those things. A theological naturalist might identify nature with God, and it would be a misreading to say that you do that, though you are careful not to say everything you think needs to be said about the relation between nature and God.

Gustafson: Or maybe I am not smart enough to say it.

Audi: I don't doubt there is a lot more to be said that you can say. In any case, I think this affects the ethics too. If you are not a naturalist across the board, it would be surprising if you turned out to be an ethical naturalist.

Gustafson: I think we understand each other on that.

Audi: I might add, I don't really think the notion of naturalism is itself clear. If we ask the difference between naturalistic and normative vocabulary, we can say that typical descriptive terms used in a chemistry laboratory are naturalistic, and "ought" and "ought not" are normative. But to give a general characterization of a firm distinction is extremely difficult.

Gustafson: One of those boxes, isn't it?

Audi: Well said. Now, you said something very interesting about enabling and requiring, and this elicits my second question. You are certainly right that we can talk of the beautiful soil enabling one to grow a certain kind of crop and . . .

Gustafson: . . . enabling a crop to grow.

Audi: OK, but it also enables us to grow a crop too, doesn't it?

Gustafson: That is true, but it also enables the crop to grow.

Audi: All right. Do you want to keep unnatural objects like us out of it?

Gustafson: No.

Audi: I was going to say that there is a sense in which the soil and the winter weather require us to have dwellings, and so forth, at least if we want to live. These examples of enabling and requiring, however, don't seem to have the normative force I think you want in asking us to pursue what God is enabling and requiring us to do. I want to return to the question of the extent to which you must resist the vocabulary of agency. Every system is entitled to some primitive terms, some terms that are undefined in that system. Moreover, a primitive term need not be inexplicable, though we could forgive some inexplicables in theology. They may even be appropriate at certain points. An inexplicable, of course, is not an incoherence. What if you simply said that you are taking the terms *enabling* and *requiring* to express just so much agency as is needed for them to have the appropriate normative force in your system, and not define that? Or perhaps give some examples of the wrong and right interpretation. I think you could find a way to work by example and without definition to a position that some people would find comfortable as providing for a personal God—a position that would link the theocentric elements to the ethical elements a little more strongly than they are explicitly linked now. Are you thinking there is something you must give up if you allow us to put some agency into these notions?

Gustafson: Gordon Kaufman and I were deeply influenced by our mentor, H. Richard Niebuhr, who talked about God acting in every action upon you. That is agency with a vengeance! It gets hard after that not to go to Calvin when Calvin says that God is not simply the determiner of a course of events, but the agent determining virtually the cause-effect sequence of every particular event in accordance with God's purposes. If you get clobbered going home, if a limb falls off your tree and falls on your head, God is the intentional agent in that act in certain forms of Protestant theology. That is something to worry about.

Audi: It is indeed, but I would think there are any number of ways to avoid this slippery slope.

Gustafson: But you understand why I have got a slope to worry about?

Audi: I do, but I guess various hypotheses about stopping that kind of excessive generalization must have occurred to you. I was puzzled about why you thought the job was so hard. I guess it is hard to do it all systematically.

Gustafson: I am so incorrigibly empirical. I have to think about corn and dirt and all that stuff. I can say, you see, that the fact that black acres of farms in Iowa have this highly productive soil depends upon enabling conditions of the deity's creation, just as somewhere else there isn't any soil like that. I am sure God didn't create that fertile soil so that my father-in-law could come from Sweden and have a good life on that farm, though he worked hard too. If I say that those conditions are enabling conditions for human responsibility, then my good father-in-law and others, who went out there and took over that land, accepted that not only as a requirement on their vocations but as an enablement. For what? For ends that, if they are not in the narrow sense moral ends, are at least human values. I want to play this out in quite silly language perhaps. If my father-in-law were seeking to know what God was enabling and requiring him to do with that quarter section of land, what he probably discerned was an obligation to use that land not only for the benefit of his family but for the benefit of portions of the human community. And it wasn't simply an obligation to use it that laid certain requirements on him as an agent. It was an enablement. It was a gift of God. He could have the vocation to do those things because that was part of what was given to him. I can say, whether it is metaphorical or not metaphorical, that God enabled and required my father-in-law to care diligently for that land for all those years. And I can say for what ends—for the end of the well-being of his family, for the end of assisting others in the human community to have food, for the end of pleasure and the flourishing of being on a farm and going out there and talking to those cows in the morning as if they were his friends. A whole host of ends were enabled. I can talk about God enabling and requiring. If that means I am using personalistic language in a stronger way than I seem to want to admit in my book, I am ready to do that.

Johann: I wasn't trying to put you in between Aristotle and Nietzsche (though most people are somewhere in between). I want to put both of them on one side, and you on the other. My whole point about deliberation is whether or not we can justify our judgments only in terms of some antecedent normative order that is knowable. I want to say that this normative order itself is a product of deliberative process. I was interpreting your discernment as deliberation. I find it a bit hard when you say I am too creative in the sense that I am not taking the facts into account. At least that is the way I understood you. I am not trying to be rationalistic in the sense of deducing something. I was trying to do it the way you were doing it.

Gustafson: Well, Bob, I think we have to get down to examples to see whether and how we differ on this sort of thing. I thought your ethics would be more inventive and creative than mine. However, if you are taking the relevant facts and things other than the relevant facts into being, or enlarging the notion of that in terms of what processes are going on, to which we don't conform but take into account in discerning creatively what we ought to do, I don't think there is a great deal of difficulty. When you moved from rationality to universalization in your paper . . . that's where being comes in for you, isn't it?

Johann: Let me interpret being in the sense of possibilities for flourishing in experience, which you seem to accept. The language of being is an older part of my heritage I've moved beyond.

Gustafson: But you used it in your paper.

Johann: Because you had Edwards saying consent to being.

Gustafson: That is fair enough. That side of Edwards is embedded and not explicated in my work. We have to consent to being, and being presses upon us and we participate in being. I can use that language. But I think that is also an element in the spirit of living theocentrically, in terms not only of a pressure toward universalization and possibilities of creativity and restraints and limitations on it, but a sense of participating in a vast cosmic process (you guys will all get me on this) of divine ordering in which I am participating. I mean the wonder as well as the awe and obligation of that. And then I have to consider and think about that with reference to the particular requirements of being. We are probably not far apart on that.

Johann: I would take the idea of deliberation precisely in those cosmic terms. I would also say that your examples in the second volume strike me as precisely processes of deliberation.

Gustafson: That's what they are intended to be.

Midgley: What we are calling anthropocentrism is just bad. What people call anthropomorphism can be bad or good according to whether it is done in a disciplined and careful way or just carelessly and slapdash. If by anthropomorphism one means using categories and concepts drawn from human life and experience to describe things not human, and one thinks this has always got to be bad, then one could not say anything about the life of animals. In fact, people simply assume that because people are different from animals in some ways, there is no possibility of knowing what is going on in an animal's experience. This seems to me ludicrous, since the behavioral psychologists concede that the people who live and work with animals, like the chaps who drive elephants, always treat them as if they did understand what the elephants were thinking. They find here a life in some sense akin to theirs, though they know it is different in some ways and have to discipline themselves about that. They could not be safe if they did not treat the animals in that way. It has been tried sometimes in laboratories; you make great efforts not to describe the animals in that way, but to do it by numbers. It isn't only that your work then goes to pieces, you get bitten! I know that this is a different problem from the problem about God, but they seem to have something in common. The presumption that concepts drawn from human life couldn't be used for anything nonhuman simply doesn't turn out right.

If we use this word *anthropomorphism*, we better ask what the *morph* is. In the first use of this term, the *morph* was the actual shape, the outward body. People talked about having idols in the form of an ox and that kind of thing. But it has been extended to cover everything that is part of the perceiving subjects that we are. When we have this negative theology, which there has been frequently, which denies we are in any position to use any of the concepts about God that we would use about people, we would end up saying that we really knew nothing about God. But we do know that God is not the Third Reich, and he is not a spotty balloon, and there are a lot of other things that he is not.

Jim, if I may make your life a little more unbearable, I entirely take your point that there are some situations in which God must not be viewed as agent, for instance, when it comes to dropping branches on people and similar things. On the other hand, you were inviting me to cross the river and believe in a slightly more positive kind of God. Even on the side of the river where I now am, gratitude is a very important concept. But gratitude almost implies agency, doesn't it? I thank whatever powers there be for having done all the many things they have done. Enabling and requiring may be among the things that they do. I don't think there can be anything wrong with that use of words. Of course, I must discipline this.

May I just note a rather touching thing in Darwin's memoirs? Darwin says how he seems to be losing his faith. He has by no means altogether lost it. He still finds in his old age that he has a strong tendency to think that the world is organized by some kind of good spirit in some kind of way. But, says Darwin, when I feel like that I realize that it is only because of the faculties that I happen to have, so perhaps I oughtn't to take notice of it. Now everything that Darwin was thinking, including that thought, came from the faculties he happened to have. Had he rejected all of them, he would have just stopped writing and working. It doesn't seem that he ought to have restrained himself at this point. We have no choice but to use the categories of thought that are natural to us, including the category of agency. This category seems to be imperative where one talks of gratitude (or indeed of resentment, as Job did). So I think it is necessary—and therefore legitimate—for me as well as you to think of gratitude as a response to agency.

Gustafson: Just note, though, when you uttered that little prayer of thanksgiving, you thanked whatever powers that be. I think for some people that would be very impersonal and nonagential language.

Midgley: Well, if you thank them, I don't think their role can be altogether nonagential.

Audi: You have already ruled out a committee.

Midgley: I don't think I would have used the plural really.

Gustafson: You did.

Midgley: I quoted this because I was thinking of your language. Sorry, I don't mean to be carping, but it is not important to me to use the plural.

Bellah: I just wanted to interject to Mary's charming example of working with animals that actually there are social scientists who attack other social scientists for being anthropomorphic.

Midgley: Oh yes.

Bellah: Which means that they are trying to understand human behavior in terms of intentionality rather than in terms of impersonal variables. . . . I will just raise one point that I was a little pained by in Jim's riposte. He put me and Lindbeck together as rooting our understanding of . . .

Gustafson: There were modal qualifiers in what I said . . .

Bellah: All right, I am not even sure if I got it right. But it seemed as if Lindbeck and I were concerned with identity and, therefore, had a social scientific understanding of the religious community rather than a theological one, which would mean to argue for the truth of . . . I can't speak for Lindbeck, but I don't see myself that way at all.

What I would like to raise, though, is a more general issue. A contrast has been posed between confessionalism and some kind of universal discourse in our discussions, as if confessionalism locks you within your tribe and the other allows you to talk to other tribes. I cannot understand that at all. There is nothing but confessional communities as far as I am concerned. The person who is in a tradition that begins with Immanuel Kant is no more universal than a person who is in a tradition that begins with Jesus Christ. I don't think that would convince John Rawls. That is John Rawls's problem; he is stuck with a lot of strange presuppositions that have not been shared by most people most of the time in the history of the world.

I would like to point out autobiographically that qua sociologist I am a member of a confessional community. Graduate students at the two departments where I have spent my life, at Harvard and Berkeley, could not get their Ph.D.s unless they knew certain books. We are a community of the book. If you didn't know Marx and Weber and Durkheim pretty well, and couldn't speak those languages, you were out. Did that mean we had some tribal loyalties to these peculiar books and their peculiar way of putting it? In one sense yes, but not in the sense that we felt that there was not something here that was true and that applied not only to Western society but to human society. Through our particularity we were engaging with the world. Furthermore, we felt in no sense that we could not engage with political scientists or philosophers or people in other disciplines. So the understanding of the Christian tradition that I hold takes tradition very seriously. There was a point in Ed Farley's paper that took Gustafson to task for not taking tradition as a source of truth.

Gustafson: That's where he was accusing me of using it social scientifically rather than theologically.

Bellah: Well, I was just reversing the language. Yet in your reply, when you indicated certain moments when monotheism comes in, that somehow comes from the confessional background.

Gustafson: It comes from historical tradition. I have been a social relativist all my life. You couldn't grow up in an ethnic immigrant community in the United States without first finding out that you were different from everybody else in your neighborhood. You spoke a different second language, went to a different church, and ate different kinds of food. Cultural and social relativism has always been there; I never had to discover it. So I don't think you are quarreling with me when you say that Kant works in traditions or that other people work in traditions. I think that the question comes in how we can move across the limitations of the languages of the particular communities to which we belong so that there is some communication. From my perspective it is not a matter of finding the universal out there, and then everybody coming to it. It is a matter of a process of communication and exchange between communities, not only trying to find but establishing the criteria of communication. That has to be particularistic too, because it is different depending on what other community you are trying to communicate with. The other thing I wonder about, Bob, is whether you and I really belong to a community. We belong to several traditions.

Bellah: Oh, absolutely!

Gustafson: Absolutely! We belong to several traditions. Part of what has got to go on has got to go on in our own heads.

Bellah: But it is a complex process of ongoing translation. It is not the effort to find the simple Esperanto into which everything else will finally be transferred.

Gustafson: No, I have never argued that. I don't think I have ever said that.

Bellah: Then I don't quite understand why you were putting me into this specially particularistic category.

Gustafson: I was putting you in this specially particularistic category because you agreed with Geertz's understanding of the nature of religious language as a set of concepts that come out of a highly particular community. You did say you didn't go all the way with Lindbeck. Lindbeck says we have to absorb this universe into the biblical language. That ends communication as far as I am concerned. That's assimilation and absorption that would make it very difficult for me to have lunch with Jim Shapiro and a lot of other people I eat lunch with at the University of Chicago. If I have got to absorb the world of molecular biology into the biblical view, we can't talk to each other. I didn't mean to put you in that box. That's a box I see Lindbeck going into.

Reeder: Just for the record to Bob Bellah, I don't think that Rawls would object to Jim's epistemology. I think the best reading of Rawls is that he begins with a particular community and moves from that, making certain basic kinds of assumptions . . .

Bellah: I was just questioning whether or not something would convince Rawls as a criterion.

Reeder: So the question is not whether that epistemology would convince Rawls, but whether a certain theory of the good would. Indeed, he belongs to a different community, if you will, in regard to the nature of human good. What he doesn't belong to is MacIntyre's proposed type of community or tradition.

Kaufman: I think this conversation may have given me a clue to an answer to the question I put to Jim about the respects in which the image of God involves something beyond nature. I would like to try it out. I have been thinking about your father-in-law working on his farm of good rich black loam. I think we couldn't really talk about nature enabling and requiring your father-in-law to do some of the things he was doing there.

Gustafson: No, not nature by itself.

Kaufman: No, nature certainly enabled him . . .

Gustafson: . . . enabled weeds to grow . . .

Kaufman: . . . but also enabled the soil to be rich, and the seeds that he put down to grow, and so on. But nature didn't have much to do with enabling and requiring him to be producing food for his fellow human beings. I sometimes use the phrase, "God is the ultimate point of reference that unifies and brings together all of the spheres of life." It seems to me, that is the way God might be functioning here. God is enabling and requiring both the relationships to nature in which your father-in-law stood and also the obligations and services in the historical order to his fellow human beings and to the wider human world. So God is really One that is enabling and requiring through both the natural and historical order.

Gustafson: I think you and I are not all that far apart on the nature-history thing. But first, there is another point where nature would come in with that particular example. By golly, food has to be present for human beings to live. It is not simply a radical choice for my father-in-law to say, "Here is good soil, and now I choose." The requirement of food itself is part of the ordering of life that somebody has got to pay attention to. Given the development of culture and the development of human capacities to make choices and intervene into nature, human responsibility is different from when you went out and picked berries in the woods. I think we would have to talk more before I agree that "ultimate point of reference" would be fully satisfactory language for me.

Kaufman: In his piety and in his activity, your father-in-law was able to think both of his working of the soil and of his producing food for some other human beings as in some way responding to what God enabled and required. And he didn't have to separate these out as responses to different powers that be. This unifies all the powers . . .

Gustafson: I understand. I like that. I may not like it tomorrow morning, but I like it now.

Richard Miller (University of Indiana): I am a bit puzzled by Kaufman's efforts to ally himself with Gustafson on a number of points. I would like to call attention to the conclusion of his paper where he criticized the adequacy of Gustafson's theocentric ethics because it doesn't provide sufficient grounds for the kinds of ethical or human aspirations to which most people devote themselves. Perhaps this isn't fair, but the judgment seems to be that Gustafson's theology is inadequate because it somehow doesn't cohere very well with ethics that are generally characteristic of Gordon Kaufman. What is peculiar is that Gustafson would never turn to an ethical criterion to test the adequacy of his theology. I think that's a dramatic divergence in both method and substance. Is that a fair reading of the division?

Gustafson: I raised that issue with reference to Gordon in volume one, and because of friendship I allowed myself some intemperate language. I got scolded by Mrs. Kaufman the next time I talked with her. That is an issue between Gordon and me, although I think it is not one that is absolutely impossible to overcome. As someone said last night, "Kaufman really sounds like Feuerbach in this regard." The question I have to ask Gordon is whether these constructs refer to more than a postulate of practical reason, which is necessary to support a moral view of life. If they refer to more than that, then other criteria have to be looked at to judge their adequacy. If the sufficient justification for them is that they support a practical reason that supports a moral view of life, then theology becomes too instrumental to suit me. It becomes a concept that backs our views rather than adding any kind of significant objective references by which it is tested. I think that is the issue between us.

Kaufman: This is a very complicated question. Let me just make a small remark. In the concession I thought Jim made a moment ago, it seemed that an ethical criterion came into the conception of God. Maybe he wants to withdraw that. But the way Jim's father-in-law relates to and has a concern about feeding the hungry with the food that he grows is certainly connected with his moral stance to what it is to be a human being and what it is to serve human beings.

Gustafson: . . . what it is to serve God by participating in this natural order in such a way that certain ends are met.

Kaufman: But not just participating in the natural order, participating also in the human order in such a way that certain human moral requirements are met. If that is part of what God enables and requires, I have got all I need from Jim on using a moral criterion also as a basis for understanding who God is, and what the divine ordering is as well. The moral criterion seems to be implied.

Miller: It seems to me the logic would include one more step that would mitigate the moral criteria. This man's father-in-law is farming these crops and feeding these people, and that would be seen as an exercise of stewardship. That is developed at length in the last four chapters of Gustafson's second volume. Stewardship is a response to the kinds of ordering processes that we see operating within the world. There is a middle term that has got to be inserted; that includes this element of responsiveness that doesn't serve as an ethical criterion. I think that would be folded into the dough and would save the argument from turning on an ethical standard in order to stand up.

Kaufman: May I say that if stewardship . . .

Gustafson: You didn't like that term.

Kaufman: Well, if stewardship is understood not to be just stewardship of the land, but stewardship of the needs of the people that his father-in-law is serving, then stewardship also has built into it an ethical dimension. If we may use this more traditional language, it has built into it God's concern for human flourishing.

Gustafson: Also God's concern for the flourishing of that Iowa soil, so that part of the stewardship is not just to ruin that soil . . .

Kaufman: Absolutely. I am not trying to subtract from that at all. I just want to make sure that the other is also there.

Paul Ramsey (Princeton University): What I want to say may very well be based on an antecedent mistake. I refer to the moment in your presentation where you were saying that many people haven't paid careful attention to your statements about what you were doing, what your authorities were, what place Scripture and tradition had. I think you actually said you felt a little lonely recently. I read the book carefully and I . . .

Gustafson: . . . and you wrote a sixty-two-page response to it.

Ramsey: I want to say this, Jim, and I want to ask you, what has happened here? What is the case? I felt that a line was being drawn. I felt that in reading the book, and some of H. Richard Niebuhr's students and some of your former students felt in reading the book, that it is not they who are drawing the line that leaves you out, but that the clear statement of your sources is drawing a line that leaves us out.

The question is about theology because the ethics have to come after that. If I believe that theology is a reflection upon the faith of the church, its explication and its re-statement, then to understand your authorities is to understand that a line has been drawn so far as theology is concerned. I know I share with you, all these former students share with you, things far more important than theology. We go to the Lord's table together. You are a preacher; I am a layman in the church. The creeds of the church, the tradition and the Scripture of the church, are community-forming. Now as I read your book, the issue here is that I feel lonely at the drawing of a theological enterprise that does not center upon the things that we had thought we shared with you at the level of first-order discourse, namely, prayer, worship, liturgy, the confessions of the church, and going to the Lord's table. I think I knew Gordon Kaufman had reacted against his professor, but your book came as something of a surprise.

I perhaps should not have spoken in this way, but I do want it to be understood that there are different ways of drawing lines. What has mostly been discussed here is your splendid accomplishment in taking a stance on authorities other than the primacy of Scripture and tradition and liturgy and so forth. As I say, this may be based upon an antecedent misunderstanding that we were together more in theology. We certainly still are and will remain together in the first-order action of Christians within the Christian community. Now, I wonder if you have any comment that would be a response to that. If not, I'd love to do it over many long evenings, but unfortunately modern life does not afford us that.

Gustafson: That is hard, Paul. I could respond biographically, and that's not an explanation. I could respond in terms of what I think my vocation is, and that would be a explanation but not a justification. In my life, in trying to be a faithful religious person in the midst of an exceedingly high-powered aggressive community of intellectuals, I discern profound religious sensibilities, and I discern moral sensitivities that put most of the churches to shame. When I meet with these people over lunch or in meetings, I find that the institution of the church and its confinement to its traditional language is simply not accessible to them. It is repulsive to them. When I delivered my Ryerson Lecture at the University of Chicago in 1981, a distinguished philosopher, recently deceased, said to me, "Jim, I believe everything you said, but I can't stand that goddamned institution." That was more vehement than it needed to be, but I think there's a population out there.

Now, I live in a very parochial world. I am not trying to universalize Hyde Park, or downtown New Haven, or anywhere else I have lived. I don't think it is simply among intellectuals. I think it is among people in the professions. I think it is among common people who are not at all interested in being theological. I think the tradition has sold people short, Paul Ramsey. It has led them to expect things in the primary language of the tradition that failed over and over again. There are experiences of suffering in the world, Paul. There are experiences of suffering of the innocent in the world, and traditional religious language has a way of just putting syrup on that stuff— and not suffering with the suffering, and not being in pain with those who are in pain! I am sorry I am preaching.

I think that at least for some of us there is a community out there that the church is not able to address meaningfully precisely because of its identification with the traditional sources that determine the basic frame of reference of its language. It is not able to tap what I think is their natural piety and their natural moral sentiment and to help them see and clarify that theirs is a legitimate form of life under God! Now that may be drawing a line, and perhaps we are not in the same community any more. I am not trying to say that I do what I am talking about well. But there is a population out there that I identify with, and I see a role here for me and maybe for others.

We go back to our mentor. One of the last things H. Richard Niebuhr ever did was to deliver the Cole Lectures at Vanderbilt on the need for the resymbolization of Christianity. I read that manuscript. I don't know fully what our mentor was really going to do finally with that. I am not only concerned with the resymbolization of Christianity so that these traditional symbols can be meaningful. I think Gordon Kaufman is trying to do that more than I am. I am concerned that we recognize a certain kind of authenticity, a religious sensibility and moral profundity and sensitivity. At least some of us should find a way of talking to and nurturing that, of helping that become self-critical, and not building barriers that in my judgment are not essential to the ultimate thing that life is about—which is not preserving that damn tradition, but it is service to God.

Afterword

The Response I delivered to the papers at the symposium stands in its own right. In the months following that event some distance has been gained both from the two volumes and from the symposium. I have benefited from conversations about the book and the papers with Tod Swanson, Mary Potter Engel, Martin Cook, William Schweiker, and most intensively with David Smigelskis of the Committee on Ideas and Methods at the University of Chicago. This essay is an Afterword. Its agenda may appear somewhat random; it results as much from matters that have provoked personal pondering after the symposium as from a systematic effort to address all relevant issues. I offer here reflections on items on which I am now prepared to make clarifications and amplifications. Whether I shall ever write a more complete defense of my work is not now certain.

The book itself is a process of discernment, as Johann notes in his paper. Its rhetoric and style, in many parts, fosters that for some readers. (Elmer Johnson's address at the symposium banquet is one evidence of this.) It is not an argument for the truth of religious or moral propositions in the sense that John Henry Newman develops in *A Grammar of Assent*. It is an argument worked out in piety and in the context of human action. The piety itself, and particularly the sense of awe evoked both by the radical contingency of all that is and by the reliable ordering of much of life, occurs within the human experiences of choosing and acting. The book begins and ends with discussions of circumstances to which it is a response. The book is an effort to discern what it means to *be* human persons and human communities, to be dependent and interdependent participants in and through (Smigelskis noted the use of the preposition *through* in my symposium Response, rather than *in,* and the choice is better) the patterns and processes of life in the world. The book is an effort to discern what it means to *act* as human persons and human communities, to act as dependent and interdependent participants in and through those processes. This is what I intended to suggest when I wrote that the book is not simply about theology and ethics, that is, the relations between ideas and concepts of God on the one hand and moral principles and human values on the other, but also about religion and morality, that is, about human beings' experiences of what I call piety evoked by the powerful other (who would be God whether there was life as we know it or not) in human choices and conduct. I was not as successful as I desired to be in developing the interpenetration of piety, theology, morality, and ethical ideas throughout the book. The tones of piety, and particularly the *sense* of dependence and awe, are muted in some sections of the book in ways that make plausible an undesired separation between piety and moral choosing and acting, and between piety and theological thinking. What is expressed in the Coda is intended to have impregnated the whole book. I need to stress again, then, that piety is not evoked by traditional modes of contemplation so much as by participation or action. The book seeks to discern a way of being and doing in the contingencies and the reliabilities of life in the world.

The first book written by a theologian that I ever read was John Baillie's *Invitation to Pilgrimage;* it was loaned to me by an army chaplain in Assam in October 1945. There is a sense in which the purpose of my book is an invitation to participate in a process of discerning. That my book, like that of any other author writing a systematic account of theology and ethics, comes from *my* years of study and *my* reflections on events and experiences is patently clear and acknowledged in the Preface. But it is not a "faith statement" if that means it is simply a personal testimony to some idiosyncratic individual experience. It contains a basically coherent argument; the elements of ambiguity and incoherence pointed out by my critics in this volume, I think, are not devastating to the morphology of the book. By the time of this writing, what I anticipated has been confirmed: there are those whose perspectives make it difficult or impossible for various reasons even to empathize with what I have written; there are very, very few who are wholeheartedly persuaded that my discerning is correct in every respect; and there are those (including all but Yoder among the authors of this volume) who take my discerning seriously though they reject aspects of what I have written. I attempted to show why what I wrote *ought* to be taken seriously by others; it is not one of our contemporary maudlin invitations "to share" in my discernment. It is an effort to be persuasive, to show in a convincing way why my account is (in my judgment) better than other contemporary accounts. (A literary critic commented orally to me that volume one was "a very moving book.") One would only embark on a project of the magnitude of the two volumes if one were deeply convinced that it resolved some issues that other writings and ways of living do not. It is, of course, not without its flaws and thus correctable; it is also, of course, subject to rejection upon the development of alternative descriptions and counterarguments.

This Afterword is organized around four themes. To my critics they may not be the most important ones. I have already been called upon to write more about what I have written than I prefer to do; I shall have to do still more if I am to address adequately questions that are outstanding.

Deliberation and Discernment

Deliberation is an aspect of discernment, but discernment is more than deliberation. Here I wish to amplify my response to matters raised in several of the critical articles. Johann and I are certainly not far apart in our accounts of the practical choice, but I continue to see a significant difference between us; it is the importance of piety. Clarification of the difference is all the more difficult since he heads a section of his paper "The Piety of Reason." Reeder indicates that there is an aesthetic aspect to my view of discernment, and Johann is not unmindful of the affections. The aesthetic and affectional dimensions distinguish markedly my work from Rawls, Wong, and some other authors cited by Reeder. It is also the case that discernment is the proper name for the more specifically theological aspects of my book; and it might be the stone called fideism or confessionalism on which Farley and Kaufman think I stumble in their critical arguments. I noted in my symposium Response that piety comes, in a sense, at the beginning of my theological argument and is not introduced to close a gap in a rational trail.

What most distinguishes discerning from deliberating is the presence of piety. Discerning is an act of piety, that is, a process conducted and experienced with a sense of awe, contingency, gratitude, conscientiousness, and devotion to God. Piety is evoked and informed by "others," objective to ourselves. An act of choice is an act of piety. The formula of discerning what God is enabling and requiring us to be and to do is intended to keep that in view. It has been made clear to me that there are sections in the book that lend themselves to an interpretation of deliberation more than discernment, that is, to viewing what I wrote as an alternative description of the ways in which factual matters, moral principles, human values, and so forth, are taken into account as points to be considered in coming to a choice. The division in the final chapter between being and doing and the way in which the section on doing is explicated are more in the mode of deliberating. Particularly the chapter on allocation of funding for biomedical research seems to have dropped some of the tones of what I wish to signal with the idea of discernment. The sense of awe and dependence in what Smigelskis calls my "triplet" of dependence, interdependence, and participation is muted, if not omitted, in some of these passages. It is more evident in the chapters on suicide and the family. Reeder's inclusion of an aesthetic element in a deliberate process only in part evokes what I intend to convey; it does get at a kind of discerning *gestaltlich* aspect of choice but does not necessarily convey a quality of contingency and awe. Reeder, I think, may miss these because he tends to abstract my ethics from its theological and religious attitudinal aspects.

Perhaps deliberation can properly connote the more rational aspects of coming to a moral choice. Deliberating is an exercise of our capacities to reason, to envision alternative courses of actions, and to anticipate outcomes and the sequences of events that might follow from them. I think Johann and I agree on the importance of deliberating. What I miss to some degree in Johann's essay is the attitudinal context that my interpretation of piety seeks to convey. This context is evoked by the consciousness that it is God with whom we are ultimately dealing in all our actions. If not for Johann, at least for some pragmatists, secular and Christian, one has done the best one can and, therefore, can rest with a kind of certainty. One might feel some purely subjective unease about how well one has done, but this is not a matter of great significance. Discernment seeks to connote other aspects. It is cognizant of the high probability that one's choice and action eliminate the possibility of some future good being realized, and thus objectively the consequences have a tragic character. Lincoln's Second Inaugural Address, with its "The ways of the Almighty are His own," evokes a sense of the possibility of a radical disharmony between loyalties, actions, and outcomes, each of which has plausible justification. And the actions in pursuit of rationally justifiable ends too often lead to the destruction of good and values. Remorse results from our morally conscientious participation in a sequence of events that has objectively evil as well as good outcomes.

The affinities between my work and pragmatism are brought out by both Johann and Reeder; they are clearly there. What awe or piety do to pragmatic deliberation is not without significance; they alter the framework of meaning and significance given to actions that come from deliberation. Not only are actions and their outcomes interpreted differently, but also the condition of our participation as persons and communities is altered.

As Calvin says, it is with God we have to deal in all our living. It is now clear to me that in my discussion of "the human fault" I did not sufficiently attend to the impediments we all put in the way of living, deliberating, and acting with a proper piety: for example, the ways in which our success in life bolsters an exaggerated sense of self-sufficiency or blurs the realities of human suffering, or the ways in which we (even in moral deliberation) subsume too many things only to technical reason—not only in the restricted sense of reasoning of means to ends but also in the sense of reducing persons and events to information and data to which moral reasoning is applied. I am perplexed, for example, by those ethical writers who highly value respect for persons and who, to establish this point, made a *case* out of Karen Quinlan before her final expiration.

Religion and Theology,
Other and Others, and So Forth

There are a number of distinctions and relations in *Ethics from a Theocentric Perspective* that have led to misunderstandings of my intentions and that need greater clarification than is present in the book. Part of the difficulty I have in making myself clear is that various distinctions are related to each other in very complex ways. It may be the case that I should now lift out more systematically the "method" that is more implicit than explicit in the book and, thus, respond to one of Kaufman's criticisms. In my symposium Response I addressed some of these difficulties; appropriate limits of space for this Afterword do not permit the full treatment that I now know is required. Let me simply itemize major distinctions, which needless to say are not separations, and describe some significant relations.

Religion and Theology. Religion refers to two distinct aspects of my work: piety and historic traditions. Theology refers to the activity of reflection that seeks to indicate some things about God and God's relations to life in the world. The activity of theology is undertaken in piety and from a standpoint in a particular historic religious tradition; it also informs piety by its interpretation of God and corrects aspects of the tradition. There is religious language and there is theological language; in some parts of my work I have made a very clear distinction between them, for example, in the use of traditional terms about God as Creator, and so forth, and in the discussion of prayer and worship. In other places the distinction is blurred in such a way that confusion occurs. And it is the case that a separation of the two languages is something I desire to avoid. This can be illustrated from my activity as a clergyman; in composing prayers and in preaching I sometimes paraphrase Augustine: God who never was not, who always is, and who never will not be. This language is primarily theological: it says some things about God. Augustine's language evokes piety, is an expression of piety, and is grounded in the Western monotheistic tradition.

Distinctions between Theology, Ethics, Religion, and Morality. (a) My distinction between ethics and morality (as I use the terms) is parallel to that between theology and religion. Ethics is an activity of reflection upon the form or forms of moral activity, providing reasons for choices and actions, justifying a way of being moral in the world. (I have for many years used Henry David Aiken's essay "Levels of Moral Discourse" as a pedagogical device to clarify this.) Morality is the activity of engagement and forebearance in life in the world. The focus of ethical reflection is on how we discern what God is enabling and requiring us to be and to do, how we justify that discernment; morality is being and doing. Ethics and morality are to each other as theology and religion are to each other. Persons gain knowledge about ethics from their lives as moral beings, and ethics informs and gives direction to their moral lives. (b) Theology is related to both ethics and morality. For ethics it provides the ultimate backing for principles and values; it is the *basis* of ethics.[1] For moral life, theology articulates and depicts the power and powers with which human life has to deal. How God and God's relations to the world are construed make a difference in moral being and doing. Moral life contributes to theology; moral experience is data for reflection upon the world's relations to God. (c) Religion is related not only to theology but to morality. Moral life occurs in piety. That makes the difference between discernment and deliberation discussed above, and it makes a difference in our dispositions toward others. Moral life also evokes and sustains piety; it is in activity that we confront limits and possibilities of life. (d) Both theological and ethical language have mediating functions. Though I am concerned with the plausibility of both sorts of language, I am primarily concerned with their capacities to inform and direct human being and doing in the world. The theologian has to make a case for his or her choice of theological and ethical language; indeed, that is the critical intellectual task of theology and of ethics. But the primary function of theological and ethical language is to aid us in discerning what God is enabling and requiring us to be and to do.

Other and Others. In both my Response to the symposium papers and in the discussion that followed I attempted, with little success, to clarify all that is involved in this terminology. Kaufman charges me with a Wholly Other similar to the early writings of Barth. Others have read my work as an explication of God as *anima mundi,* though no one has specifically used that term. Other, or Ultimate Power, functions in a way similar to "the principle of Being" (in contrast to "Being"), but I have not carefully explored that alternative and am not prepared to do so here. Other is basically theological language; I do not compose prayers that refer to Other, though I have invoked the term in preaching after more particular expressions and experiences have been used. The impersonal connotation of Other is intentional; I have argued in the book against personal agency language about God because of its excessive anthropomorphism. I reject a kind of Feuerbachian turn Kaufman takes. The Other refers to that which is the source of all that is, the Ultimate Orderer of all that is, and that which would be if everything *as we know it,* including our world and life in it, did not exist.

"No person has seen God." No person or community could sense and describe relations to the Other except through "others," through human ex-

---

[1]For one discussion of *basis,* see James M. Gustafson, *Ethics and Theology,* vol. 2 of *Ethics from a Theocentric Perspective* (Chicago: University of Chicago Press, 1984) 298.

periences of many sorts including perceptions of persistent patterns and processes of life. As I indicate in the book, this is my way of accounting for the biblical materials; they are the record of a particular community's interpretation of many areas of human experience as media of an experience of Yahweh, of the presence of the Ultimate Other. (I do not intend to imply that the religion of Israel was always monotheistic.) The presence of the Other is discerned through others—for examples, historic events, natural events, the ordering of nature, the activities and presence of particular persons. While I use the language of parts and wholes, I deliberately do not use that language in relation to God and the world, as if all the "parts" of the world made up the "whole" of God. Nor do I engage in a discussion of similarities and differences between what I attempt to express about God and the world and the distinction between the primordial and consequent natures of God. My theology is not a "natural theology" in the sense of a purely rational argument for God's existence, or for specific characteristics of God *a se*. It is also strikingly different from a book published since mine, namely Moltmann's *God in Creation*, trinitarian theology based on the Bible and the tradition that, in an exceedingly speculative way, interprets the internal relations of the persons of the Trinity to each other and the relations of the Trinity to the creation. (I continue to be amazed at how much some theologians know about God.) In my exposition I have also sought to avoid views of the divine determination of each particular event; I distinguish myself from, for example, Edwards in this respect.

Different "things" are indications of different ways through which one discerns God's presence, and what one articulates about that presence is grounded in those different "things"; there are different ways through which one discerns the Other through others. What is confusing to some readers is my failure to make clear whether the language of ordering, sustaining, creating conditions of possibility, patterns and processes of interdependence of life in the world, and so forth, is primarily theological or primarily religious in the senses stated above.

I did argue that for practical religious purposes it is appropriate to use more immediate language of a religious tradition and its piety and thus to speak of God as Creator, Sustainer, and, even in a very restricted sense, as Redeemer. This claim for practical appropriateness without clarification of how that language does or does not refer to the same things as ordering, and so forth, may be a specific source of confusion. I attempted in my response to the *Journal of Religious Ethics* articles to make clear that our language about God is a linguistic construct, a very human enterprise. I have sometimes been tempted to take recourse to a point in Calvin's discussion of the mode of Christ's presence in the Eucharist; after making it as clear as possible, he seems to sigh and say that it is a mystery. "And, to speak more plainly, I rather experience than understand it."[2]

Our languages about God all have a mediating function, whether the affectively laden language that personalizes God in practical religious life, the abstract language that speaks of God as Ultimate Power and Other, or the language that attempts to show how we discern God's presence and requirements in and through patterns and processes of interdependence. That does not mean they are arbitrary, but the criteria of adequacy are multiple, and there has to be a fittingness of all the terms to each other within a single coherent effort to speak of God and God's relations to the world, of the Other and the presence of the Other discerned in and through others.

Science and the Sciences, Theology, and Ethics. Audi's paper attends most carefully to the ways in which science and the sciences function in my book. In partial response to his paper and in response to other comments, I attempt here to clarify some of the obscurities in the book.

Sometimes I wrote about science and at others about sciences. When I wrote in the plural at some points I stressed the importance of being informed by and responding to particular scientific investigations. In the first volume the most general use of science is to provide background "facts" or general scientific theories that are part of the context for interpreting life and thinking about it theocentrically. It is not my place to defend an evolutionary view of life any more than it is my place to expound the arguments that continue about aspects of evolutionary theory. I assumed, I think defensibly, that as a general interpretation there is not any important dispute among reasonably educated persons. Similarly, it is not my place to defend proposals about the long-range future of the universe of which we are a part, though I know that proposals about both the origins and the temporal end of the universe are subject to alteration in the course of further investigations. I also assume the relative accuracy of accounts of certain human drives such as hunger, sexuality, and sociality that are directed differently by different persons and in different cultures. Thus, I stressed our continuities with other animals.

This use of science as a source of background "facts" or well-grounded beliefs about the world provides backing for such notions as ordering and sustaining processes in which our senses of dependence, gratitude, and obligation are evoked. Thus, it informs both piety and ways in which I attempt to write about God. It also is a basis for criticism and revision of many traditional religious accounts of life in the world, for example, those I call anthropocentric.

---

[2]John Calvin, *Institutes of Christian Religion,* 2 vols., trans. Ford Lewis Battles, ed. John T. McNeill (Philadelphia: Westminster Press, 1955) 2:1403.

In the second volume I more often adduce materials from particular sciences with reference to moral choices, as in the chapters on population and nutrition and on biomedical research funding. The relevance there is more directly to ethics and morality than to theology and religion. Particularly in the chapter on nutrition I cite a number of very contemporary investigations, the results of which must be taken into account in considering alternative courses of actions. On these particular "facts" relevant to nutrition, the scientific jury, so to speak, is still out; the very particular conclusions are more disputed than are the general themes from science adduced in volume one. The moralist does not naively accept these "facts" on the basis of "expert" authority. Yet for purposes of making responsible policy choices, the theological moralist needs to be informed by them.

Perhaps I can generalize in this way: the more settled scientific beliefs inform piety and theological construal, and thus our being; the more contingent studies inform our morality and ethical reflection, thus our doing. Both inform, consequently, our discerning of what God is enabling and requiring us to be and to do as participants in and through the patterns and processes of interdependence.

Whether this section of the Afterword further clarifies obscurities in my book or more satisfactorily responds to my critics, I am uncertain. That still further development and clarification remains to be done, however, I am certain.

Service and Human Flourishing

From a number of sources, I know that the overall impression of the book to, I think, hasty readers is that the view of life I provide is totally grim, bound to self-denying service, devoid of the erotic, joyless, repressive to human flourishing, and the like. In oral discussions I have noted that Julian Hartt's and my language of powers that bear down upon us is sometimes referred to as if I had said nothing about the powers that sustain life and create conditions of possibilities for it. I do not write with rhapsodic flourishes about hope and an open universe, and the term *hope* is discussed most in a chapter on suicide. I state that "Long Friday" discloses more about life in relation to God than does Easter. With Smigelskis and Engel I have had the most intensive discussion of the fittingness of this impression, and there can be no denying that evidence for it is present in the book. Nor is the perceived emphasis the result of heedlessness and absence of intention on my part, though evidences that would modify distorted exaggerations are amply present in both volumes.

I will not modify the critique of radical individualism nor my concern for obligations arising not only from our interrelatedness but also from the need to consider the common good more than is usually done. It may be the case that some current manifestations of what I deplore both in the way persons live and in some theological and other literature will themselves be corrected in time; indeed, that may well be occurring more as an outcome of the specific forms of "divine judgment" of exaggerations than the outcome of anything anyone has published. The number of philosophical critiques of contractarianism steadily increases. (I heard a baccalaureate sermon in May 1986 that cogently addressed these matters and, from what I could tell, was appreciatively received by both parents and graduates.) I will not modify my fundamental critique of theologically supported anthropocentrism, nor my claim that life is to be lived in the service of God.

It is the case, however, that what are more muted themes in the book could be developed without, I think, undercutting the emphasis on service and on restraints of self-interest for the sake of others. I will not take space here to cite passages in which I develop themes that careless readers find missing: joy in the beauties of nature and in aspects of human culture, gratitude for technologies that relieve drudgery and pain, the fulfillments that can come in the life of a family, the need for development of personal resources and self-esteem even as a condition of being of service to others, the occasion of events that bring new possibilities for self and communities, and so forth. And I do note the debilitating outcomes of utter self-denial that others often suffer. There are many surprising "signs of grace" in human experience: recoveries from deep despair to a life of participation and meaning; reflecting on disasters so that some benefits can come from them in the future; recreative abandonment of occupations and preoccupations in the sheer joy of music, art, literature, and for some of us fishing and working crossword puzzles; capacities to celebrate life in the midst of conditions many persons would find nauseating, as described in Dominique Lapierre's remarkable account of a Calcutta slum he can rightfully call *The City of Joy;* relishing in the presence of one's most beloved and in his or her love; the freedom to be more creative when persons are released from the erosive effects of particular institutions or human relationships; indeed, absorptions in objects and activities that are of no intended service to God or any person or community. To remember these and similar things is not to be carried away theologically or morally, for while life is sustained, maintained, and fructified a very long list of specific events and of continuing debilitations that threaten deeply the ordering and preservation (not to mention the flourishing) of societies and persons, culture and nature could also be written.

Reeder, in the first draft of his paper, called my work an ethics of human flourishing; he subsequently qualified that and correctly so. But the critical comments adduced above indicate that the issue of human flourishing as individuals and communities is a matter that I should develop further with greater care and precision. The pinch comes for me in ways I noted in the book.

There is no automatic harmony between not only desired but desirable degrees of flourishing among related individuals, among related communities, and between individuals and communities to which they belong. Quandaries arise when we face competing goods, when we must choose between active pursuits of goods and relationships and proper forbearance, when we experience tensions between human loyalties that cannot be fully resolved and rational deliberation about the proper actions, and so forth. These are not only "objective" quandaries but also human suffering in the face of them is unavoidable. My discussion of proper objects of love, and of loving even proper objects neither in excess nor in defect, is related to this matter. I have argued that no fixed hierarchy developed a priori is satisfactory for resolving such conflicts. I did not undertake to comment on and extend the long Christian discussion of the "double love commandment," and particularly the relations between proper self-love and love of neighbor and of God, though I made clear in the use of Jonathan Edwards's *Charity and Its Fruits* that I agreed with him that happiness is a natural end that is not to be condemned. The matter of proper proportions between various objects of love was discussed as well.

There are resources in theology as well as in some of the human sciences in relation to which more extensive development of what I shall call here the issue of "human flourishing" can and ought to be developed more than I have done. Tillich's notion of a "centered self" is one; H. Richard Niebuhr's discussions of the struggle for integrity of self is another; Karl Barth's description of joy is a third. Surely Augustine's *Confessions* and his more abstract discussions of love and its proper objects is yet another. There are also one's own experiences, those of others one knows well, the depiction of these things in literature (as I noted, for example, in Mary Gordon's *Final Payments*), and other powerfully depicted accounts. It is not only the case that persons and communities need a significant amount of self-esteem and flourishing in order to be of service to others, that self-hatred is an impediment to freely loving others, that we have duties to ourselves as a condition of fulfilling our duties to others; it is also the case that joy is a good in its own right. As Lapierre so powerfully shows in his account of a Calcutta slum, celebration can occur in conditions of human degradation; joy is not merely a respite from suffering that gives strength to renew one's struggles. There are occasions of rich meaning that satisfy something deep in the human spirit. Ecstasy occurs and properly so.

I will not pursue this more in this Afterword, and I again call attention to the presence of concerns for human flourishing, indeed as Reeder indicates, for the flourishing of life, in the book to those who seem to have missed it. Joy can flourish in the fulfilling of our obligations, but it is not guaranteed. I think I will not find reasons in further pursuit of this theme to shift the weight of my work from the prior and ultimate claim that the vocation of human beings and communities is to serve the purposes of God as they can be discerned. It may be that I have understated that proper human flourishing is one of God's purposes, as something in accord with the divine ordering of life in the world. And it may be that participating in life in accord with the purposes of God brings the most profound joy of all.

Conservation and Innovation

Whether my book supports radical social and cultural criticism and proposals for revolutionary change has been the subject of both published and unpublished comment. In my Response to the papers delivered at the symposium, I addressed this issue, particularly in relation to Bellah's paper, but also in commenting on Midgley's paper. Recall that I indicated that the view of living in the world that I develop can be the basis for severe criticisms of culture, and that (to use Farley's term) the "commonsense ontology" Midgley and I share is one example of this. Her paper, whether she would like the term or not, is profoundly "prophetic" in the way it calls attention to what has been disastrously ignored in the course of the development of technical humanism. Recall also that I indicated that on the basis of the theology I have developed one cannot be satisfied with only an indicting disclosure of destructive and evil tendencies in culture and society, nor can one be satisfied only with proposing a vision of a better world. Discernment and intervention took place in very particular circumstances, and thus the moralist is obliged to address specific matters of policy. My illustrative chapters were intended to show how this can be done. In the book I made a plea for competence in the matters that have to be taken into account by persons responsible for policy and action in a way that often is not present in ecclesiastical pronouncements. This is necessary for the sake of being understood, being taken seriously by responsible persons, and having more specific effects on courses of actions. To some, as I noted in the book, this seems like rearranging the deck chairs on the *Titanic* as the ship is going down. At a number of points I argued that forbearance rather than intervention is the proper response. All of this has the effect of restraint upon highly activistic approaches that have, I think, dominated much of recent Christian ecclesiastical life in many parts of the world. My acute awareness of the complexity of the world appears to some readers to sustain only gradual processes of change; it is incremental rather than radical.

The peril of such emphases is involvement in the immediate circumstances of life so that one fails to detach oneself and gain a view from a more distant point of perspective. That peril, per se, however, is generalizable; deeply activistic engagements or radical prophetic stances can contract our vision of reality as well. I recall having addressed this issue in my presidential address to the American Society of Christian Ethics in January 1970 at its meeting in Atlanta. The choice of topic was determined by my audience, our occupation with civil rights struggles and the Vietnam War, and the fact that we met on the west side of Atlanta. There are correctives to such contractions in what I have written.

One correction of this peril in my book is the importance of discernment as a communal activity based on shared considerations, that is, on communities of moral discourse. From a theocentric perspective, communal discernment requires the inclusion of persons who have various competencies relevant to the issues at hand, various moral sensibilities, and various interpretations of ends to be sought. To be effective, a community of moral discourse has to break the bounds of limited class interests, ethnocentrism, and other restrictive features that drastically limit the points to be considered. Participants need to be informed by relevant literature that sheds light on the issues and enlarges the human spirit. Breadth of study is a condition for proper moral detachment: study of relevant materials from various disciplines, study of history, study of ethical theory, study of the classics of human cultures, and particularly for the churches, study of the biblical and theological traditions. Diversity of participants is a condition for moral detachment: participants should be open to expansion, and sometimes radical transformation, of perspective in the light of the distinctive insights of others.

If, as I have long believed, the import of rigorous moral and theological reflections is its capacity to deepen and broaden human capacities to make sound judgments and engage in appropriate action (or forbearance), then persons who are located and function in very dense and particular circumstances need to be deepened and broadened by visions and arguments that take a broader and more radically critical view. In the moral community, disclosure of radically new possibilities is important, and circumstances and events occur in which discerning what God is enabling and requiring responds to those possibilities. I have illustrated such things in the book, for example, in my interpretation of the general course of the civil rights movement in recent decades.

Intervention and innovation in times and places of possible radical openness can, however, lead to tyranny as well as to more humane institutions. Perhaps Hitler was one of the most perceptive and effective persons in our century in responding to discontents, nourishing them, and marshaling them in support of a visionary program. The founding fathers of the United States of America were also perceptive and active; they established institutions that, while excluding some persons from full human rights, have become the basis for developments that are fundamentally praiseworthy. A trite commonplace must be recalled: openness to new possibilities in itself does not guarantee beneficial outcomes.

I can also argue, more strongly than I have, that the theocentric perspective itself alerts persons to possibilities for radical change. More than many proposals in theology and ethics, it distances persons and communities from immediacies and requires openness to seeing particulars within larger wholes, more inclusive contexts. From it one can demonstrate the need for radical transformations of human valuations, for example, from the anthropocentrism that dominates both the religious and secular traditions of the West. One can see how loves need to be expanded and sensibilities intensified, how class interests, ethnocentrisms, and sexism need to be altered. One can criticize present institutions and conventional wisdoms for the narrowness of what they perceive to be their proper interests and for the ruttedness of their procedures of thinking. There is backing for rearrangement of institutions and for reform within them as well as the introduction of new institutions required to sustain and realize proper ends. What should temper aspirations is that proposals for change, whether gradual or revolutionary, cannot begin de novo and must anticipate and take into account the inevitable "costs" that accompany the pursuit of some special goods. Yet, I see no reason why, from the perspective of my work as a whole, radical revolutions, including the use of violence, cannot under certain circumstances be justified, but I do not think they can be pursued with joyful abandon as Luther admonished with reference to the conduct of war once one's cause is just.

The brevity of these comments under the heading "Conservation and Innovation" does not do justice to the issues, but it does indicate my consciousness that more or other illustrative chapters might have shown how discerning what God is enabling and requiring us to be and to do could under certain circumstances lead to more radical innovations than is apparent to some critics.

In the debates in Swedish scholarly journals, there is a time when an article is headed by an editor as *Slut replik,* final reply. Of course no reply is final; there are many other matters that have been brought to my attention or that I have generated from my own pondering in recent months that could receive attention. Indeed, what I feared when I undertook the writing of *Ethics from a Theocentric Perspective* is occurring, namely that I would become occupied with defending, revising, responding to critics. I have no desire to spend my remaining years simply doing those things. Yet the greatest tribute an author can receive is demonstrated by the fact that my fear has come to pass, namely that what I have written has been read, with varying degrees of seriousness and care, and deemed worthy of attention from my peers. I am obliged and pleased to make responses. *Slut replik*—at least to the papers prepared for the Washington and Lee Symposium!

James M. Gustafson

Contributors

Robert Audi   is Professor of Philosophy at the University of Nebraska.

Robert N. Bellah   is Ford Professor of Sociology and Comparative Studies and Vice-Chair of the Center for Japanese Studies at the University of California at Berkeley.

Edward Farley   is Professor of Theology at the Vanderbilt University Divinity School.

James M. Gustafson   is Henry R. Luce Professor of Humanities and Comparative Studies at Emory University.

Robert O. Johann   is Chair of the Philosophy Department at Fordham University.

Gordon D. Kaufman   is Professor of Theology at the Harvard University Divinity School.

Mary Midgley   now retired, was Senior Lecturer at the University of Newcastle, United Kingdom.

John P. Reeder, Jr.   is Chair of the Religious Studies Department at Brown University.

John Howard Yoder   is Professor of Theology at the University of Notre Dame.

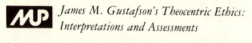 *James M. Gustafson's Theocentric Ethics: Interpretations and Assessments*

Interior typography by Margaret Jordan Brown

Binding designed by Alesa Jones

Composition by MUP Composition Department

Production Specifications

    text paper—50-lb. Glatfelter, Natural Smooth

    endpapers—Rainbow Antique, Cayenne

    cover—(on .088 binders boards) Holliston Roxite #57603, linen finish, red

    dust jacket—80-lb. enamel, printed PMS 200 (red), and PMS 872 (gold)
        film laminated

Printing (offset lithography) and binding by Braun-Brumfield, Inc.,
Ann Arbor, Michigan